C000056069

CAROLINE
CHISHOLM

CAROLINE CHISHOLM

Margaret Kiddle

With an Introduction by
PATRICIA GRIMSHAW

Melbourne University Press

First published 1950
Second edition 1957
Abridged edition 1969
Reprinted with new introduction 1990

This edition (MUP Australian Lives series) 1996

Cover designed by Mark Davis
Printed in Malaysia by SRM Production Services Sdn. Bhd. for
Melbourne University Press
PO Box 278, Carlton South, Victoria 3053, Australia

National Library of Australia Cataloguing-in-Publication entry
Kiddle, Margaret, 1914–1958.
    Caroline Chisholm.
    Includes index.
    ISBN 0 522 84733 1
    1. Chisholm, Caroline, 1808–1877. 2. Women
philanthropists – Australia – Biography. 3. Women social
reformers – Australia – Biography. 4. Australia –
history – 1788–1851. 5. Australia – Emigration and
immigration – History. I. Title.
994.02092

This book is dedicated
to the memory of all the women
who helped to pioneer Australia
especially to that of my own great-grandmothers
Elizabeth Kiddle, Eliza Loch, Janet Burrett
and Margaret von Hill

TO MRS CHISHOLM

The guardian angel of her helpless sex,
Whom no fatigue could daunt, no crosses vex,
With manly reason and with spirit pure,
Crown'd with the blessings of the grateful poor,
For them with unrepining love she bore
The boarded cottage and the earthern floor.
The sultry day in tedious labour spent,
The endless tale of whining discontent
Bore noonday's burning sun, and midnight's chill,
The scanty meal, the journey lengthening still;
Lavished her scanty store on their distress,
And sought no other guerdon than success.
Say ye who hold the balance and the sword,
Into your lap the wealth of nations poured,
What have you done with all your hireling brood,
Compared with her the generous and the good?
Much ye receive and little ye dispense,
Your alms are paltry, and your debts immense;
Your toil's reluctant — freely hers is given;
You toil for earth, she labors still for Heaven.

ROBERT LOWE
Spectator (Sydney),
28 February 1846

Foreword

This is the story of a brave woman bravely told. Caroline
Chisholm was a pioneer in many senses of the word, and not
least in establishing a place for women in public affairs. In this
enterprise she was alone in Australia where the conditions under
which she worked were even more forbidding than those that
confronted her only real rival at the time, Elizabeth Fry in
England. Apart from the deep-seated conventional objection to
the intervention of women in public affairs, an obstacle common
to all societies in the second quarter of the nineteenth century,
Mrs Chisholm had to contend with the primitive conditions of a
colonial society and a bitter religious controversy. She was
handicapped by lack of material resources, but she had great
personal assets. She had energy, human sympathy, administrative
ability of a high order, personal charm and dignity, a husband
unobtrusively devoted to her work, and undying faith in the
cause to which she had so unselfishly put her hand. Without
these qualities it would have been impossible for her to have
commenced her work, let alone to have carried it through with
so large a measure of success. Caroline Chisholm was a great
pioneer, the greatest of women pioneers in the history of
Australia, and all the greater because she did not look for
material reward or public position. On the contrary she spurned
both, perhaps to a degree that injured her cause towards the end.
She died in poverty and obscurity.

Miss Kiddle has succeeded to a marked degree in making Mrs
Chisholm's work live again. Her book contains both historical
research of high quality and a restrained judgment on a
character that must often have tempted a writer with the author's
imagination to dramatize the story. In her search for material
Miss Kiddle has shown an energy and enthusiasm not less
remarkable than that possessed by her heroine. She has
thoroughly probed every source that would yield fresh material
on the activities of Caroline Chisholm, and she has fitted this

material into a story of Australia's economic development for nearly three decades commencing in the middle 'thirties of last century. This has involved judgment not only on the character and actions of the central figure in the story, but on many other leading personalities in both Australia and the British Isles, and on the main economic problems associated with land settlement and immigration in Australia. The book is thus more than a biography of Mrs Chisholm. It is a contribution from original sources to the economic history of Australia. Nevertheless, it will be received by historians and the public of Australia as a biography, and as such it will be surprising if it is not rated as one of the great Australian biographies. I have derived great pleasure and profit in reading and commenting on the work, and I have no doubt that it will quicken the interest of others, as it has mine, in the character and achievements of an extraordinary woman, as well as in the economic problems of her period.

Mrs Chisholm was essentially a woman of action and not, as Miss Kiddle is careful to point out, an original thinker. Her life exemplified the view that people with energy have a great advantage over others in the influence they exert in their own day. Her writing and speaking had reference exclusively to the problems that were at her hand, and were designed to promote the things in which she was interested. There was nothing original about them, though they formed a necessary part of her armour. She was restrained in controversy until towards the end when she attacked the squatting interests, but she never departed from restraint in anything pertaining to religion, though she had good reason to do so. It may be said that her best writing was done in refuting the contentions of Dr Lang that she was working to proselytize the Roman Catholic religion to which she was a convert in her adolescence, and a devoted adherent to the end of her life. She was persuasive in argument, both in writing and in personal discussion, and there is little doubt that had she lived half a century later she would inevitably have played a great part in Australian politics. Her capacity for work was enormous, and she was able to maintain active leadership in her advocacy of a sound and vigorous immigration policy whilst bringing up a large family to whom she was a devoted mother. All this is brought vividly before the reader in Miss Kiddle's well-balanced study. But the outstanding impression made by the book is of a woman who combined great energy with many finer human qualities, and above all a noble femininity.

Of great interest is the development of certain radical traits in her thought and actions in her later years. After spending eight years revisiting England, she returned to Victoria in 1854 at a time when the first fruits of the gold discoveries had been easily gathered, and the 'diggers' were turning their attention to land settlement. Immigration to Mrs Chisholm had always been the settlement of the family unit on the land, and now she found that the land was held all too firmly by the squatters. This appears to have marked a turning point in her thought. More and more she joined with those who were clamouring for a liberal land policy, and to an increasing extent she criticized the influence of the squatters, sometimes with bitterness. This is the only evidence of a bitter trait in a character that must have been sorely tried on many occasions when she met with indifference and opposition in plans that seemed obvious to her, as well as being of deep humanitarian interest. What is astonishing about Mrs Chisholm is that she achieved so much for so long without breaking with the powerful interests in the colonies. Though averse to any display of force, her thinking had been influenced by the Chartists during her stay in England, and in public lectures on her return to Australia she supported part of their platform. This again demonstrated her basic courage as well as her response to the aspirations of the immigrants who had first call on her public sympathies from the very beginning of her work.

In this book Caroline Chisholm stands again before us in all her strength and weakness. It is published at a time when many Australian women feel a sense of frustration, largely because we seem to have lost the pioneering spirit of which Mrs Chisholm was the living embodiment. For devoted and unselfish service to a great cause her life has no parallel in Australian history. As such, the book should be an inspiration at a time when inspiration is needed, and I have no doubt that its author would desire that it should be received in this spirit.

DOUGLAS COPLAND

Preface to the Abridged Edition

In the year after the publication of the second editon of this book, Margaret Kiddle died at the early age of forty-two. A short memoir of her will be found at the beginning of her *Men of Yesterday* (M. U. P., 1961 etc.). This third edition of her *Caroline Chisholm* has been slightly abridged. No material alteration has been made to the text except to shorten it by reducing or omitting material which is either repetitive or of interest only to specialist students. These last may readily consult the earlier editions in libraries, and it is hoped that abbreviation may make it possible in an age of rising costs to keep in print a book of interest to the general reader. I wish to thank Mrs Sylvia Morrissey for preparing for this abbreviation, and Mr G. F. James for producing the final text as printed here.

R. M. CRAWFORD

1968

Acknowledgments

This is not the personal biography of Caroline Chisholm which I once hoped to write because, after an eight years' search, I have been unable to trace her private papers. If these still exist, the publication of this book may lead to their discovery.

In the long search for Caroline I have had many generous helpers. The first was Mr G. F. James under whose guidance, and with whose unfailing encouragement, I began the research for a Master of Arts thesis.

I cannot make an individual acknowledgment here to all the libraries and historical societies in Australia and overseas which gave me information; many of them are mentioned in my notes. In particular, however, I acknowledge the untiring assistance given me by the librarians and staffs of the University, Public, and Parliamentary Libraries, Melbourne, and the Mitchell Library, Sydney.

Caroline's descendants, the late Mr E. Chisholm of Sydney and his sister, Miss Mary Chisholm, as well as their cousin, Mrs Langton, gave me what information they could, but they had no family records. Through the good offices of Mr H. A. Pitt, I met another of her grandsons, the late Mr E. Dwyer Gray. As a child he had known his grandmother and could tell me something of the end of her life. His sister, Sister Mary Philomena (Ursuline Convent, Waterford, Ireland), was able to tell me a little about the lost portrait of Caroline. Mr H. Chisholm, of Sydney, provided the photograph of the bust.

At a time when I was finding it increasingly difficult to continue the research the late Father George O'Neill, S.J., wrote to me. He had begun a biography of Caroline Chisholm but, with his other activities, found it too arduous. He heard of my work in a round-about way, and offered me his material. We corresponded regularly, and it is a profound regret to me that he did not live to see the book completed.

It was Father O'Neill who insisted that Mrs Jellyby in *Bleak*

xii

House was in part a caricature of Mrs Chisholm. I could find no evidence for this in any Dickens' literature until Mr Humphrey House, author of *The Dickens World,* gave me a list of references to the *Household Words* articles.

Besides those I have already mentioned there are many others I would like to thank for their assistance: Miss Margaret Swann (Granville, N.S.W.); Miss Barbara Armstrong (Kyneton, Victoria); Miss Lucy Drucker (Institute of Historical Research, London); Miss Logan (Melbourne); Sister Claver (The Sisters of Charity, Melbourne); Mrs Collingridge (Sydney); Professor E. L. Woodward (Oxford); Professor W. K. Hancock (Oxford); Mr G. M. Young (Marlborough, England); Mr Leslie C. Staples (editor of the *Dickensian,* London); Sir Henry Hake (National Portrait Gallery, London); Professor Thomas Bodkin (University of Birmingham); Mr B. McNamara (National Gallery of Ireland, Dublin); The Rev. Charles O'Conor, S.J. (Dublin); the Rev. L. H. C. Hopkins (Wootton Rectory, Northampton, England); Mr R. Brooke-Caws (Curator of Messrs Coutts & Co.'s Museum, London); Mr A. R. Wiltshire (Superintendent, Bank of Australasia, Melbourne); Dr T. F. Ryan (Melbourne); the Rev. James Murtagh (editor of the *Advocate,* Melbourne); Mr A. T. Smithers (Victorian Treasury); Mr Stapleton (Lands Department, Melbourne); Mr R. L. Williams (Maitland Hospital, N.S.W.); the Rev. Frank Hanlin (Sydney); the Rev. J. W. Doyle, S.J. (Canisius College, Sydney); Major Warren Perry (Archivist, Canberra War Memorial); the Rev. J. McGovern (Granville, N.S.W.); the Rev. N. M. McNally (Sydney); the Rev. Maurice Kingsford (Oxford); Dr Ian McCallum (Melbourne); the Registrars-General of Sydney, Melbourne, Adelaide and London; the Shire Secretaries of Melton, Gisborne, Keilor, and Metcalfe; the Town Clerk of Essendon, Victoria; the Port Phillip Pilots' Association, Melbourne; the Public Record Office, London; and the Keeper of the Records, Commonwealth Relations Office, London.

Father O'Neill devoted many hours to reading and criticizing the typescript. He enlisted the help of the Most Rev. Dr Eris O'Brien, who gave me generously of his time and knowledge. Mr Manning Clark gave me advice with some of the chapters in which he had a specialized knowledge of the subject matter. Professor R. M. Crawford must know every sentence I have written here almost as well as I do myself. I shall always be grateful for his sympathetic understanding both of Caroline's problems and my own.

Professor Douglas Copland has read and re-read the type-script. As so many times before, his whole-hearted encouragement has urged me to complete a task which sometimes seemed too difficult. In the midst of beginning exacting work of his own he has also found time to write a preface in which he gives me much more praise than I deserve. But I thank him most sincerely for it, and on behalf of Caroline I thank him for his praise of her. She deserves all of it.

Lastly, I thank Miss Elsa Troedel for her patience in typing the much-corrected manuscript. And I thank my mother and father for the encouragement and support without which this book would not have been completed.

MARGARET KIDDLE

August 1948

Since the first edition of this book was published I have visited Ireland and searched for the records of Caroline Chisholm which I hoped might still exist there. I am convinced they have been destroyed. There is no trace even of the large portrait of her painted by A. C. Hayter. It is most unlikely now that any more substantial information concerning her will be discovered. Therefore, though this new edition has been revised, the revisions do not make any alteration in the actual story of her work; they are revisions and corrections of detail. In making them I have been guided by suggestions from Professor J. A. La Nauze, Professor S. J. Butlin, and Mr Humphrey House, to all of whom I am very grateful.

MARGARET KIDDLE

1957

Contents

Abbreviations

H. of L.	House of Lords Sessional Papers
H.R.A.	*Historical Records of Australia,* first series
ML	Mitchell Library, Sydney
S.M.H.	*Sydney Morning Herald*
V. & P.	*Votes and Proceedings*
Emigrants' Guide	Eneas Mackenzie, *The Emigrants' Guide to Australia, with a Memoir of Mrs. Chisholm* (1853)
Female Immigration	Caroline Chisholm, *Female Immigration considered in a Brief Account of the Sydney Immigrants' Home* (1842)
Memoirs	Eneas Mackenzie, *Memoirs of Mrs. Chisholm with an Account of her Philanthropic Labours in India, Australia and England, to which is added a History of the Family Colonization Loan Society* (2nd ed., 1852)
Therry, *Reminiscences*	Roger Therry, *Reminiscences of Thirty Years' Residence in New South Wales and Victoria* (1863)

CONVERSIONS

1 mile	= 1.61 kilometres
1 acre	= 0.405 hectares
1 ounce (oz)	= 28.3 grams
1 pound (lb)	= 454 grams
1 hundredweight (cwt)	= 50.8 kilograms
1 ton	= 1.02 tonnes
1 pint	= 0.568 litres
1 penny (d.)	= 0.83¢
1 shilling (s.)	= $0.10
1 pound (£)	= $2.00
(12d. = 1s.; 20s. = £1)	

Introduction to the 1990 Edition

by PATRICIA GRIMSHAW

Caroline Chisholm was one of those people, renowned in their life-times, the recording of whose life has undergone considerable shifts of fate at the hands of historians. At the peak of her public activism she was accorded respect, amounting at times to sheer adulation, by the Australian colonial and the British public. She was regarded in Victorian Britain as comparable with two other great female reformers, Elizabeth Fry and Florence Nightingale, and the latter cited Caroline Chisholm along with Elizabeth Fry as a model for her own foray into nursing in the Crimea. Yet, like many other women famous in their time, Chisholm was quite swiftly dropped from historical memory. For the Mother Country, her activism was increasingly linked with the fate of a distant new nation, rapidly establishing its own indigenous historical tradition, while Australian history-making made scant place for women in its tale of conquest of land and attainment of liberty for its migrant European population.

It was the work of one of Australia's first female academic historians, Margaret Kiddle, that changed this situation. Her biography of Caroline Chisholm, published in 1950, established Chisholm's importance in a decided and authoritative fashion. Chisholm entered the fabric of Australian historical consciousness in a positive way, an acknowledgement accorded to the rare woman. Few general histories of Australia after 1950 failed to mention Chisholm, while public bodies attached her name to a growing number of institutions – a college at La Trobe University, the Chisholm Institute of Technology, two Catholic senior schools, a federal government electorate. A drawing of her appears on the five dollar note. Kiddle's biography sold well, and was twice reprinted. Chisholm was generally written of with genuine respect. Yet, with another shift of the historical scales, the new women's history that emerged in the wake of the feminist move-

ment in the early 1970s, and which challenged so many assumptions underlying earlier Australian historiography, brought the
implications of Chisholm's reform agenda for her own sex under a
sceptical eye. It was not so much the significance of Chisholm as a
historical actor that feminists questioned, but the meaning of her
activism in terms of social equity for women. Within current
Australian history, therefore, Chisholm stands as a key figure in
debate and discussion, a situation that makes the reprinting of
Margaret Kiddle's biography timely. An appreciation of Kiddle's
interpretation of Caroline Chisholm's life, and the significance of
that interpretation for current debates on women's history in the
early 1990s, rests on an exploration of the successive chroniclers
who have told Chisholm's story, and of the shifting portrayal of
'true womanhood' their tales reveal.

Margaret Kiddle began her study of Caroline Chisholm for a
Master of Arts thesis at the University of Melbourne at the beginning of World War II. After several years in teaching and the public
service during the war, she returned to complete the thesis in 1947
and was employed first as a tutor, then as senior tutor, in the
History Department from 1946 till her death in 1958. That she
should have entered university and proceeded to an honours
degree followed by postgraduate research and a teaching position
was by no means a usual set of chances and choices for a young
middle-class woman in the Melbourne of the 1930s and 1940s. In
their autobiographical essays in the collection *The Half-Open Door*,
published to commemorate one hundred years of women's
education at the University of Melbourne, two of Margaret Kiddle's
colleagues in the post-war History Department, Kathleen Fitzpatrick and Alison Patrick, described the influences against high
academic achievement and professional employment experienced
by women of their class, although they, like Margaret Kiddle, had
resisted them. As was the case for virtually all women who entered
university in the 1930s, Margaret Kiddle had attended a private
girls' secondary school, in her case the Melbourne Church of
England Girls' Grammar School. Her father, John Kiddle, was a
solicitor; his wife, Mauna Loa Kiddle, the mother of four children
(of whom Margaret Loch, born in 1914, was the eldest) kept her
daughter under prudent and careful surveillance. An entry in
Margaret's 'Progress Book' on her seventh birthday read, under the
heading 'Any marked hereditary pecularities': 'Self-willed and
persistent; power of concentration. Quick at learning'. The parents
were swift to find resemblances in character extending back over

generations: the family was proud of its pioneering forebears, who had 'made good' in the colonies, and Margaret herself dedicated *Caroline Chisholm* 'to the memory of all the women who helped to pioneer Australia', but in particular to her own four great-grandmothers, Elizabeth Kiddle, Eliza Loch, Janet Burrett and Margaret von Hill. She knew something of all her ancestors, and was filled with admiration for their exploits, women and men alike. 'I wish you had known some of the others', she wrote once to a friend, 'they were a tall, swift-moving, laughing crowd, superb on horseback'.

Margaret Kiddle's praise for the physical prowess of her kinfolk was undoubtedly tinged with a muted envy. In her teens she grew into a tall, thin, young woman, with, at seventeen, a 'pronounced chin development' that certainly in her mother's eye denoted character development. She had already, alas, developed a severe chronic kidney complaint. In a school where a hearty interest in sport was a mark of 'school spirit', Margaret was to be found loyally and bravely cheering the fit and able from the sidelines. In the school magazine she described herself wryly thus in Gilbert and Sullivan style: 'M. L. K.: I know the Kings of England and I quote the fights historical'. Indeed, her bouts of disability left her a good deal of time for reading, and with her family's keen interest in Australia's settlement and development, more pronounced at that time among the well-to-do, Margaret's growing scholarly interest was engaged by history. In the History Department she found stimulation from the teaching of two academics, Professor Ernest Scott and Miss Jessie Webb. Leadership of the department was assumed in 1937 by a man who had a profound influence on the teaching of history in Australia, Professor R. M. Crawford. Scott had already encouraged students in the use of original sources. Crawford continued this tradition, as well as initiating heroic efforts to preserve local Australian records, which stimulated interest in the hitherto underdeveloped area of Australian history. It was Crawford who encouraged Margaret Kiddle to rewrite her master's thesis on Chisholm for publication by Melbourne University Press.

Margaret Kiddle won for herself a special place in the historiography of Australian women with her biography of Chisholm and her subsequent important work, *Men of Yesterday: A Social History of the Western District of Victoria*, which, despite its unpromising title, explored a good deal about the lives of squatters' wives and daughters along with the central narrative that focused on the male squatters. *Caroline Chisholm* was the first study about an Australian woman to emerge from an academic context. Since the time of the earliest historians of Australia, the narrative of Australia's past had centred on a particular set of central themes: the taking of a continent, the economic development of the colonies as successive enterprises waxed and waned, the establishment of a political system and a society which represented an improved version of British life. The alignment of these first historians of themselves as Australian men, with their version of the Australian past, established a tradition of pursuing the origins of Australian national identity along a path that quite decidedly ignored the experiences of women. Women did not appear as movers and shakers in this drama; at first women posed a problem because there simply weren't enough of them; then they got married, had children, and apparently became historically irrelevant except for the population question. Ernest Scott's 1912 textbook history of Australia did acknowledge at least the success of female suffrage and the entry of women to the university. (He was married to Mabel Besant, the daughter of the famous English theosophist, Annie Besant.) But Professor Crawford's history published in 1952 (in the preface of which he thanked Margaret Kiddle for her 'digging', or research assistance work) did not deviate far from the accepted path, although his work now had the two world wars and the great depression to add to the text. And so it was with other Australian history writing, largely a male preserve. There were very few women who held lectureships in Australian universities before 1950, and those few had not turned any special attention to their sex.

Women's past had certainly been recorded in Australia, but outside the influential academic mainstream. The shelves of public libraries abound with histories of women, published throughout the century, written by women, largely for women. Many middle-class women sensed the omission of their sex from the dominant record, and hastened to make good the gap, with memoirs, auto-biographies, biographies and accounts of women's organizations. These female writers, too, had a tale to tell, of brave pioneer women building homes in the bush alongside men, of women leading their sex to civil rights and into public life, of women sustaining an altruistic concern for the poor and underprivileged: 'worthy women' all. Some were novelists: Kylie Tennant, Eleanor Dark, Marjorie Barnard, Flora Eldershaw. These writers were not often listened to, however, by those who held positions of influence and prestige in universities. Academic history emphasized the dramatic event, political change, economic transformations, and the men whose names and activities were associated with them. Australia had been less diversified by class than Britain, and there were as a consequence few 'great women' to be discussed. In northern countries, prominent women were usually also rich women, high-born women, women with others of their sex of lower status at home attending to their household's mundane needs.

And yet there was one easily identified great woman in Australian history who awaited a scholarly study, and that was Caroline Chisholm. Her career, as Margaret Kiddle proceeded to describe it, was extraordinary. But Kiddle also demonstrated graphically the way in which Chisholm's activities intersected with two of the major themes of the central questions of Australian historiography: how to increase the European population in Australia, and how to encourage closer settlement of the land. Chisholm's concerns meshed narrowly with that interaction of British colonial policy makers and local colonial authorities that so preoccupied analysts of the Australian colonial period.

The story which Kiddle told was a compelling one. Caroline Chisholm's means had not been ample, far less so than most prominent women of Victorian England, since the income of her husband, a captain in the British army, was not princely; it was adequate enough, however, to enable her some freedom from continual domestic labour for themselves and their children, eventually six in all. Within a few years of her arrival in the colony of New South Wales in 1838, Caroline Chisholm's attention had been drawn to the appalling state of penury into which so many single female migrants fell on their arrival. She persuaded Governor Gipps to allow her premises to house the women, successfully solicited donations for their temporary upkeep, and was soon well on the way to establishing networks of information and support for finding employment not only for single women, but for married women and men with large families, similarly disadvantaged by the labour conditions of the colony. Chisholm personally found land and settled a number of families in a co-operative farming venture. As a side issue she pressed the prosecution of the captain and surgeon of a migrant ship who had cruelly mistreated a young woman for her resistance to sexual overtures. These first endeavours were followed by a trip to Britain during which she determinedly advised the Colonial Secretary, Earl Grey, on emigration policy (the dissemination of necessary information, the selection of migrants, the conditions for safe passage and arrival) and gained financial backup for her own preferred emigration programme. Previously she had settled some eleven thousand people in rural New South Wales; now she assisted around twenty thousand more to migrate. Back in the colonies in 1854 she took up the cause of the deserted wives and children of diggers, established shelters for families travelling to the diggings, and espoused the diggers' call for the unlocking of the lands from the squatters' grasp. Margaret Kiddle portrayed Chisholm as a woman of unusual courage and resolution, with exceptional organizational abilities, as persuasive with her voice as with her pen. One would have thought it hard for historians before Kiddle to have ignored such a figure.

Margaret Kiddle prefaced her book with a frank statement: 'This is not the personal biography of Caroline Chisholm which I once hoped to write because, after an eight years' search, I have been unable to trace her private papers'. Like most biographers, in other words, she had initially aimed to explore, along with the 'life and times' of Chisholm, the interaction of the personal with the public face of her subject. Here, like so many later biographers of prominent women, her purpose was frustrated, either because Caroline Chisholm had kept no private papers, or because they had been destroyed. The nearest Margaret Kiddle could come to some personal statement by Chisholm herself was a simple brief memoir she wrote about the circumstances of establishing the Female Immigrants' Home in Sydney. Chisholm herself was aware that women publishing under their own names was a rare event and thought herself probably the first woman to do so in the colony. She wrote a good deal more than that, but these other writings were her vehicles for publicizing her ideas on the need for support services for migrants, for improved knowledge of colonial conditions, for a more humane basis for selection of prospective settlers. Her views on immigration, and incidentally on many other issues, including religious tolerance, were thus widely aired through her own authorship. While her publications indicated something of Chisholm's vigour, courage and liberalism, they do not provide an entry to the intimate understanding of her subject that Kiddle sought. This was true, too, of the bulk of commentary that Chisholm's activities elicited, in the press and journals of her day both in Britain and the colonies. While Kiddle did trace descendants of Chisholm, they had no papers, only vague memories, few family myths about her to hand on. (Chisholm actually ended her life in straitened means and isolation, never a hopeful indication for biographers who seek personal papers.)

There were only a few sources that offered some hints

concerning Chisholm's personal situation and private responses. One was fictional, the character 'Mrs Jellyby' drawn by Charles Dickens in *Bleak House*. Dickens knew Caroline Chisholm well, and had visited her home in London. While clearly a great admirer and supporter of Chisholm, Charles Dickens, Kiddle concluded, was certainly not above incorporating aspects of Chisholm's existence (her inevitably somewhat disordered domestic arrangements, for example) into an otherwise fictional creation. Fiction is a two-edged sword as a source for the historian, and Kiddle accepted this evidence with cautious evaluation.

A second source of personal insight was a memoir of Caroline Chisholm written in 1852 by a London Nonconformist publisher and writer, Eneas Mackenzie, two years before her return to the colonies. The work might have proved gold to Kiddle, but unfortunately the intimate details it provided were patchy. Mackenzie, whose admiration for Chisholm knew no bounds, was convinced that she would attract the attention of future biographers: he would do his duty for posterity by recording her life. He knew Chisholm well, as a member of her colonization society, and was acquainted with many of her friends. He saw himself to be in a special position to collect 'the interesting documents relative to the distinguishing features of her career' while such information was readily available, and to record oral testimony about her to ensure that any 'inaccuracies' that might exist about her life would be corrected promptly by 'living witnesses'. Unfortunately for the twentieth-century biographer, he then disclaimed any intention of prying into the intimate details of Chisholm's private life. He wanted to attend more to 'positive facts than to minute personal illustrations, as during the lifetime of an individual, more especially a lady, there is ever a feeling of delicacy against gratifying a mere morbid taste by rudely peering behind the veil of domestic life . . .'. Mackenzie offered probably only two slight but valuable details, one concerning the inspiration from a visitor for a young Chisholm's interest in emigration, the other her stipulation, before her consent to marriage, that she be allowed freedom as a married woman to pursue public activities of a charitable nature. The historian Anne Summers was later to castigate biographers of Australian women for concentrating too much on the personal, for adopting a 'chatty' style because they knew in advance that their work would not be taken seriously. This was not a temptation Kiddle could fall into, even if she was likely to: the material was simply not there.

Where Mackenzie was invaluable, however, was in offering a sense of the basis for Caroline Chisholm's fame in this most active period of her career. Mackenzie himself gave prominence to Chisholm's activities for the protection of single women from male sexual predatoriness, in the light of revised attitudes to sexual morality under his admired Queen Victoria. Did any of his readers, he asked, recall the lax days of old, when the roué was a glorified figure, and women prized for decorativeness and passion rather than for intellect? This was the 'miasmatic moral depravity' which had wafted to the colonies to flourish freely. There girls and young women, 'the unprotected children of poverty and of crime', were deemed the rightful spoil of 'degraded-minded men' with a callousness scarcely credited back in England. But the new Victorian age had seen a marked change in women's position: '. . . the domestic, social, and intellectual virtues are cultivated, reverenced and esteemed as a duty that womankind not only owes to herself but to society'. It was this new message, this reformed morality, that Caroline Chisholm had taken to the colony of New South Wales. In terms of emigration, Mrs Chisholm had

> found the stream polluted, and she has purified it. The weak she has protected, and the poor she has sheltered tenderly and affectionately. With a woman's courage and resolution she has asserted the dignity of her sex, and caused the unscrupulous voluptuary to shrink appalled, and respect nature's loveliest creation, although in want and in rags.

His verdict? 'PHILANTHROPIST! A word mighty in significance, encircles with humanizing radiance the name of CAROLINE CHISHOLM.' Mackenzie's eulogy was echoed by Samuel Sidney, another prominent London Nonconformist, whom Mackenzie cited. Chisholm's philanthropy, asserted Sidney,

> . . . was not a mere amusement to be taken up at odd hours, like a new romance – to be laid down as quickly as it was taken up – to be satisfied by a distribution of cheap tracts, or, at most, of cheap superfluous guineas – by capricious visits to poor cottages, whose misery renders the change from the luxurious drawing room a pleasing excitement. It is a part of her life – of her daily duty. For the cause she embraced, she has chosen to abandon the luxuries, nay, the comforts, to which her fortune and station entitled her; to wear stuff instead of silk; to work hard, to live hard, to save, that she may spend upon the poor . . . We find her not like Mrs. Fry – descending from the drawing room to the prison, to return, carriage borne, to that drawing room, when

her errand of mercy was done – but in the small room of a small house, in an obscure suburb . . .

Chisholm, Sidney continued, possessed organizational ability that almost amounted to genius, combined 'with energy and perseverance.

Mackenzie's memoir elicited commendation from an unlikely source, the *Westminster Review,* which admitted that it had small respect for professional philanthropists in general, or for ladies of Mrs Jellyby's type in particular – and indeed, philanthropy was usually only noted in connection with a crown or coronet. But the *Review* warmly recommended Mackenzie's work 'to every friend of progress, and every lover of humanity'. Mrs Chisholm had done more for the

> moral regeneration of the Australian colonies than *all their clergy, with their four or five bishops to boot.* She did, moreover, what they could not do – what you feel no one could have done but herself. Like other moral heroines, she seemed born just for that work which she did, and which waited for her to do it.

The *Review,* like Samuel Sidney, pointed to Chisholm's 'extraordinary faculties for organisation and government'. For another commentator, the French historian Jules Michelet, the fifth continent of the world had thrown up one saint, one legend, who had done more for Australia than all the emigration societies and the British government put together. They had failed in colonization 'where a simple woman succeeded by her force of character and vigour of soul'. This was adulation, indeed, but somewhat devoid of the substantial detail about Chisholm that contemporaries might have recorded.

Subsequent writings about Caroline Chisholm were also of little practical use to Margaret Kiddle, since they were not only slight in substance, but derivative of Mackenzie's initial biographical sketch. (That does not mean that they are not now of interest to us, of course, in terms of locating Margaret Kiddle's own biography within a historiographical context of writing about women.) After the flurry of writing about Chisholm mid-century, one further British foray was made by G. Elliot Anstruther, who produced a biographical essay in a series called 'Women-workers', published by the Catholic Truth Society in London. Chisholm was, for the last time within British historiography, discussed in a context of pious British female reformers. Clearly, while Fry and Nightingale would sustain a strong place in British historical consciousness, the onus for further serious acknowledgement was now on the historians of Chisholm's adopted home.

Two further biographical sketches of Chisholm appeared in Australia before Margaret Kiddle's work, both produced by women outside academic life. Writing in 1925, Margaret Swann, a local history enthusiast, was clearly impressed with a specifically Australian reading of Chisholm's work. At the height of Australian public concern over the lowering of the Australian birth-rate, and the supposed need to fill up the empty spaces for security reasons, Swann admired Chisholm's facilitation of the entry of Europeans to populate the continent. Was there not a continuing need to welcome the surplus population of the 'Motherland' for Australia's vast unpopulated tracts of land? Australia was rich, maintained Swann, in everything that went to make wealth and prosperity, except 'the one essential element – labour'. Of all the many snippets of good advice that Chisholm offered in her time, Margaret Swann selected with approval her response when some settlers expressed their pressing need of a school and a church: ' "Do not ask what will the Government do for us," Chisholm exhorted, "but let your question be, "What shall we do for ourselves?" ' Margaret Swann, as an educated Australian woman of the 1920s, was aware of the significance of Chisholm's stepping outside the bounds of expected mid nineteenth-century female behaviour. Swann saw that both Chisholm's public work and her public speaking in Australia in the late 1850s, together with her explicit justification of both, amounted to an attack on the traditional prejudice against a woman taking a public part in politics. Eleanor Dark, the novelist, wrote on Chisholm in *The Peaceful Army: A Memorial to the Pioneer Women of Australia 1788 to 1938*, the volume on Australian women produced for the country's sesquicentenary in 1938. For her, the same aspect of Chisholm's life was uppermost, as she joined with other women to thrust women at least marginally into the historical record. For Eleanor Dark, 'not half-a-dozen books by Mary Wollstonecraft could have been more effective "vindication" than the life of this indomitable woman'.

There was clearly some luck involved in Margaret Kiddle's engagement in her study of Caroline Chisholm. Very few women anywhere in Australia had undertaken postgraduate theses, and in an anti-intellectual masculine cultural climate, men faced social difficulties simply undertaking humanities studies. The choice of a woman's life as a research focus was highly unlikely. But secondly, the necessity of a biography of Chisholm had been pointed to by

none other than the eminent historian, Keith Hancock, in his highly
regarded history of Australia published in 1930. Hancock acknowledged Chisholm's importance, but knew little about her. 'It is
surprising', commented Hancock (undoubtedly referring to Lytton
Strachey's school, which had taken Florence Nightingale as a
target) 'that her story has not been pounced upon by one of our
clever modern specialists in the short biography; but probably her
character is too substantial and balanced to lend itself to their
mildly malicious irony'. Here was a challenge for a 'balanced'
historian to assume, ideally without the malicious irony. But
Hancock did more. He suggested, in his brief treatment of Chisholm, another theme that might be pursued through an examination of her life (not, one must say, a theme that he did anything
more than raise here). This 'extraordinary' woman, through her
amazing ability to influence men of power, through her practical
compassion that was worth the work of a thousand indiscriminate
philanthropists, had succeeded in raising New South Wales from a
'trough of iniquity'. He quoted approvingly Chisholm's statement
to Earl Grey: 'For all the clergy you can appoint, all the churches
you can build, and all the books you can export, will never do much
good without what a gentleman in that colony calls "God's police"
– wives and little children'. Further, it was not exaggeration to
assert that 'Mrs Chisholm established the dignity of womanhood
and of the family in New South Wales'. Hancock, in effect, not only
suggested that Caroline Chisholm was a figure of stature, but indicated issues of women's agency, and of gender relations, that a
study of her life might open up. Margaret Kiddle assumed this
biographical task; the second challenge, to contextualize
Chisholm's life within a framework of gender analysis, she
attempted, but only hesitantly.

Margaret Kiddle herself was by no means unaware of issues of
gender relations and of women's status at the time of her
researching Caroline Chisholm's life and of her own career in the
History Department at the University of Melbourne. While the
radical feminism of the 1970s offered a particular, sharp critique of
gender relations that we have come to equate with feminism,
another style of feminism of a liberal colour had informed the
world view of many educated Australian women throughout the
twentieth century. It had been the efforts of liberal turn-of-the-
century feminists that had established, not only such civil rights for
Australian women as the parliamentary franchise, but a legitimate
place for women in higher education and in the professions. Not all

women who prospered in such careers acknowledged the work of these pioneers, or thought about the continuing restraints on women's autonomy, but some, quietly but firmly, continued to discuss these concerns. In his foreword to the first edition of Kiddle's biography of Chisholm, Professor (later Sir Douglas) Copland referred directly to the feminist issue. The book, he writes, appeared at a time

> when many Australian women feel a sense of frustration, largely because we seem to have lost the pioneering spirit of which Mrs Chisholm was the living embodiment . . . the book should be an inspiration at a time when inspiration is needed, and I have no doubt that its author would desire that it should be received in this spirit.

Professor Kathleen Fitzpatrick, a highly regarded historian who was Margaret Kiddle's colleague in the History Department, said in a speech to women graduates in 1958 that women had a legal right to do almost anything, 'but they are in fact hedged in with invisible barriers which keep them, as it were, on the outer of our national life'. Such ideas were part of Kiddle's cultural environment. In her assessment of Caroline Chisholm, Margaret Kiddle is constantly reflective about the meaning of Chisholm's career in the context of the changing status of women in the Victorian period, a perception clearly rooted in her own preoccupations as a woman living in the Australia of the late 1940s.

And so Margaret Kiddle wrote this biography, the first full-length study of Caroline Chisholm, and the first account of her life based upon an exhaustive, meticulous examination of all records by and about her subject, interpreted within the confines of an academic, scholarly environment. Under the influence of British historiography, Australian history writing was essentially empiricist, eclectic in its attachment to theory, the organizing assumptions underlying interpretation implicit, seldom explicitly revealed and discussed. What Kiddle was able to do, unlike the amateurs before her in the biographical field, was to establish the narrative of Chisholm's life firmly within the political and economic context of immigration to and settlement of Australia, providing an important, and fresh, perspective on these central issues. At the same time she offered a judicious and careful commentary on Chisholm's work as a reformer, as an advocate for poor women and for parents of young children, as befitted the twentieth-century scholar's style, trained to mediate spontaneous personal responses with the 'irony', if not the 'malicious irony', that Hancock observed. (Of course Kiddle came first to this work within the restricted boundaries of the thesis where unwritten rules discourage the bold or colourful statement; examiners in turn bewail the dullness of academic prose!) Kiddle was certainly restrained by the necessary conventions of close footnoting, and of avoiding speculation that could not be neatly substantiated. Not for Kiddle the eulogies of Mackenzie, nor even the freedom of interpretation of Hancock in his *Australia*.

As Margaret Kiddle's first foray into extensive research into documentary evidence, Caroline Chisholm is a fine book. By any standards, it is a sound piece of historical scholarship. Kiddle took a person, famous for a period of her lifetime, all but removed from the historical consciousness of the country where her prominent work took place, and promoted this figure to the fore of Australian colonial history. If Kiddle is reticent about her personal responses to Chisholm (Copland's foreword suggests she showed 'a restrained judgement on a character that must often have tempted a writer with the author's imagination to dramatize the story') she clearly found Chisholm's work constructive, positive and effective. In places Kiddle makes value judgements which reveal something of her own world view as a middle-class woman raised in the 1920s and 1930s. She writes, for example, of some migrants as being of 'poor quality', of others as 'the best types', or 'of superior type'. In discussing sexuality and prostitution her choice of language is circumspect in keeping with polite conventions. She writes of a predominantly criminal population 'causing grave moral evils', of young orphan and workhouse girls whose 'moral character was questionable'. (Chisholm herself made a spirited defence at times of Irish orphans and the morality of emancipists, and spoke carefully yet actually more frankly about the sexual question.) Kiddle applauds Chisholm's pragmatism, attributing her success to her lack of attachment to any particular theory of immigration. At the end she criticizes Chisholm for apparently abandoning pragmatism by embracing so wholeheartedly the diggers' radical causes: Chisholm 'refused to see that the middle way between the two extremes of squatter and miner was the only hope of solution'

On 'the woman question', Margaret Kiddle is dissatisfied with her subject's performance, but takes pains to avoid appearing too partisan. When describing Chisholm pitted against the Governor of New South Wales himself in her determination to support Margaret Bolton's suit against the captain and surgeon of the *Carthaginian* for cruel maltreatment, Kiddle points out that the Immigration

Committee had described Bolton as ' "a correct, but peevish girl" ' – characteristics, says Kiddle, 'which possibly explain all her troubles'. Margaret Kiddle focuses upon the extent to which Chisholm stepped beyond the boundaries of proper Victorian femininity, and what Chisholm herself made of it. 'The astonishing thing about her', comments Kiddle, 'is that she did such work at a time when women were still imprisoned in the strait-jacket of Victorian convention'. Kiddle presumes that Chisholm would have been thereby forced to look at other women like herself, and feel anger at their lack of opportunities. But Kiddle is forced to accept that Chisholm was no rebel and no theorist. She was too occupied with immediate practical concerns 'to consider the rights and wrongs of the conditions she saw about her . . .'; in spite of her own career Chisholm believed that 'a woman's place was in the home', and that it was the 'design of nature' for women to be supported by their husbands. Chisholm felt the inconvenience of the Victorian attitude towards women. Yet, observes Kiddle, she never denounced this crippling handicap.

Margaret Kiddle's preoccupation with Chisholm, therefore, revolves around a search for the reason her subject did not extrapolate from personal experience to early feminist understanding of the broader structures underpinning the restricted behaviour of women of her class. Kiddle does not proceed to analyse the meaning of Chisholm's agenda for poorer single women, namely, their movement into household service and then into matrimony. Kiddle agrees with Hancock's version of Chisholm's work for the poor, and for families. Chisholm, she writes, proved to the people of New South Wales that 'female immigration need not be attended with immorality if the women were given proper protection. By proving this, she altered the attitude of the community to female immigration, and by fostering family life, she raised the social standard of the whole colony'. It was an interpretation of Chisholm's work that was reiterated by Manning Clark, Kiddle's fellow student and close friend, in his own history of Australia, which undoubtedly extended the influence of the biography.

Yet Chisholm's advocacy of the family was the very issue that later feminists would seize upon as problematic. The germinal revision of Chisholm came in 1975, in Anne Summers' radical feminist account of Australian history, *Damned Whores and God's Police: The Colonization of Women in Australia*. Two years previously, the desire to see women appropriately honoured within the Catholic Church had actually prompted another full-length biography of Chisholm, written by a Catholic activist from Kyneton, Mary Hoban, and entitled *Fifty-one Pieces of Wedding Cake* (a reference to wedding-tokens Chisholm received from grateful brides). Mary Hoban's aim was a pious one, that 'the Church will come to see Caroline as one whose life richly reflected the love of God'. She hoped that, ultimately, Chisholm would be raised to sainthood: 'While the ranks of the saints include queens and martyrs and holy widows a plenty, there is not, I think, a married woman from the ordinary walks of life'. Hoban, then, presented a hagiography, filling out her study with extensive quotations from Chisholm's writing, though Hoban was also unable to discover intimate journals or letters. While distant theoretically from the secular radical feminism that was shaking accepted views of femininity in Australia in the early 1970s Mary Hoban's quest was ultimately linked to those changing attitudes to gender which were not to leave religious institutions untouched. Her biography, however, had little impact on academic attitudes.

Anne Summers' general history of women touched only briefly on Caroline Chisholm, yet her critique was extremely significant for the development of the historiography of women, since *Damned Whores and God's Police* shaped feminist historical consciousness for the next decade. Of women's biographies, she wrote: 'Scholarly works like Margaret Kiddle's *Caroline Chisholm* . . . are read by fairly select groups and are occasionally referred to by historians of the period but they too generally fail to be integrated into any tradition because the subject of their research is too often relegated to a footnote in the more general studies'. Kiddle had promoted Chisholm as an individual on to the historical stage, yet it was true that no thematic discussion of women had ensued. What Summers succeeded in doing was to provide a sustained thematic framework for women and gender relations in Australian society within which Chisholm herself, and her reform agenda, could be understood. Ironically, Summers' own interpretation was one which stood at odds with current mainstream Australian history: Summers therefore did not provide a model for viewing Chisholm that superseded Kiddle's but, rather, one which stood as an alternative. To understand Summers' interpretation is to appreciate the challenge she offered to mainstream history, as part of a New Left, and radical feminist, critique of the assumptions underlying accepted views of Australia's past.

The late 1960s and early 1970s witnessed the emergence of radical political movements which developed critiques of

Australian society, as well as a broad revision of both public and personal political practices. The New Left began a reinterpretation of Marxist orthodoxies; radical and socialist feminists dissociated themselves from what they viewed as the male-dominated New Left, to form groups in which they could evaluate their lives as women and the social structures that endorsed current work, sexuality and child-rearing arrangements. Since the time when Margaret Kiddle's *Caroline Chisholm* appeared, there had been a diversification in the presentation of Australia's past by academic writers. Whereas a group of historians known as radical nationalists (Russel Ward, Robin Gollan, Ian Turner, Brian Fitzpatrick) presented a version of Australia's past which stressed the country's egalitarianism and sought causal explanations in indigenous factors (the nature of the Australian frontier, the reliance of workers on collective action, the need to harness the state for welfare ends) the New Left stressed, by contrast, the continuing anomalies of wealth and poverty in the country, the persistent inequalities based on race, ethnicity and class.

The radical feminists, in turn, pointed to another oppressive political hegemony, that of men over women. Their starting point was the question: if women won civil rights at the turn of the century, and the right to an independent wage, why were they still for the most part unwaged housewives, or workers in the lowest paid, least desirable jobs, outside arenas of overt power, and represented at an ideological and symbolic level in demeaning ways? Such injustice was maintained in the last analysis, said the feminists, by the threat, or use of, physical force, but in usual conditions by the promotion of stereotypes of femininity. Women's personalities and expectations of life were such that they were easily contained by male power; women, very often, even rejoiced in their situation. It was in the arena of the family that children learned, and internalized early, notions of a gendered identity; it was the family that provided women with lifelong, repetitive, thankless, unpaid work on behalf of men and their children. While a political revolution was needed to usher in the equality and justice of a socialist society, another revolution was needed to free women from sexual tyranny by men, and this was the overthrow of bourgeois family structures. The most impressive of the feminist revisionists, Anne Summers, wrote in a style accessible to a readership far beyond the usual academic texts, and strongly influenced the academy through the young feminists who entered research and teaching in tertiary institutions.

It was Anne Summers who seized upon two words quoted by Caroline Chisholm – 'God's police' – and thereby gave both the words, and Chisholm, a new prominence, for 'God's police' came to represent an idea that went to the heart of the new feminist history. Anne Summers pointed in *Damned Whores and God's Police* to a difficult and demeaning start for women in the Australian colonies, from convictism to the harshness of climate and isolation endured by pioneering women. Despite apparent gains as established urban centres appeared, women continued to be oppressed by the manipulation of two stereotypes of femininity, that of sexually deviant prostitute, or of upright matron who was accorded a respected place only as long as she sustained, and insisted upon others sustaining, a rigidly conventional path. Should she appear to stray, a woman was threatened with condemnation as 'damned whore'. Women as wives of men and mothers of children were entrusted with the policing, the moral guardianship of society, in that they were expected to curb restlessness and rebelliousness in men and instil virtues of civic loyalty and submission in children. Both these functions were exercised primarily through family relationships. Few women left the safe track. Margaret Kiddle had expressed mild scepticism about Chisholm's contribution to the status of middle-class women. Her reasoning was most unlikely to have taken Summers' route, writing as Kiddle did twenty-five years earlier and totally outside the context of 1970s feminism, which was at a considerable distance theoretically from the liberal 'women's rights' feminism her own circle espoused.

For Summers, then, Caroline Chisholm saw the civilizing and moderating role that married women could play in a frontier environment: women's supposedly 'innate desires for marriage, children and homes would, if encouraged by the authorities, secure a reversal of the Damned Whore stereotype'. But what Chisholm did not understand, Summers continued, was one vital fact: 'that the God's Police stereotype was just as much an imposition on women as the one it replaced'. Chisholm, who herself epitomized the God's police stereotype, was permitted and even encouraged in the public sphere because she used her considerable influence for social control over the lives of poor women and the working class in general, in the interests of capital, and the wealthy. Chisholm's public career, Summers concluded, did not set a precedent for other women. Her philosophy of women's role in the family was, in fact, 'rapidly and widely accepted for she was voicing a view which was evidently compatible with the rapid and stable growth of

colonial society'. Summers herself did not deny Chisholm's extraordinary abilities; yet Summers succeeded in promoting the
importance of Chisholm only to leave her stamped with a decidedly negative image.

Fifteen years later Anne Summers' work, in turn, stands as an
important landmark in Australian history, yet attached to a political
outlook and agenda that has been subjected once again to revision.
Later feminist historians have stressed a certain shrewd pragmatism in nineteenth-century reformers like Chisholm, as they have
for the feminists of the later part of the century, in their manipulation of existing ideologies to win for women stronger social
power. Chisholm's work preceded the mass activism of the feminists but in many ways her approach was qualitatively the same. The
Evangelicals in Britain in the 1820s and 1830s promoted the moral
authority of women in the family in their efforts to find a utility
model of femininity to replace one of decoration, decadence and
frivolity. Most of these reformers looked to the middle class. Chisholm was one of the first of her contemporaries to impute moral
power to working-class wives and mothers: there was surely something heroic in her trumpet call for the very women more often
despised and degraded by bourgeois society. The alternative prospects of poor colonial women for any dignified independent existence in the paid workforce were wretched, particularly in a period
of barely restricted fertility. Summers recognized that the attempt
to enhance the status of wives and mothers offered women some
new authority, and that male patriarchal power was thereby dimin-
ished. She underestimated the obstacles to alternative avenues for
improved life chances: few were possible in the colonies of
Chisholm's day. It must be remembered that Chisholm did not
view wifehood and motherhood as in any way inconsistent with
constructive participation in the affairs of a community but as
parallel to it.

When the ideology of woman as moral and spiritual guide of the
family became widely accepted among the middle class by the late
nineteenth century, feminists argued from this basis that women's
influence was needed everywhere, in the body politic as it was in
the family. They did not, even then, equate full citizenship with
independent paid employment; for first-wave feminists, unwaged
mothers had as much right to citizenship as paid workers. These
feminists, like Chisholm, saw most married wives and mothers as
having a different, but equally important, essential task in terms of
reproduction and productive labour. From the perspective of the

situation in which Chisholm found herself, and the ideas at her command, one could validly argue that she demonstrated a shrewd pragmatism, even if her actions had unexpected outcomes. To use the mechanism she chose for protecting single girls and women from the hazards of a heavily male frontier was not unconstructive; to speak up for the poverty of young children and the needs of families was a reasonable advocacy given the priority given to male needs and male labour in the colonies. Chisholm's suspicion of male sexual predatoriness was acute, honest, and well-founded: to turn male attention to woman as co-worker and mother of his children, to himself as sturdy protector and provider (certainly not a lazy man living off a wife's wages) looks highly restrictive from the perspective of modern Australia. It was arguably a positive step in the 1840s.

Even Kiddle's disappointment that Chisholm did not articulate a feminist position with regard to women of her own class must be looked at in terms of Chisholm's own times. In the 1830s, 1840s and 1850s there were only a handful of women, committed radicals, attempting to push the boundaries of feminine behaviour, among them a small group whose own experiences of sexism led them to generalize from their personal situations of the unequal gender order of their society. The likes of Angelina and Sarah Grimké, the American abolitionists, were women frustrated in their reform endeavours: Chisholm was not. Moreover, in New South Wales she was isolated from discussion of such issues. John Stuart Mill's essay, *The Subjection of Women*, which underpinned Victorian liberal feminist activism, was not published until 1869. Chisholm did reflect on her career and, certainly when she gave public lectures in New South Wales in the late 1850s and early 1860s, felt obliged to preface her speeches with some justification for public speaking. Her first public work had been in the cause of charity, she said. She did not think then 'of laws about land, nor of the state, nor non-payment of members'. Some people seriously objected to a lady appearing in public and 'spoke as if a woman should not have any opinion whatever with regard to politics'; she, Chisholm, did have them, and believed she had the right to be heard. But in fact no one stopped her, no one objected enough, and audiences paid good money to hear her. By 1861 she was lecturing on early closing. Chisholm (unlike many reformers) was by now far more radical politically than at the outset of her career. If a more spirited defence of her own politicking had been called for, it is not unreasonable to believe that she would have proceeded to develop it.

Margaret Kiddle's was a brief academic career, no more than twelve years from her appointment as a tutor in 1946 to her death in 1958 at the age of forty-four years, when still a senior tutor. It is ironical, in retrospect, that her undergraduate record was undistinguished, and that the very masters thesis from which *Caroline Chisholm* emerged was awarded a lowly second-class (lower division) honours grade by her examiners. For *Caroline Chisholm* and *Men of Yesterday* promoted her immediately among the eminent historians of Australia, and with that deep respect she is still regarded. She was a pioneer in women's history at a time when few saw women as a serious focus of inquiry, and she proved herself in an intellectual climate not conducive of female excellence. Her senior male colleagues were clearly supportive of her work, but a distinct paternalism coloured their evaluation of her that she must have sensed, and responded to in the way she presented herself in the academic environment. In a kindly memoir he wrote after her death, Professor Crawford made some comments on Margaret Kiddle revealing of his own attitudes toward her. Alluding to her serious health disability, he commented on her writing of children's novels; (in one, *West of Sunset*, Caroline Chisholm appeared briefly as a motherly, all-wise and all-knowing benevolent figure). Such activity, he said, was

> . . . close to her heart. Knowing that she would not have children of her own, she wrote for the children of others. Margaret, who worked for her own living, was not opposed to careers for women; but having denied herself what she valued most in life, she knew the limits, at least for her, of alternative ambitions.

He suggested, in other words, that she was a reluctant academic, not ambitious to rise up the academic hierarchy; she would in fact, have preferred the lot of the housewife and mother. He continued in the same vein with a comment on Margaret Kiddle's response to her reception at the Australian National University where she was awarded a fellowship in 1954.

> Her undoubted success in Canberra amused as well as pleased her, for she was accustomed to say that she was not really an academic, which was not only her serious assessment of herself, but also as near as she came to admitting that the things she most valued in life were those which life denied her, except vicariously.

Yet in *Men of Yesterday* and *Caroline Chisholm*, Margaret Kiddle demonstrated historical skills the equal of any of her elders and betters. However historians today may interpret the significance of Caroline Chisholm's life, she remains central to current debates about colonial Australia and women within it. Kiddle's work stands as the classic biography offering entry to understanding this important historical figure. It is not likely in the near future to be superseded.

Melbourne
January 1990

Introduction

SYDNEY IN THE EARLY 'FORTIES

Australia was founded not because of an ideal of empire, but mainly as a matter of sordid necessity. The transportation of felons overseas was practised most of the time the American colonies were under British rule, and when those colonies declared their independence the problem of what to do with the redundant criminals became urgent. It was only then that the favourable descriptions of the great southern land, which Captain Cook had visited, were remembered. And so, after much discussion, it was decided to send the prisoners to the unoccupied country. The First Fleet arrived in January 1788, and the settlement at Sydney Cove was established.

The convicts were mostly of poor physique, disease-stricken and hopeless; taken from familiar places to the vast, grey silence of the Australian bush where, with little more than their hands to help them, they had to make their home. Their warders, the soldiers of the New South Wales Corps, had small interest in the planting of such a miserable settlement. But Governor Phillip, surrounded by indifference and despair, could see the vision of the future and, driven on by his courage, these poorest of colonizers somehow survived.

They did more than survive; they founded a prosperous colony, so that when free immigrants began to come to New South Wales they found comfort and plenty. But it was not until the beginning of the 1820s, a few years after the end of the Napoleonic Wars, that these immigrants began to arrive in steadily increasing numbers. And many found the fortunes they sought, for during the next twenty years, with only one brief period of depression, the prosperity of the colony grew as its numbers increased.

During these years Sydney became a thriving city, very different from the forlorn encampment of tents pitched on the edge of the unknown a half-century before. There were many fine

I

buildings. In 1838 Governor Gipps, writing to Lord Glenelg, Secretary of State for the Colonies, mentions the existence of 'one Government House, eleven Churches, four Gaols, one Lunatic Asylum, one Watch-house, three Courthouses, one National School, one Signal House, one Police Office, and numerous other places of separate confinement'. In a few weeks he hoped to begin 'another Gaol, three or four more Courthouses, two Watch-houses, a Police Station, and another Church'.[1] But these stone structures were often isolated in the midst of grassy spaces, or cramped by tumble-down hovels.

The roads of the colony had been marked out as, year after year, the country settlers brought their produce to Sydney. These tracks were quagmires in winter, and masked by clouds of dust in summer. Sometimes it was almost impossible for drays to enter the city with their loads of wool and dairy produce.[2] Then sweating draymen shouted and cursed, while their whips cracked over the backs of the straining bullocks.

There were no watercourses along the sides of the streets, and even in dry weather pools of 'stagnant filth'[3] were found in the main thoroughfares. Paving stones had been placed around the principal pavements by 1840, but the narrow, winding streets were unnamed, and the houses unnumbered. At the end of 1841 the roads were being levelled and metalled by a gang of about forty convicts, but it was not until four years later that they were continued down to Circular Quay.

There was no sewerage and the insanitary conditions were appalling. Goats, pigs and cattle strayed about as they pleased; homeless mongrels wandered at will. The streets were supposed to be swept by convicts who were too sickly for heavy work, but to be put to do this was regarded as a heaven-sent opportunity to sleep in the sun. No one scrupled to leave dead animals in the roadway to be cleared away by someone else, when they became too noisome for endurance. An indignant letter in the *Herald* complained that a dead horse had been left in the neighbourhood of Sherry's Gardens, close to the South Head Road. The carcass, brought there several days before, had been skinned by the men who brought it. The writer had hoped the fly-blown remains would be removed when he saw a policeman come in sight, but the policeman had only come to cut off some meat for his dog.[4]

At that time the police had just received their new uniforms

[1] *H.R.A.* xix. 481.
[3] *Ibid.* 2 October 1841.
[2] *Herald*, 25 November 1840.
[4] *Ibid.* 19 November 1841.

—blue jackets with inner breastings of velvet, fine yellow cashmere waistcoats, and greenish-brown trousers. The buttons on their jackets were silver, and they carried blue truncheons. As the *Herald* remarked,[5] the uniform must have been far too heavy for the climate. There was need for police, especially at night, for the streets were only dimly lighted, and there were far too many opportunities for violence and robbery.

The convicts and ex-convicts were chiefly responsible for the constant undercurrent of crime, drunkenness, and immorality. The press complained continually of the 'large numbers of disorderly houses'[6] which were found all over the city, but 'particularly at the south end of Elizabeth Street'.[7] The sly-grog shops flourished, while brutal sports, like organized dog-fighting, were popular with the baser element of the population. Drunken carters and draymen were a menace to the safety of sober citizens, and there were protests against the practice of many masters lending their assigned servants their horses after sundown. The men made a habit of galloping furiously through the streets, 'to the great danger of the populace'.[8]

It was a city of sharp contrasts of wealth and poverty. Great landowners, like William Charles Wentworth, lived in almost feudal magnificence. Their shining carriages bumped and swayed through the streets, and their womenfolk enjoyed the leisurely life made possible by assigned labour. But the old lags went begging and kicked through the dust, careless of the beauty of the blue harbour which lay before them.

It was the harbour which, then as now, gave the city its indestructible beauty. Travellers compared it to the Bay of Naples, or the Lakes of Killarney, and became lyrical in describing 'a panoramic landscape as vast, varied and magnificent as any the world contains'.[9] The graceful sailing ships dipped and glided across its waters, before anchoring beside the crowded quays. And among the white sails moving over the harbour one golden spring day in September 1838, were those of the *Emerald Isle*. She was at the end of a voyage from India, and on board were Captain and Mrs Chisholm with their two little sons.

Caroline Chisholm was thirty years old, tall and stately, with a serene face lit by grey eyes. There could have been little that her eyes did not see as she looked about her. The shuffling old

[5]*Ibid.* 20 November 1840. [6]*Ibid.* 17 July 1840.
[7]*Australian*, 20 November 1841. [8]*Herald*, 28 August 1840
[9]Sir Roger Therry, *Reminiscences* (1863), p. 38.

lags dressed in shameful yellow; the vigorous free colonists; and
the fine gentlemen with well-brushed side-whiskers. And in the
motley throng were a few free immigrants who had not yet found
work, and were without food or shelter. It was Captain Chisholm,
a Scotsman, who heard the voices of some Highlanders. They
could speak no English, but he was able to talk with them in
Gaelic. He gave them money to buy food, but it was his wife, with
quick common-sense, who suggested they should buy axes and
ropes, so that they could become wood-cutters. This they did and
were most successful.[10]

The Chisholms saw few other unemployed immigrants, for the
colony was then enjoying unclouded prosperity. That day of their
meeting with the Highlanders, Caroline Chisholm must have
looked beyond the dust and the depraved, hopeless faces of the
old lags to the blue harbour. There, with sails furled, lay the
rows of ships beside the wharves. Some had brought free immigrants to a colony which had first been founded for prisoners. It
was only two years later that the last convicts were to be disembarked. After that, immigrant ships alone would bring the
free labour which was to give New South Wales strength and
greatness. Caroline Chisholm was far-sighted, and during her
first days in Sydney she probably saw something of the future.
Her own future was to become bound to that of the colony, and
of all cities Sydney was to be the one 'of her heart's choice'.[11]

[10]Eneas Mackenzie, *Memoirs of Mrs. Caroline Chisholm*, p. 23.
[11]As quoted by E. Dwyer Gray, *S.M.H.*, 16 February 1924.

1

Early Years, 1808-40

ENGLAND AND INDIA

Mrs Chisholm was born in or near Northampton in 1808. Her
father, William Jones, was a yeoman farmer and the family seem
to have been comfortably well-to-do. Very little is known of her
early life, though in later years she told one charming story of her
childhood. Her father had invited an old soldier to stay with
the family and his exciting tales of distant lands inspired Caroline
to invent a migration game. Using a wash-hand basin she 'made
boats of broad-beans; expended all [her] money in touchwood
dolls, removed families, located them in the bed-quilt and sent
the boats, filled with wheat, back to their friends'. Having upset
the basin, which was supposed to be the sea, she was punished
and forced to carry on the game afterwards in a dark cellar 'with
a rushlight stuck upon a tin kettle'.[1] The most remarkable part
of the game was that she had a Wesleyan minister and a Catholic
priest in the same boat, and she spent hours settling the disputes
of two quarrelsome colonists. This was her first attempt at colonization, and it was made before she was seven years old.

Her father died early and left her mother to educate Caroline,
and her brothers and sisters. I have found it impossible to discover how many children there were, and whether they were
older or younger than Caroline; but it is recorded that as a girl
she visited the sick of the village, and helped them when they
were in need. She was brought up to look on philanthropic labour
as a part of her everyday life. And in this upbringing of the North-
hampton farmer's young daughter is seen evidence of the
quickened social conscience of that time. The moral sense which
in the eighteenth century had driven John Howard and Elizabeth
Fry to try to improve the state of the prisons was by then stirring

[1]Eneas Mackenzie, *Memoirs*, pp. 3-4. Mackenzie, who seems to have
known her well, quotes the story from a letter she wrote to a friend
in Sydney.

the rich and comparatively well-to-do. There was scope for their labours in the misery which then prevailed; for, disrupting the social structure and adding to the confusion of post-war conditions, were the effects of the rapid growth of industry, and the final stages of enclosure.

It was not remarkable then, that Caroline Jones should have been reared in philanthropic ways, but it was remarkable that she should have taken her philanthropic work so seriously. Suffering of any kind always moved her to indignant pity, and the suffering she saw about her made her resolve to devote her life to philanthropy. In an ordinary young woman this resolve might have been cast aside to take its place among lost dreams, but Caroline Jones was no ordinary young woman. When she was twenty-two her resolve was so strong that after 'other advantageous offers for her hand' had been refused, and Captain Archibald Chisholm of the East India Company asked her to marry him, she consented only on condition that he should leave her free to do any philanthropic work she wished.[2]

He consented willingly, though she insisted he should think over the proposition for a month. The agreement was loyally kept through a long lifetime, for he not only left her free to work herself but helped her with a selfless devotion.

Either just before, or immediately after, her marriage she became a convert to the Roman Catholic Church. Captain Chisholm was a Catholic; he was thirteen years her senior, and she was very much in love with him; his influence was probably the final factor in her decision. They would have wished to avoid the possible family complications which often arise in a marriage of mixed religions; but certainly hers was no mere conversion of convenience. It was not in Caroline Chisholm's character to make such a change of faith unless her whole heart was behind it. In a young woman who had been brought up a Protestant in an intolerant age her decision must have taken great moral courage.

For two years after their marriage the Chisholms lived at Brighton; then Captain Chisholm sailed for Madras at the beginning of 1832, and his wife followed him a few months later. There she found an outlet for her energies. The daughters of the soldiers in the barracks were running wild, and she determined to establish a school where they could be given useful training. As the wife of a junior officer she must have found it difficult to put her plan into effect, but at this time sweet voiced

[2]Eneas Mackenzie, *Emigrants' Guide to Australia* (1853), p. 5.

Mrs Chisholm, with her dark red hair, began to prove the power of that persuasive charm for which she was later to be famed. She enlisted the help of friends, and in five days the sum of two thousand rupees was raised by 'a few gentlemen'. The Governor of Madras, Sir Frederick Adams, gave £20.[3] All difficulties were overcome, and 'The Female School of Industry for the Daughters of European Soldiers' was founded.[4]

The school was a great success, and the government soon gave assistance by subsidies. It was a forerunner of the 'homecraft' school of to-day, though the 'three R's' were taught as well as cooking and housekeeping. The organization and teaching were amazingly modern. There was a school mistress and a matron, but the pupils governed themselves by a system of committees.

During the six years she spent in Madras, her two eldest sons were born, and their care, as well as the running of the school, kept Mrs Chisholm well occupied. At the end of those years her husband was granted sick leave, and he and his wife decided to spend it in Australia with their family, instead of returning to England like most other Anglo-Indians. The *Emerald Isle*, in which they sailed, was chartered by the Australian Association of Bengal, a body formed to encourage 'facilitation of communication with, and resort to the Australian colonies'[5] at that time, for Indian interest in New South Wales was growing. Caroline Chisholm was always eager to visit new lands, and meet new people. The woman who, as a child, had played a game of colonization, could have needed little urging to set out on a voyage to the antipodes, where she would see the youngest English colonies.

They embarked at Madras on 23 March 1838. The *Emerald Isle* was a new ship of 551 tons and, grossly overloaded, had to put into Mauritius for repairs. Here she stayed over a month while her passengers found lodging on shore. Adelaide, the capital of South Australia, was sighted on 24 July, and there again the *Emerald Isle* was laid up for a month. That time spent in Adelaide may well have had a significant effect on Mrs Chisholm's later attitude towards the Wakefield system of colonization. South Australia was founded under Wakefield's influence and when the Chisholms were in Adelaide the faults in the model colony had become evident. They went on from Adelaide to spend three

[3] *Sidney's Emigrants' Journal* (Sydney, 1850), p. 262.
[4] By 1853 this school had become 'the noble Orphanage that graces Madras' (*Emigrants' Guide*, p. 73).
[5] Journal of John Dickson Loch (1837-39) passenger on the *Emerald Isle*, now in the possession of Mrs Evelyn Snodgrass, Melbourne.

weeks in Hobart Town before making sail for Sydney. It was a long seven months' voyage, and the Chisholm family must have been glad to leave their cramped quarters and unpack their boxes.

After spending the few days in the city, during which they met the Highlanders, Captain and Mrs Chisholm found a small cottage at Windsor, and set up house there. For the next year they lived quietly, making many friends, and learning a great deal about conditions in the colony. During this time they enjoyed the peace of happy family life; they were never to find that peace again until Caroline Chisholm was old and ill, and her husband impoverished. Their third son was born at the end of the year and, at the beginning of 1840, Captain Chisholm was recalled to active service in the Chinese 'Opium War'. By then his wife and children were so contentedly settled that there seems to have been no thought of their returning to either India or England.

At the time Captain Chisholm left New South Wales the prosperity which the colony had enjoyed was passing; Caroline Chisholm saw many signs of the coming depression and, whenever she visited Sydney, was most concerned by the numbers of unemployed immigrants wandering the streets.

THE IMMIGRATION SYSTEM

It was not until 1831 that the British government had instituted a scheme of assisted emigration. Before then all the free immigrants who arrived in New South Wales were people of independent means who paid their own passages. In England there was a widespread ignorance of the colony and indifference to its future. Those who thought about colonies at all believed that all other dependencies would follow the example of the United States. Moreover, Adam Smith, the father of British economics, considered that under the mercantile system then prevailing, though the colonial trade was valuable, England 'derives nothing but loss from the dominion she assumes over her colonies'.[1] Therefore, argued the government, what was the use in encouraging a profitless colonial empire if it was bound in the very nature of things to disintegrate. The disintegration of the Spanish and Portuguese colonial empires after the Napoleonic Wars gave point to this argument.

But there was one way in which colonies were useful; they were a place to which unwanted people could be sent. The convicts had been dumped in New South Wales and now

[1]Adam Smith, *The Wealth of Nations* (1934 ed.), ii. 112.

England, with a rapidly increasing population, was burdened
with unemployed. And despite the steady supply of convicts
provided by the harsh penal code and discontent in England,
the colony was in urgent need of labour. But the official mind
moved slowly; it was not until Edward Gibbon Wakefield
interested the government in his theory of colonization that it
was decided to send numbers of assisted emigrants to New
South Wales.

The gist of Wakefield's theory was 'firstly the sale of colonial
waste land at a uniform fixed price. Secondly, the use of the
whole or a fixed proportion of the revenue from land sales in
emigration. Thirdly, a judicious selection of emigrants on the
grounds of age, sex and social position, preference being given
to young married couples.'[2]

The 'progressive element' in the scheme was the relationship
between land sales and emigration. This appealed to the thrifty
home government, which saw the opportunity for removing some
of the surplus English·population, and at the same time of supply-
ing the demand for labour in New South Wales. But the home
government was not wholly concerned with such mercenary
considerations. By the scheme of assisted emigration it also hoped
to correct the disparity between the sexes in the colony, since
one of the many unfortunate results of transportation was
the disproportionate number of men to women in the population
of New South Wales.[3] Fewer female than male convicts were
sent out; for women were generally given lighter sentences. Then,
during the 'twenties, when the free immigrants began to arrive
in larger numbers, the majority of the newcomers were still men
— as was natural where pioneering had to be done. This disparity
between the sexes in a predominantly criminal population was
causing grave moral evils, and so the home government resolved
to send large numbers of female emigrants to New South Wales.

The praiseworthy resolve was rather spoilt by its poor execution for, as most of the women sent were from orphanages and
workhouses, their moral character was questionable. Moreover,
if they were of good character when they set out, they were often
corrupted on board ship, because of the insufficient protection
given them on the long voyage. However, the government per-

[2]R. C. Mills, *The Colonization of Australia, 1829-42* (1915), p. 120.
[3]In 1821 the ratio of males to females was 100 to 37. By 1833 it was
100 to 36. In 1841, although the influx of free immigrants had begun,
the ratio was still 100 to 50. (Ralph Mansfield, *Analytical View of the
Census of New South Wales*, 1841.)

sisted in its effort, and during the next few years succeeded in sending large numbers of both male and female emigrants to New South Wales.

By the time Caroline Chisholm arrived in the colony there were two systems of assisted immigration operating concurrently. There was the old government scheme instituted in 1831, by which, from 1835 onwards, immigration of both women and men was entirely free; and there was the bounty system, introduced in 1835 because of the complaints made of the older scheme.

When first introduced the idea was that bounties should be given to individual settlers to bring out the number of suitable immigrants they desired. In this way it was hoped to temper the supply of immigrants to the demand. But it was soon found that the settlers could not introduce the immigrants they wanted. To do so individually was costly and they could not select the immigrants in far-away England. They had to depend on agents in the homeland, and gradually the bounty permits were transferred. The shipping agents applied for, and were granted, permits in their own names, and no mention was made of the colonists.

It was when the bounties were substantially increased that the system was abused; for it was a profitable source of income to the shipowners, and the ships were crowded as full as possible, often regardless of the suitability of the immigrants, or of their comfort. There was an Immigration Board which met in Sydney, and could refuse to authorize the payment of bounty on any particular immigrant. The immigrants were supposed to bring certificates of character with them, but these were sometimes forged, and the Board had no means of proving the forgery.

Nevertheless, the colonists found the bounty system more satisfactory than the government scheme, chiefly because it was less costly and, on the whole, brought out a better type of immigrant.[4] The British government favoured the older system, but when a very large number of bounty orders was issued from the colony it was forced to put 'an entire stop . . . to the Emigration managed by Government Officers'.[5] The last government ship berthed in Port Jackson in February 1840.

One of the worst faults in the immigration system had been the lack of any plan for dispersing the immigrants after their arrival in Sydney. There was an Immigration Barracks, and there the government immigrants had been maintained for a month,

[4] Gipps to Stanley, 14 May 1842, Memorandum on Immigration (*H.R.A.* xxii. 47).

[5] Stanley to Gipps, 14 October 1841 (*H.R.A.* xxi. 545).

if necessary, after they disembarked, so that potential employers had an opportunity to engage them. The bounty immigrants were only allowed to stay on board ship for forty-eight hours after berthing and then, if not engaged, were put off to find work as best they could. According to the bounty regulations, every single woman was supposed to be under the protection of a married couple and to remain in their care until otherwise provided for, but these regulations were often evaded.

When the older government scheme of immigration was discontinued, the method of dealing with the bounty immigrants was altered. They were allowed to stay on board ship with full rations for ten days, or else the captain had to find them suitable accommodation on shore. After the ten days' grace, if still unemployed, they were turned loose in Sydney.

Although there were to be no more government immigrants the Immigration Barracks was still occupied by the Government Immigration Agent. He gave the bounty immigrants any information they needed, and told them where they were most likely to find work. Prospective employers, too, could enquire from the agent whether he knew of any immigrants who might suit them, but there was no registry office, and no system of country dispersion.

While conditions were good and the demand for labour was insistent, this defect does not seem to have been evident. Individual immigrants, especially women, sometimes suffered; and the men with large families of small children, who were unproductive of labour but needed extra rations, sometimes found it difficult to get work. But the great majority seem to have found employment. Indeed, it was the settlers, rather than the immigrants, who suffered because of the lack of dispersion. They had to make a long, expensive trip to Sydney to try to engage immigrants, and if the ship came in early they were often disappointed, so great was the demand for labour.[6]

This demand increased during the period of prosperity at the end of the 'thirties. There had been good seasons, and many inexperienced newcomers took up land without much knowledge of farming. Prices were high, and over-optimistic graziers began to buy stock and speculate in the expectation that the good times would last indefinitely.

The speculation in land was encouraged by the introduction of Wakefield's system in South Australia. There, land was sold

[6]Report of the Immigration Agent, I. D. Pinnock, March 1840 (Immigration Papers, La Trobe Library, Melbourne).

at 12s. an acre, and it became necessary to raise the price in New South Wales so that sales of South Australian land would not be affected. It was raised from 5s. to 12s. as a minimum price for the acre in 1839, the regulation to take effect when the remaining 300,000 acres of land offered at 5s. had been sold. The result was a frantic rush to buy the remaining 5s. lots, and a burst of hectic speculation.

During the first two years after Caroline Chisholm came to New South Wales the colony was passing through this time of feverish prosperity; but speculation was succeeded by depression and drought. The second colonial boom had broken. It was then that the lack of a system of dispersion of the immigrants began to cause widespread distress. The demand for labour declined sharply; and even old hands were thrown out of employment. During the boom Governor Gipps had been 'surrounded and solicited' by the colonists to increase the supply of labour by issuing large numbers of bounty orders. Gipps knew that transportation of convicts to New South Wales was to cease in 1840, and this, as well as 'the great apparent prosperity'[7] had influenced his decision to accede to the importunate demands.

In 1841, troubles in Canada were diverting the stream of emigration, and 20,103 immigrants brought out on bounty orders flooded into Sydney—as compared with the 6,637 who had arrived the year before.[8] Even without the depression such a number would have been too great for a population of 130,856 to absorb quickly, but most of them arrived after the bubble of speculation had burst. When the ten days' grace allowed on the bounty ships was past, those who were unengaged crowded into Sydney. Some found casual work, others did not find even that. There was still a demand for labour in the interior, but the immigrants were largely taken from urban populations and often preferred to starve in the city rather than brave the terrors of the unknown bush. Those who suffered most were the men with large families of small children, and the immigrant girls. It was the plight of these girls, cast adrift in a strange city, that aroused the compassion of Caroline Chisholm.

THE CONQUEST OF PREJUDICE

After Captain Chisholm had sailed for China, the misfortunes of the homeless immigrant girls troubled her so greatly that she

[7]Gipps to Russell, 24 December 1841 (*H.R.A.* xxi. 607).
[8]R. B. Madgwick, *Immigration into Eastern Australia* (1937), p. 223.

took some of them into her own small home at Windsor. She gave
shelter to as many as nine at one time, and found positions for
them among her growing circle of friends. She also found immediate work for others, but those she managed to help were an
infinitesimal number compared with the hundreds still in urgent
need. To be effective, assistance had to be given on a large, public
scale.

She saw this very clearly, and yet she hesitated; 'as a female
and almost a stranger in the Colony [she] felt diffident'.[1] Caroline
Chisholm knew that if she was to help the homeless immigrant
women it could be done in no half-hearted fashion. She would
have to go into the streets and argue with procuresses and reclaim
prostitutes. She knew, too, that such an undertaking would be
considered so outrageous that it would call forth a storm of condemnation. The prejudice of the time against women taking any
part in public affairs was so strong that only the bravest dared
to flout it. And at heart she was conventional, and had no wish
to flout public prejudice. Added to this was the fact that she
was a Roman Catholic, and the animosity towards Catholics was
intense, as any reader of the contemporary press is often reminded.

She later made little mention of it, but the thought of her
children's welfare must have troubled her most. If she began
public work they would lose something of the care which only
she could give them.

As she hesitated, torn by doubts, the depression was advancing,
and the numbers of unemployed in the streets were more notice-
able. In her pity for the women Mrs Chisholm began to feel
that when any girl abandoned the struggle to find work and fell
a prey to the procuresses of the brothels, she herself was 'not
clear of her sin',[2] because she had not done all she could to
prevent it.

At last, in January 1841, her conscience drove her to write to
Lady Gipps, the wife of the Governor, and ask her for help.
'From that time,' she wrote later, 'I never ceased in my exertions.'[3]
She met every immigrant ship which anchored in the harbour
and, 'gathering the unprotected girls around her [gave] them
sound motherly advice, and when necessary sheltered and protected them in her own home'.[4] At the busy wharves she was
soon well known — a dignified figure wearing a black brocaded

[1] Caroline Chisholm, *Female Immigration*, p. 2.
[2] *Ibid*. p. 4.   [3] *Ibid*. p. 3.
[4] J. F. Hogan, *The Irish in Australia* (Melbourne, 1888), p. 131.

silk dress with a white lace collar. She had decided that the best way to provide for the girls would be to establish a 'home' from which they could find good positions. She herself would care for them in this home and, true to her ideals, she intended that her services should be given without payment to all in need, whatever their race or religion.

This was her plan, and she knew it would encounter 'the opposition of some, and the lukewarmness or actual hostility of others'.[5] After writing to Lady Gipps she wrote several letters to the Governor, explaining what she hoped to do, and asking his help, but the letters were 'merely acknowledged with the severest official brevity'.[6]

Then she thought of soliciting the aid of the press in winning public sympathy for her venture. Two of her friends, however, refused to visit the *Sydney Herald* office and her own distaste for such publicity is apparent from her statement that for three weeks she 'hesitated and suffered much'.[7] At the end of that time she found courage to see the proprietors of the *Sydney Herald* herself and impressed them with her personality and her plan. But they were reluctant to give open support until she had won the consent of the governor.

By this time her proposal to found the 'home' had become fairly well known in official circles. The general opinion seems to have been that Mrs Chisholm was a lunatic,[8] for who in their senses would go out into the streets of Sydney and gather in homeless girls unless they were paid to do it? As well as this contemptuous general indifference there was extreme Protestant and Catholic opposition. The many ardent Protestants were afraid of her 'Popish Plot', and the ardent Catholics were afraid she would not proselytize for their faith. As for Governor Gipps, he probably thought he had troubles enough without becoming involved in such a controversial proposition.

Gipps was a shrewd man but, like many others, he was deceived by the false prosperity of the boom. His large issue of bounty orders was a blunder for which he was severely censured by the Colonial Office,[9] and he honestly admitted his fault in 'having trusted too much to chances which could not be correctly calcu-

[5]*Female Immigration*, p. 4.
[6]Hogan, *op. cit.* p. 133.
[7]*Female Immigration*, p. 4.
[8]*Sidney's Emigrants' Journal* (1850), p. 270.
[9]Russell to Gipps, 16 July 1841, and Stanley to Gipps, 14 October 1841 (*H.R.A.* xxi. 429, 550).

lated, or with safety relied on'.[10] He was confident, however, that the large numbers of immigrants would be quickly absorbed, and though the government evidently provided the newcomers with tents and some rations there was no systematic effort made to disperse them inland.[11]

The Governor seems to have thought he could manage well enough without Mrs Chisholm's help, and he shared the prejudice of the time against the entry of women into public affairs. Sir George believed that woman's place was in the home, and it took a great deal to shake any of his beliefs. Nevertheless, Mrs Chisholm's persistence at last gained an interview with him.

It was a momentous meeting, and it also had its humorous side. Mrs Chisholm must often have seen the governor at public functions; his appearance was no surprise to her. He has been described as 'a stern but handsome man with keen black eyes and bushy black eyebrows. He looked every inch a Governor.'[12] In his portraits the character of the man is stamped on his face. It is an arresting face, keenly intelligent and shrewd; the face of a man who would stand no nonsense. But if Caroline Chisholm knew what Sir George looked like, she had the advantage of him. Sir George was quite unprepared for the appearance of a poised, charming young woman, who carried herself with gracious dignity. He later told a friend[13] that he 'expected to have seen an old lady in white cap and spectacles, who would have talked to me about my soul. I was amazed when my aide introduced a handsome, stately young woman who proceeded to reason the question as if she thought her reason and experience, too, worth as much as mine.' But though the Governor was impressed, he was not won over. When she insisted later on a second interview, he told her frankly that she had 'overrated the powers of [her] own mind'.[14] It is to his credit, however, that in spite of the anti-Catholic feeling of the time, he believed her to be disinterested in her aims. Sir George evidently did not want to commit himself to the support of what he considered a quixotic scheme. He tried to delay making a decision, though Mrs Chisholm says she thought 'that under the existing circumstances [the desperate situation of

[10]Gipps to Russell, 24 December 1841 (*ibid.* p. 607).

[11]Gipps to Stanley, 2 April 1842, 14 May 1842, 23 May 1842 (*ibid.* xxi. 3, 43, 67).

[12]George Gordon McCrae, 'Some Recollections of Early Melbourne in the 'Forties', *Victorian Historical Magazine*, i (1911-12), 114.

[13]*Sidney's Emigrants' Journal* (1850), p. 271.

[14]*Ibid.*

the immigrant girls] he would not refuse my request though he would rather not grant it'.[15]

Mrs Chisholm was not to be put off—she was determined to carry out her plan and, as always, whenever she was in doubt or trouble, she prayed most earnestly for divine guidance. Her religion was the mainspring of her life, and during this testing time she felt herself very close to her God. While in church on Easter Sunday, 1841, she was given strength to make a great vow. In her own words, she 'was enabled at the altar of our Lord, to make an offering of my talents to the God who gave them. I promised to know neither country nor creed, but to serve all justly and impartially. I asked only to be enabled to keep these poor girls from being tempted by their need to mortal sin, and resolved that to accomplish this, I would in every way sacrifice my feelings — surrender all comfort — nor, in fact, consider my own wishes or feelings, but wholly devote myself to the work I had in hand.'[16] From that moment she believed she had the divine blessing for her work and a mission to fulfil. It was from this belief that she drew strength to struggle against all discouragements.

She considered the idea of publishing about forty letters, 'detailing the miseries of some of the young women', but she decided against this, for in the interests of the colony she would have 'lamented making a passing and transient distress known in England'.[17] She managed to gain a hearing with the women who were later to form the Ladies' Committee for the home. Lady Gipps was one, and others were Lady O'Connell, Lady Dowling, Mrs Richard Jones, Mrs Roger Therry, Mrs W. Mackenzie, Mrs J. Wallace and Miss E. Chambers. They gave her no material help, but lent an aura of propriety to her design.

The opposition of some members of her own church especially saddened her at this time, for when they knew that she was determined to work 'for all and through all', several of the leading Catholics threw 'every possible obstacle in her way'. She was 'daily and hourly requested to give up all thoughts of the Home'.[18]

In desperation she determined to spend a few days by herself at Parramatta to win some peace of mind. She missed the boat, and decided to walk quietly for a little while. Her feelings 'had been used as a doormat' and she wished to confront her friends

[15]*Female Immigration*, p. 5.
[16]*Ibid.* p. 4. 　　　　　　　[17]*Ibid.* p. 5.
[18]*Sidney's Emigrants' Journal* (1850), p. 270; *Female Immigration*, p. 6.

again with a brave face. As she walked past Petty's Hotel she
came upon 'a frail beauty' and found that she knew the girl. She
was a very beautiful Highlander named Flora, and the last time
Mrs Chisholm had seen her she had been living with the other
bounty immigrants, camped in tents around the Immigration
Barracks. Mrs Chisholm had noticed then that a wealthy married
settler had been attracted to the girl, and she had tried to warn
her of the danger, but Flora was heedless. Now she was flushed
with rum, and bent on suicide. For an hour Mrs Chisholm paced
beside her up and down the beach expostulating and comforting.
In the end she found her lodgings and at last left the girl after
she had promised not to throw herself in the river. The incident
had proved to her, better than anything else could have done,
that she was right and her critics were wrong. She turned
back to the city; from that moment fear left her.[19]

The distress of the immigrant girls was beginning to cause a
public outcry. The *Chronicle* of 11 September 1841 reported that
2,557 immigrants had arrived during the preceding seventeen
days, and published an indignant letter telling the story of one of
them, Mary Teague. She was charged with drunkenness, though
she protested she was not drunk, but faint with hunger, as she
had had no food since the day before, when she was put off the
ship. Because she had no money to pay the fine, she was placed
in the stocks, and three days later she was found in a ditch by
the roadside, too weak to move.

Suggestions followed that the government should give the
bounty immigrants shelter in the Immigration Barracks, particularly, says one correspondent, 'as part of the Immigration Barracks is put to no earthly use'.[20]

While public feeling was growing Mrs Chisholm persisted in
reminding the Governor of her plan, and she at last won his
consent to establish the home — but only on the condition that
the government was to be put to no expense; and for this she
had to give a written guarantee.[21] Gipps was taking no chances;
extra expenditure inevitably called down the wrath of the home
government upon him.

On 26 October the *Chronicle* announced that a 'Female Immigrants Home' was to be established under 'the prudent and experienced direction of Mrs. Chisholm'. She was granted the use

[19]*Female Immigration*, p. 9.
[20]*Chronicle*, 14 September 1841; *Herald*, 15 September 1841.
[21]*Report*, Select Committee on Colonization from Ireland, H. of L.
(1847), xxiii. 408.

of a part of the old wooden Immigration Barracks which stood in Bent Street, near the present Government Printing Office. A storeroom fourteen feet square was cleared for her accommodation, and when she took possession of her 'Office', closed the door, and 'reflected on what [she] had been compelled to endure' for this, her first feelings were those of indignation that such a trifle should have been so long withheld, but, characteristically, she shrugged away her anger and 'better feelings followed'.

Her description of how she spent that first night is so eloquent both of her courage and resource, that I give it in her own words: 'I retired, weary, to rest. Scarce was the light out, when I fancied from the noise I heard that dogs must be in the room, and in some terror I got a light. What I experienced at seeing rats in all directions I cannot describe. My first act was to throw on a cloak, and get at the door with the intent of leaving the building. My second thoughts were, if I did so, my desertion would cause much amusement and ruin my plan. I therefore lighted a second candle, and seating myself on my bed, kept there until three rats descending from the roof alighted on my shoulders. I felt that I was getting into a fever, and that in fact I should be very ill before morning; but to be out-generalled by rats was too bad. I got up with some resolution. I had two loaves and some butter (for my office, bedroom and pantry were one). I cut the bread into slices, placed the whole in the middle of the room, put a dish of water convenient, and with a light by my side I kept my seat on the bed reading "Abercrombie" and watching the rats until four in the morning. I at one time counted thirteen, and never less than seven did I observe at the dish during the entire night. The following night I gave them a similar treat, with the addition of arsenic, and, in this manner passed my first four nights at the home.'[22]

[22]*Female Immigration*, pp. 10-11.

The Female Immigrants' Home

THE HOME ESTABLISHED

Caroline Chisholm was no rebel against established conventions. She was too occupied with practical difficulties to consider the rights and wrongs of the conditions she saw about her, too busy to think of any but the affairs of the moment. First, she had to decide how her own family was to be managed. She had hoped to have her three little boys living near her, but she found this would not do, and after a short time sent the two elder children back to Windsor, where they were well looked after by Miss M. Galvin, of whom she speaks with heartfelt gratitude. She still kept the youngest with her, though several friends advised her to send him away. Then an epidemic broke out among the immigrants and she saw that if she was to continue her work, she must part with him. This realization troubled her greatly, and for a few hours she was again racked with indecision. By this time, besides the rat-ridden storeroom, she had been granted four more rooms in the Barracks, and these had been thrown into one for the home. In this large room she had ninety-four women sleeping and, that night of her indecision, she says: 'as was usual with me I saw the girls after they retired to rest . . . I asked if they had any place to go to if I turned them out; not one had a place of shelter. On my return to the office, I found a poor woman waiting for a white gown, "to make her dead bairn decent". I went into my room, packed up my little fellow's wardrobe, and the next day he was at Windsor. This was the last sacrifice it was God's will to demand.'[1]

In her published letters and pamphlets this is the only reference she makes to that great personal sacrifice. During her later work one day each week was 'inviolably set apart'[2] for her family, and probably she was able to make some such arrangement while she managed the home.

[1] *Memoirs*, p. 43. [2] *Emigrants' Guide*, pp. 28-29.

Her children in later years all seem to have had a great love and admiration for their mother. If they had been neglected critics would certainly have flung the accusation against her. But after she sent her 'little fellow' away to Windsor, her family had to take second place because, to Caroline Chisholm, the work which was intended to give others domestic happiness had to come first.

She arranged for a committee of fourteen women to help in the management of the home, and among these were those she had first interested in her plan. In particular, she mentioned Lady Gipps as giving her 'kind and generous support'.[3] Committee members, however, had little to do beyond allowing their names to be associated with the home; it was Mrs Chisholm who was the hard-working secretary.

She was an unpaid secretary. She seems to have had no income beyond what her husband earned as a captain in the East India Company's service, and her work was wholly dependent on public subscription. Governor Gipps had made it quite clear that she could expect no financial help from the government. Nevertheless, so convinced was she of the justice of her cause that she does not seem to have felt any qualms about embarking upon what was really a gamble. She went into the venture with the serene assurance that the Lord would provide, and later the Lord did provide, in the shape of donations from a grateful public; but it was her own courage and ability which were to win that public support.

The women at the home had been brought into shelter entirely by her own efforts. She took some of them from the streets, and ventured alone at night into the notorious 'Rocks' region to gather them in. Sometimes she was given unexpected help; one rough man came and told her where she might find a girl who was in danger. He was fearful his good deed would become known and asked her to keep it secret, stammering, 'I should be jeered at past bearing; but somehow it lay on my mind — I ought to tell you'.[4] Mrs Chisholm found this girl and brought her to the Barracks. She found other women in Hyde Park, and many more came directly from the immigrant ships. When she began her work she estimated that there were six hundred unemployed women in the city. Many of those she received into the home had 'slept for nights in the Government Domain . . . seeking the sheltered recesses of the Rocks rather than encounter

[3]*Female Immigration*, p. 10.
[4]*Ibid.* p. 59.

the Dangers of the Streets'.[5] One party of sixty-four girls had only
14s. 3d. among them.[6]

She established a registry office at the Barracks, the only free
one in Sydney at the time. She was able to find positions for some
of the women in Sydney, but her chief object was to take them
into the country where, despite depressed conditions, there was
still a steady demand for labour. The majority of the women
themselves were better fitted for rough country labour than for
work in the town. From the very beginning, when Governor
Gipps had granted her the use of the Immigration Barracks, she
had set about systematically discovering the demand for labour
in the different country districts. To do this she had sent out
hundreds of copies of a circular to clergymen, police magistrates
and other responsible members of the country communities. The
text[7] deserves quoting in full, for it shows both her organizing
ability and her understanding of the labour problems.

Sir,
    I am endeavouring to establish a Home for Female Immi-
grants and have little doubt but funds will soon be raised to
enable me to accomplish this; and as my first object is to facilitate their obtaining employment in the country, I shall feel
obliged if you will favour my intention (should you *approve*
of the same) by giving me the information I require regarding
your district and any suggestions you may think useful will be
considered a favour.
    1st. Whether girls who at home have merely been accus-
tomed to milk cows, wash and the common household work
about a farm would readily get places? At what wages? and how
many do you think would in the course of the next two years be
required?
    2nd. Good servants, such as housemaids and cooks — the
rate of wages and the probable number required for the same
period?
    3rd. Married couples with small families, say two or three
children, ditto?
    4th. Could employment and protection be found for boys and
girls from 7 to 14 years of age?
    5th. Have you had opportunities of observing if the young
women can save any part of their wages? for they are generally
of opinion that nothing can be saved in the country, every

[5] *Report*, Colonization from Ireland, H. of L. (1847), xxiii. 407.
[6] *Memoirs*, p. 53.
[7] *Sidney's Emigrants' Journal* (1850), pp. 276-7.

article of wearing apparel being so much dearer than in town?

6th. What would be the cheapest and the best way of conveying the young women to your district?

I have to observe that the servants will be classed according to their qualifications, and distributed fairly so that those who are absent will have an equal chance of getting a good servant with those who are present. Subscribers of one pound will have servants selected and sent to them without trouble; it will, however, be necessary that an order should be sent to cover the expense of their conveyance.

I require by donations to raise what will furnish a house and by subscriptions I expect to support the institution. I am of opinion that when families in the interior can get servants sent them, we shall not hear of young women suffering distress and losing character for the want of a situation. I shall feel obliged if you will favour me with a reply by the tenth of November next.

I have taken the liberty to annnex a subscription list, and I shall feel obliged if you would leave it in the hands of some person to receive subscriptions and acquaint me with the same that it may appear in the papers.

This circular is dated 21 October 1841, a few days before it was publicly announced that she had begun her work. There are several interesting points to be noted in it. She stressed the fact that she was depending on the public for subscription and support for the home. Those in the country who wanted to have a servant selected for them had to subscribe £1, and pay the expenses of the servant's conveyance to the interior. This was a fee for a special arrangement; no charge was made later when parties of immigrants were taken inland and engagements made after they had already arrived in the country. It is significant that from the very beginning Mrs Chisholm intended to help *all* immigrants and not only the immigrant girls. This is shown clearly by her reference to the married couples, and by the question regarding the boys and girls under fourteen. She was trying to find situations for the immigrants with large families of young children. The colonists had protested that they did not want this class of immigrant but the bounty agents took them to fill up the ships. She was also anxious to be able to tell the girls the exact conditions in the country, and whether they would be able to save any of their money.

Governor Gipps agreed to frank all her letters to the country,[8]

[8]*Report*, Colonization from Ireland, H. of L. (1847), xxiii. 414.

a considerable help, as in those days the postage for half an ounce
was 4d. to Parramatta, 7d. to either Windsor or Campbell Town,
10d. to Bathurst, and 1s. for three hundred miles. The governor
was being won over to her scheme, but when he discovered to
whom she was writing letters he sent for her in a great hurry,
and she found him in a state of excitement. 'Who, pray, are these
John Varleys and Dick Hogans and other people of whom I have
never heard since I've been in the Colony?' demanded Sir George.[9]
He had expected her to write to the wealthy pastoralists, who
could always afford to have a good supply of labour. When she
explained she was writing to small farmers, police magistrates,
and others who knew most about the demand for labour,
and who would employ immigrants sent to their districts,
he saw her wisdom and agreed to frank as many letters as she
wished.

Gipps was a powerful friend, and she won another, only less
important than the Governor. This was Bishop Broughton, leader
of the Church of England. Broughton, whose immense diocese
of Australia taxed all his abilities, was an old friend and school-
fellow[10] of Sir George Gipps. Mrs Chisholm probably approached
him even before the governor gave his consent to the establishment of the home. Certainly, she approached Mrs Broughton, and
Mrs Broughton may have prepared the way for her with the
bishop. At all events, after meeting Mrs Chisholm, the bishop
wrote to the Rev. Henry Stiles, his chaplain at Windsor.[11] He
was impressed both with Mrs Chisholm, and with her plans;
his letter requests the chaplain 'to assist in establishing any young
women of good character'. This letter is dated 21 October 1841,
the same day as Mrs Chisholm's general circular, and a few days
before the home was officially established. In a second letter to
Stiles, dated 17 November 1841, *after* the home was established,
Broughton shows clearly how his suspicion of anything 'Popish'
was struggling with his perception of her sincerity. He believed
that Caroline Chisholm had 'no views other than she professes' but
he feared that unconsciously she might be used 'as an agent
for others with deeper purposes'. He did not approve of the
establishment of the home, for it was a scheme which he thought
had never succeeded before, but he was 'at all times desirous of
giving aid in individual cases'. He found it impossible to give

[9] Samuel Sidney, *The Three Colonies of Australia*, p. 155.
[10] *Dictionary of National Biography*, under 'Bishop Broughton'.
[11] Bishop Broughton to Rev. H. T. Stiles, 21 October 1841. Stiles Papers
(ML).

Mrs Chisholm any open encouragement but he gave Stiles permission to act as he thought best and sent him £5 for Mrs Chisholm, with the stipulation that she should not know 'whence it comes'. The letter is a troubled one — Caroline Chisholm was a phenomenon which Broughton had rarely encountered. In his dilemma he discussed the matter with the Rev. R. Allwood, minister of St James' Church, and Allwood must have been convinced of Mrs Chisholm's sincerity, for he soon became one of her most ardent supporters.

Meanwhile, Broughton's permission to Stiles to act as he thought best had had important results. Stiles answered her circular of 21 October in terms which show the bishop's guiding hand. He wrote expressing his approval 'of a design which at the first view appears so entirely laudable', but he feared that as she was 'a devoted member of that part of the Catholic Church which renders allegiance to Rome', the immigrants in her charge 'would be *advised, restrained and protected* by the clergy of the Church of Rome'.

Mrs Chisholm's answer was such a 'frank and straight-forward avowal' of her objects,[12] that Stiles was won over, and forwarded a subscription for £2, which was almost certainly a part of the £5 Broughton had sent him. Mrs Chisholm considered Stiles 'the first honest opponent'[13] she had met with. His open championship of her cause swung the body of the Church of England to her support.

She had valuable support also from the leader of her own church. At this time the Roman Catholic Bishop, Polding, was in Europe, and the Rev. Francis Murphy had just succeeded Dr Ullathorne as Vicar-General of the diocese. It was, therefore, Murphy whom she asked to support the home. And though there is no record of how, or when, she made her request, Murphy, that 'priest of six-priest power',[14] soon became one of her staunchest supporters.

She had decided that the best way of transporting her girls from Sydney into the country was by bullock dray. The drays came into the city with wool and produce and returned empty to their various owners. She was anxious to get the first party of girls away as soon as possible, for in a few weeks she had no less than ninety-six on rations at the Barracks and, as she says,

[12]*Sidney's Emigrants' Journal* (1848), pp. 276-7.
[13]*Female Immigration*, p. 9.
[14]*Australian Encyclopaedia*, under 'Francis Murphy'.

this was 'a serious number'. Probably the government had made
some contribution to the rations, for at this early date she was
not well enough known to be supported entirely by voluntary
private donation.

She was lent a dray which was to take the first party into the
country. The morning came when the girls were to set off but,
Mrs Chisholm remarks ruefully, 'their fears overcame their good
resolutions and I had to send the dray away empty'.[15] The fear of
the town-bred for the bush was hard to overcome; there were
all manner of stories of blacks, bushrangers and bunyips to daunt
even the bravest hearts. She managed to keep her failure secret,
and the next morning she records triumphantly that she ordered
two drays and, as the girls were too afraid to go by themselves, she
went with them.

This first party probably numbered about sixteen, including
herself, for eight would have fitted comfortably into each dray
with room for their boxes. She went from farm to farm and
successfully placed every one of them. It is not clear if these girls
had situations waiting for them in the country or whether she
placed them as the drays passed through the different districts.
From the terms concerning private engagements set out in her
circular, however, it would seem as if they did not have definite
situations waiting for them when they left Sydney. If they had,
their prospective employers would have arranged their transport
themselves.

After this success she never faltered. From the time she had
first appealed to the editors of the leading newspapers they had
favoured her plan, but they had given no active support until
the governor had granted her the use of the Barracks. As soon
as she had his support, even though it was grudging in the beginning, the press, particularly the *Sydney Herald,* rallied to her side
and urged the public to support her with subscriptions and
rations.[16] It was this paper, too, which several times asked for
the co-operation of the settlers in the interior in lending their
drays. But this seems to have been after the first party had been
sent into the interior; for them she had somehow found the drays
herself.

After her first journey she established branches in several
country towns. These depots were a most important part of
her organization, and the hand-bill issued by one of them illustrates

[15] *Female Immigration,* p. 12.
[16] 23 November 1841, 2 December 1841.

their functions. It declared that 'persons requiring servants are provided with them on applying at this institution where a limited number of the most eligible class of immigrants arrive . . . from Sydney every week . . . The agent is in attendance daily between the hours of 9 and 12 in the morning and 4 to 6 in the evening'. Single women were supported at the depot, and single men were received when they were wanted. A few labourers arrived from Sydney every week. Married men were forwarded from Sydney two or three at a time 'if they were without children'.[17] The branch homes were in the charge of clergymen, and 'respectable residents'; doubtless these were the 'agents' mentioned.

Those wanting servants wrote to Mrs Chisholm stating the type of work, the wages, the description of servants required, and also the method of conveyance into the interior. The expense of transporting a servant to the Maitland district cost the employer 12s. 6d., which was 'not to be deducted from the wages of the servant unless the agreement entered into is broken on his or her part'.[18]

By December 1841, there were branches at Parramatta,[19] Liverpool and Campbell Town. The notice in the *Chronicle*[20] concerning this remarked that 'these resting places will enable families to make their way into the interior by daily marches, taking the chance of finding employment on their way'. At that time the funds of the 'parent home' — the Immigration Barracks — were 'too low to give anything more than shelter or protection with wood and water'. Mrs Chisholm hoped, therefore, that the branches would help the parent home, and this they did. It was found 'almost necessary to give one day's rations to each female at each house' but, the advertisement adds suggestively, 'money is wanted for this'. A branch was then needed at Yass, but it would have cost £60 to establish and was not founded until the next year.

The scope of the parent home had expanded. By the beginning of December a day school had been added to the registry office to keep the children of the immigrants from the streets.[21] Mrs Chisholm was now dealing with families as well as single girls.

[17]'Better Ties than Red Tape Ties', *Household Words*, iv (1852), 532.
[18]*Sidney's Emigrants' Journal* (1848), p. 57.
[19]The buildings used as the Parramatta Depot are still in existence. They are two brick cottages in what was once known as Providence Row, now Symington Terrace (information by courtesy of Miss Margaret Swann).
[20]18 December 1841.　　　　[21]*Herald*, 13 December 1841.

The expense of the school was met by the Rev. R. Allwood and the Rev. Francis Murphy. Allwood regularly visited the home twice a week to care for the religious instruction of the Anglican immigrants.[22] In this way he was able, as Broughton had suggested to Stiles, 'to guard and influence' the Anglican flock. Nevertheless, he does not seem to have had any doubts of Mrs Chisholm's sincerity and through the many years that they were associated he gave her all the support in his power. It was a friendship which testified to the Christian tolerance of both. In the same way Murphy watched over the religious education of the young Roman Catholics. The Presbyterians were also provided for, because the mistress who taught the children was a member of the Church of Scotland. There could have been little room for religious intolerance in such a school.

After Mrs Chisholm took her first parties away to the country, and organized the school and registry office at the Barracks, it seems likely that there were only a few women sleeping there. But by then she was caring for all the immigrants who were camped in tents on the grassy slopes about the ramshackle old building, and 'near Cooper's Distillery'.[23] In the description of the home given by Judge Therry, there is no mention of the big dormitory where the first homeless women had slept. He says[24] the Barracks was 'a building composed of a ground floor only, of curious construction. It was built of slabs through which the wind made free entrance by day and night, and it [the home] consisted of two rooms only, one a large, schoolroom like apartment, furnished with forms for those who came to transact business, and two or three wooden chairs, while the mistress of the Home sat at a small table, with a quire or two of paper before her, where she drew as many contracts of service in a few hours as the most expert clerk would prepare in a dozen . . . The other apartment in this rickety edifice was a small, comfortless sleeping apartment with furniture to match.'

Every contract for service was drawn up in triplicate: one copy for the immigrant, one for the employer, and one kept by Mrs Chisholm herself. In this way she ensured that those who passed through her hands should have good treatment, for there was little chance of the employer casting off his or her obligation, when there was such a complete record of the agreement made.

[22]*Ibid.* 2 December 1841.
[23]*Chronicle*, 23 November 1844; *Female Immigration*, p. 31.
[24]Therry, *Reminiscences*, p. 420.

She insisted that fair wages should be given. The average rates of wages at the time were:

For a single man, £20 a year with weekly rations:—Flour, 9 lbs.; meat, 10 lbs.; tea, 2 ozs.; sugar, 1½ lbs.[25]

For a single woman, £9 to £16 a year, with similar rations.[26]

For a married man and his wife and one child, it was £25 and weekly rations: Flour, 20 lbs.; meat, 18 lbs.; tea, 4 ozs.; sugar, 3 lbs.[27]

On 2 December 1841 the *Herald* gave a progress report of the engagements Mrs Chisholm had made since the home had opened at the end of October — a period of little more than a month. She had found situations for several families at £21 to £26 a year. Eleven children under thirteen were provided for at £2 10s. to £7 a year, and seventy-six female servants were employed at £9 to £16 a year. As fifty-eight of the latter had been taken into the country, she must have made at least two or three journeys inland in that short period. A few others had been given money and donations of bread, coffee, tea, rice, sugar and other supplies. The *Herald* again reminded settlers of her need for drays — a reminder which was repeated a week later; she had then placed fifty-four more people, and twenty-three of these were waiting to go into the interior. In the next week, sixty-three made engagements, and the majority of them went into the country.[28]

The largest numbers included in her parties were newly-arrived immigrants, but as the depression advanced, and new numbers were thrown out of work, she took 'Ticket-of-leave men, Emancipists, any persons that wanted work that would go into the country . . . English, Irish, Scotch, Episcopalians, Presbyterians, Catholics, Orangemen and Repealers'.[29]

There were more Irish than English and Scottish immigrants, because the poverty in Ireland during these years was so desperate that it was impossible for a large proportion of the population to make a living at home. A tide of immigrants flowed out to England, America and Australia from the impoverished country. During the years 1839-42, 23,705 Irish immigrants arrived in Australia

[25]*Female Immigration*, p. 50.
[26]*Report*, Colonization from Ireland, H. of L. (1847), xxiii. 410.
[27]*Female Immigration*, p. 48.
[28]*Herald*, 13 December 1841.
[29]*Report*, Colonization from Ireland, H. of L. (1847), xxiii. 411.

as compared with 5,986 Scots and 12,227 English and Welsh.[30]
There was a good deal of resentment felt towards these Irish
immigrants. They were nearly all Roman Catholics. Moreover,
as the economic organization of Ireland was much more primitive
than that of England, their standard of living was generally lower
than that of the colonists. So the term of approbrium 'dirty Irish'
came into general use, and was fiercely resented, the old, deep-
rooted hatred of the English exploiters of Ireland burning with
fresh vigour in the new country.

Caroline Chisholm was often confronted with the prejudice
against them and one girl, who refused to stay in the position
found for her, burst out in bright-cheeked defiance: 'From morning
till night my mistress is *flinging* at my country; and it's the country
to love, ma'am — ah! you have never seen it, or you would see
I could not stay.'[31]

The Irish, with their buoyant optimism, were the most easily
persuaded to go to the country — even if they knew little of
country conditions. She would talk to them, give two or three
'hope', and then 'let them loose among the others'.[32] But her
love and understanding for them gave a fresh opportunity for
criticism to those who feared her Catholicism. When the Maitland
branch home was founded in February 1842 there was 'some
opposition to the project' from this minority who believed she
favoured Catholic interests. The *Australian*[33] championed her,
and argued that it was not she who brought the Irish Catholic
immigrants to the colony; it was those who used the bounty funds.
Mrs Chisholm merely transmitted the immigrants after they had
arrived.

ON THE ROAD IN 1842

During her first year of work Mrs Chisholm founded branches
at Parramatta, Port Macquarie, Moreton Bay, Wollongong, Maitland, Scone, Liverpool, Campbell Town, Goulburn, Yass and Bong
Bong. There was also a depot in the New England district.[1] A
proper system of country dispersion had been established.

It seems almost unbelievable that she could have travelled so

[30]Madgwick, *Immigration into Eastern Australia*, p. 234.
[31]*Female Immigration*, p. 72.
[32]*Report*, Colonization from Ireland, H. of L. (1847), xxiii. 413.
[33]2 April 1842. This branch home was converted into the Benevolent
Asylum in November 1842, and from this the present Maitland Hospital
developed (information by courtesy of Mr R. L. Williams, Secretary of
the Maitland Hospital).
[1]*Female Immigration*, p. 87.

far and accomplished so much, in such a short space of time. She reached Port Macquarie, Moreton Bay, Wollongong and Maitland by boat, but for the rest she had to struggle over dreadful roads in bullock drays.

The first journey was the only one on which she took female immigrants alone; on all her other journeys she had men, women and children as well as girls. The men helped her with the yoking and unyoking of the bullocks and the driving. 'A prisoner from Hyde Park Barracks'[2] is mentioned as being with her on later journeys, and he must have given her assistance in the same way. She soon procured a saddle-horse — a white one — for herself, so that she could ride ahead of the drays to find the best camping place. The horse was given the name of 'Captain' and became as well known as his rider.

If there was no other shelter she slept beneath the drays with her people, but after she had been at work a few months, the weather became colder, and she found that the open drays were not satisfactory: 'I wish you could use your interest to try and borrow a horse and covered cart for me. I require the cart to sleep in at night and carry little children by day; I have a saddle-horse for my own use. I have now provided for seventy families; the weather is, however, very changeable, and I require a covered cart to enable me to continue my exertions.'[3]

This cart was added to the cavalcade of drays, and the noise of Mrs Chisholm's parties must have been heard by the homesteads long before they came in sight. These bush homesteads never let her want for 'provision of any kind'.[4] They were only too eager to give her parties food and shelter; and when she was given shelter in this way she insisted that she should not be separated from her people but should sleep beside them.[5]

She travelled the road to Goulburn so often that almost every tree on it must have been familiar to her. She would set out with her immigrants 'as early as five in the morning'. There were sometimes too many for all to ride in the drays, in which case they travelled slowly on the 'ride and walk' plan, taking it in turns to ride.[6] Slowly the drays jolted the length of George Street till they were out of the city. Two miles out in the cool of the early morning one of the first landmarks was Grose's Farm, on the left

[2]*Sidney's Emigrants' Journal* (1850), p. 278.
[3]*Ibid.* A quotation from a letter which must have been written to an influential friend in 1842.
[4]*Report*, Colonization from Ireland, H. of L. (1847), xxiii. 409.
[5]*Memoirs*, p. 68.   [6]Therry, *Reminiscences*, p. 418.

of the road, and adjoining it was the old Sydney racecourse. Here
they crossed the bridge over Johnston's Creek, and a mile and a
half further on passed 'Annandale', owned by Robert Johnston,
with its avenue of Norfolk Island pines leading to the house. A
mile on, and they came to 'Elswick', the 'seat' of James Norton,[7]
and soon afterwards they passed the Cherry Gardens. Mrs Chisholm knew every inn-keeper on the road, and found their wives
excellent mistresses for her girls; her parties had a vociferous
welcome from each public house. A mile further on they came to
the 'Speed the Plough Inn', and here they left the main road
which went on to Parramatta.

The immigrants turned southwards for Goulburn. The journey
began to be lonely; there were homesteads at intervals of a mile
or two, but they were off the road. They passed a few inns, and
must have spent the night at one of them, or else in the open,
for the drays could only travel about ten or twelve miles a day.
Next morning they creaked by Irish Town, a few bark huts and
hovels, fourteen miles from Sydney. There was only one public
house between this and Liverpool, almost twenty miles from
Sydney. Here, she probably spent the night at the depot, and
then set off again early the next morning with the immigrants who
were going on with her. The road became a bush track with
empty miles between the homesteads. There was no other habita-
tion until they passed the little village of Narellan, thirty-six miles
from Sydney.

Ordinary travellers were terrified of the loneliness of the road.
The country was infested with bushrangers, nearly all ex-convicts,
and ruthless in their treatment of women, as well as men. Bushrangers, like the notorious Jackey Jackey, who had at last been
captured only a few months before the Immigrants' Home opened,
held the countryside in terror and attacked many of the homesteads. Only a short time before Mrs Chisholm began her bush
journeys, an unfortunate Mrs Morris, an elderly woman, was
coming from Bathurst to Sydney with £300 to pay an account.
She was set upon by two men, beaten, knocked down, stripped,
and her corsets slit open with a knife to get at the money. She
was left naked and bleeding on the road, to be found by the next
passing dray.[8] It was stories such as this which made some of the
immigrants too terrified to leave the city.

But no bushranger ever attacked Caroline Chisholm or her

[7]*New South Wales and General Post Office Directory*, 1835.
[8]*Herald*, 17 July 1840.

parties. They may have thought that the parties would not have had much money with them but when Mrs Chisholm rode off alone, as she often did, she was never molested. She became known and loved throughout the length and breadth of the colony.

Eventually, as they travelled on to Goulburn, the immigrants came to the rolling Wollondilly and Goulburn Plains, and passed through 'Lockersleigh' — Major Lockyer's estate. To those who were used to noisy, bustling cities, or the compact, friendly little farms of England, the aloof vastness of this country was awe-inspiring. Some, especially the children, must have been captivated by the new sights and sounds around them, the strange trees, and brightly-coloured parrots. But even the few adventurous spirits quailed before the immense silence of the plains.

On her first journeys the country was new to Caroline Chisholm as well as to her people, but she says nothing of any fear she may have felt on her lonely rides between the farms. She had trained 'Captain' so that when the drays came to a ford she could sling a child on either side of the saddle, and then urge him across the river by her voice alone. In this way she got all the children over; the adults crossed either on the horse, or on the drays. Two miles beyond 'Lockersleigh' a ford crossed the Wollondilly River, and after that the party of immigrants passed through several other properties, including the famous 'Camden' — the Macarthurs' holding. Then the drays jolted through the township of Berrima, and on to Goulburn, the best part of one hundred and thirty miles from Sydney.

Sometimes Mrs Chisholm rode on to Yass before returning to Sydney. Her strength and endurance must have been phenomenal to have accomplished such journeys under such conditions. Yet during the first year she was almost continually on the road, with only one short break of a week or two in Sydney while she collected more immigrants.

There are many stories of her adventures on the journeys — some of which she tells herself. Often she was asked to find wives for lonely settlers and once, when she was riding ahead of her party along a track, 'a stout, rough bushman, clearing a few bushes at a leap',[9] caught her horse's head, and pleaded with her to find him a wife. In this case, as in all others, she refused to become a direct matrimonial agency, but her dearest

[9]*Sidney's Emigrants' Journal* (1850), p. 279.

hope for all the girls in her charge was that they should marry, and become the mothers of happy families. When placing them, she always had this in mind. One letter asking for a wife was written by a widower who asked her to choose him 'a young woman between the years of 25 and 35, English, clean in person, neat in habit, mild in manners, and an accomplished needle-woman' — in short, a perfect paragon. It says much for Mrs Chisholm's resourcefulness that the letter was endorsed in her hand — 'Managed to send a clergyman's sister as needle-woman to Mr. H. This arrangement terminated satisfactorily'.[10]

A story she tells of how once she came to a waterless camping place gives a vivid picture of some of her difficulties, and the way she overcame them. 'I had thirty women and children in the party, all tired, hungry, and thirsty, the children crying. Without saying a word, I sent one of my old bushmen off on horseback three miles to get enough milk or water for the children. In the meantime some of the immigrants came up and said in a discontented tone, "Mrs Chisholm this is a pretty job, what must we do? There is no water". I knew it would not do for them to be idle; anything was better than that in their frame of mind; so partly judging from the locality, I said to them without hesitation, "If you will dig here, I think you will find water." Directing the tools to be got out, they immediately set to work, and, providentially, they had not dug many feet when they came to water.'[11]

By such resource, by patience and inexhaustible good humour, she urged her timorous immigrants onwards to find new homes and happiness.

THE 'CARTHAGINIAN' PROSECUTION

When the home was first established Mrs Chisholm had been too occupied by the urgent task of finding employment for the immigrants to consider the lack of protection for girls on board ship, one of the greatest evils of the immigration system. She soon expressed her views strongly on this abuse, and found time during the first year she was secretary of the home to institute the prosecution of the captain and surgeon of a ship for mal-treating one of the girls in their charge. This prosecution caused a stir in the colony and at the Colonial Office in England, because it exposed the conditions on board the immigrant ships. According

[10]*Ibid.* p. 275.   [11]*Memoirs*, p. 67.

to the bounty regulations the immigrant girls were supposed to travel in the care of married families, but as they rarely met the families until they came on board, the provision was not much use as a protection for them.

The *Carthaginian* arrived in Sydney at the end of January 1842, and a number of women immigrants went to Mrs Chisholm's home. One of them, Margaret Anne Bolton, 'was in a very excited state and very unwell'.[1]

Aged about twenty-six, the description of her given to the Immigration Committee was that she was 'a correct, but peevish girl'[2] — characteristics which possibly explain all her troubles. From the beginning of the voyage she appears to have been unpopular. The other female immigrants, several of them 'women of the town', scornfully called her the 'old maid', and she was thoroughly disliked by the captain and surgeon, because she accused them both of gross immorality.

No doubt she was most aggravating, but she did not deserve the brutal treatment given her. Twice the captain and surgeon took her on deck and threw cold water over her. On the second occasion, one night about ten o'clock, there was a noise among the girls and 'a screaming at someone playing ghost'. The commotion disturbed the captain and surgeon so they determined to punish the ringleaders. Margaret Bolton swore later that she had no part in the disturbance, and certainly it was not in accord with her character to play ghosts; but the two men punished her because she did not catch those who were making the noise. They dragged her up on deck and threw several buckets of water over her. She was 'dressed in a nightdress and one petticoat and a shawl thrown over her shoulders'. After the water was thrown, her hands were handcuffed behind her, a greatcoat flung over her shoulders, and she was left on deck till well after twelve o'clock. Then the third mate helped her from the deck, for by that time she was too weak to walk by herself.[3] She could not find the key of her box to get dry clothing, and so sat shivering in her wet clothes all night. Since then she had never been well, and was unable to work.

This was the story told to Mrs Chisholm at the Barracks. She knew that similar incidents had occurred before, and the culprits had not been reprimanded. The captain, Robert Robertson, and

---

[1] *Herald*, 19 April 1842.
[2] *Report*, Immigration, *V. & P.* Leg. Council N.S.W. (1842), p. 515, evidence of Joseph Long Innes.
[3] *Australian*, 19 April 1842.

the surgeon, Richard William Nelson, did not have good records; therefore, she determined to bring them to justice.

Governor Gipps was alarmed at her temerity and warned her that a government prosecution was a serious matter. She made forthright answer: 'I am ready to prosecute: I have the necessary evidence, and if it be a risk whether I or these men shall go to prison, I am ready to go to prison'.[4] Sir George made no further protest.

Mrs Chisholm managed to interview both the surgeon and the captain at the Immigration Barracks. There she confronted them with Margaret Bolton and her accusation. The captain was silent, but the surgeon made a flat denial. Then, evidently after Mrs Chisholm had expressed a frank opinion of both their characters (she had a pretty turn of invective when aroused), they admitted the accusation was true. Coached by Mrs Chisholm, Margaret Bolton complained to the Immigration Board, three members of which were magistrates. A warrant was issued against Robertson and Nelson, and they were tried and condemned to imprisonment for six months, with a £50 fine each.[5]

The punishment was richly deserved, especially in the case of Dr Nelson. It came out that he was in the habit of throwing lime into the faces of the immigrants to stifle them, and make them go up on deck. This, and other facts were widely published in the press, and from this time stricter measures were taken in England to see that regulations were not evaded.

About a month after the trial, while speaking in the Legislative Assembly, Governor Gipps made an acknowledgment of Mrs Chisholm's work. He admitted that he had 'at first afforded but small countenance to her plans, but . . . had since found reason to change his opinion'.[6] He had good reason to, for if she had not distributed so many immigrants inland, the wrath of the Colonial Office would have been aroused. In reprimanding Gipps for his large issue of bounty orders Lord Stanley, the Secretary of State, had remarked, ominously, 'I shall expect the fullest and most accurate account of the manner in which these immigrants are disposed of'.[7]

If Mrs Chisholm had not begun her work, Sir George would not have been able to inform Stanley, with some complacency, 'that, large as has unquestionably been the supply of labour

[4]Samuel Sidney, *The Three Colonies of Australia*, p. 140.
[5]Gipps to Stanley, 13 May 1842 (*H.R.A.* xxii. 80).
[6]*Australian*, 19 May 1842.
[7]Stanley to Gipps, 14 October 1841 (*H.R.A.* xxi. 550).

which has thus been poured into the Colony, it has been absorbed without any serious inconvenience'.[8] It was her exertions which enabled him to make such a declaration, but it was not until over a year later that he acknowledged even her existence in a despatch to the home government.

At the same time that the Governor praised her work to the Legislative Assembly, he remarked that she had been able to get her immigrants into the interior at much less cost than the government could have, because no one would do anything for it except at the highest price. Her expenses of conveyance were only one-third those of the government, and were paid by contributions from the people themselves. The Immigration Agent, too, in his annual report in May 1842, was eulogistic of her work, and of her system of country depots — which he hoped would be maintained and extended so that the emigrants could be confident before they left England 'that in New South Wales they would not be left destitute in the place where they may be landed . . . but that they will at once be conveyed into those Districts where employment is ready for them'.[9]

The numbers of distressed families had so increased at the end of 1841, that Gipps had allowed them to be received into the Immigration Barracks. At the beginning of 1842 there were thirty-one married men with families, and fifteen single females sheltering there. Evidently the families were under the charge of F. L. S. Merewether, the Immigration Agent, whereas the girls were still Mrs Chisholm's particular care. These forty-six were the only immigrants whom Merewether acknowledges as unemployed at that time, but besides these there were still a good number camped in the tents near the Barracks. Towards the end of May 1842 Gipps was happy to report to Stanley that 'of the large encampment of Immigrants which was to be seen . . . a few weeks ago, all the tents, with the exception of five, have now . . . disappeared'.[10]

Neither Merewether nor Gipps knew the complete numbers of the unemployed immigrants; Caroline Chisholm could have given Lord Stanley 'the fullest and most accurate account' of their disposal, but this she was not called upon to do, though she published her own report of the first year's work of the home at the end of 1842.

[8]Gipps to Stanley, 2 April 1842 (*H.R.A.* xxii. 3).
[9]*Report*, Immigration Agent, 14 May 1842, *V. & P.* Leg. Council N.S.W. (1842), p. 222.
[10]Gipps to Stanley, 23 May 1842 (*H.R.A.* xxii. 67).

THE FIRST YEAR'S STOCKTAKING

Her report, *Female Immigration, Considered in a Brief Account of the Sydney Immigrants' Home,* was published in pamphlet form. As well as telling of the actual work accomplished, it is a trenchant indictment of the faults of the bounty system. She claimed to be 'the first lady in Australia who has ventured in the character of an author to appear before the public'. This claim has not been disputed.

Female Immigration is rambling, sometimes disconnected, and could have been much better planned, but it is intensely interesting. The interest of the tale she has to tell is enhanced by the easy, conversational style of the writing. Though the structure of the pamphlet is poor, and there are many repetitions, the reader's attention is held from the first page to the last. She begins by telling how she came to found the home. After this introduction she criticizes the bounty system, and makes several well-considered suggestions for its reform. Criticisms and suggestions are made in a haphazard fashion, strung together with anecdotes, but with a little juggling they fall into place. The pamphlet ends with a general classification of types which she had used when distributing the immigrants, and an appendix of interesting letters she had received.

The abuse which she cried out against was that of allowing immigrant girls to be engaged directly from the ship during the ten days they were permitted to stay on board. She did not hesitate to outrage Victorian delicacy by describing cases where girls had been taken from the ships to become inmates of brothels. One case was that of an orphan of fifteen, who was unconscious of her future vocation when Mrs Chisholm found her. She knew only that her mistress had told her to walk between such and such streets at certain times and 'a gentleman' would give her £2. One man, well known to the Immigration Board because he always met the ships and engaged single women from them, came to Mrs Chisholm's office to engage one but received scant courtesy from her; he immediately went to a ship just arrived in harbour and got what he wanted. Mrs Chisholm was powerless to remove the woman from his house.

She suggested that if the bounty system were to continue the 'importers ought to land the immigrants immediately or send them into the interior . . . The best plan would be to send a steamer to the side of the ship and clear off those who are drafted for Maitland, Port Macquarie, Moreton Bay, etc., at once'. Those for Sydney, Liverpool, Campbell Town, Goulburn and Bathurst should be sent to the place intended for their reception. Grose's Farm would probably be the best, for it was 'very convenient for the drays'. If the immigrants were drafted in this way, her branch homes would be in great demand, because immigrants would be sent direct to the depot in each inland township. Whatever was done, she asked that the government give the immigrant girls proper care and protection on their arrival.

She had 'no hesitation in saying that girls of bad character are shipped to these colonies and must be known at the time to be such'. In many cases, she declared, the women were without certificates and then the importers did not put in their claim for the bounty. In other cases, certificates were forged, but the Sydney Immigration Board had no means of checking them. She advised, therefore, that the Immigration Board should send an 'active superintending agent' to England, a man who knew Australia so that the immigrants would be well chosen, and there would be fewer 'bad bargains'.

To correct the immorality prevalent during the voyage she had a word to say concerning the appointment of surgeons. She considered that there should be a medical officer appointed in England to inspect the emigrants, and 'he should hand over his approved list to the surgeon of the ship. The importers should not have the liberty to select their own surgeon'. To ensure that he would know his duties thoroughly the age of the surgeon selected 'ought not to be less than twenty-six'. The duties of the captains and surgeons should be as distinct as possible, and there should be not one, but two, surgeons — one an older man who had made the voyage before. Both were to be carefully chosen for 'moral character and professional ability'. One of them was to give out the provisions, not the captain as was the prevailing custom, because, as she pointed out, the surgeon knew the physical needs of the immigrants better. As a further check, the surgeons should not be paid until they had 'submitted to a duly constituted board a journal of the voyage . . . giving a full report'. She acknowledged that for all her suggestions regarding the appointment of surgeons she was greatly indebted to advice from Dr Nicholson.[1]

[1] Afterwards Sir Charles. He had arrived in Sydney in 1834 and soon became one of the leading figures in the colony. He was elected a member of the first Legislative Assembly in 1843, was later first Chancellor

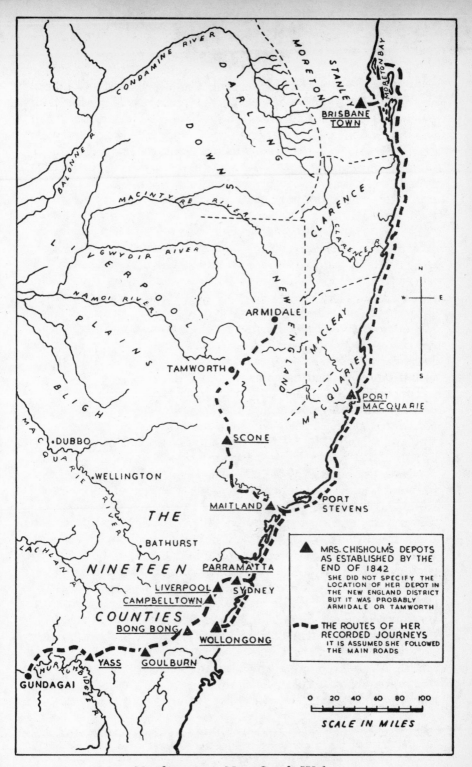

North-eastern New South Wales
(From a map by W. Baker, 1847,
now in the Mitchell Library, Sydney)

She had constructive criticism to make concerning the organization of the Immigration Barracks. There appears to have been a superintendent of immigrants who dealt with routine matters. Mrs Chisholm suggested that this superintendent should look after the rations and tents only; he should visit the tents three times a day, and he should have nothing to do with office work. The single women should be in the charge of a responsible woman who would attend the surgeon when he visited the sick. Single men should not be excluded from the immigrants' encampment, but should be allowed to have a tent near the Barracks until they had a situation offered them.

The suggestions for reform had no immediate effect, because in the next year it was decided to suspend assisted immigration. The drought and the depression, together with the high price of land, had combined to reduce land sales to a minimum. The Wakefieldians had tied immigration to the land fund by using the proceeds of land sales to pay for the introduction of immigrants. When these sales dwindled, immigration could not be financed.

Nevertheless, in spite of the drought and the beginning of depressed conditions, there was still a demand for labour which it was difficult to satisfy. There were homeless, hungry immigrants in Sydney but, as Mrs Chisholm knew, there was work to be found inland. Unemployment in Sydney was aggravated by the lack of a system of dispersion. The Immigration Committee of 1842 reported that there was no appearance of 'a superabundance of labour in any part of the territory'; there were *not* too many immigrants.[2] Until Mrs Chisholm began her work there were certainly too many immigrants in Sydney, but the committee was concerned with conditions throughout the whole colony.

That Mrs Chisholm was able to dispose of her immigrants as easily as she did proves that the supply of labour was in no way too great for the demand. This is borne out by the fact that in *Female Immigration* she reported that she was closing the home for girls, as there was no longer any urgent need for it. On 31 October 1842 the *Sydney Morning Herald* likewise reported that the home was closing. The homeless girls were provided for, and her organization of country dispersion was

---

of the University of Sydney and first president of the Queensland Legislative Council.
[2]*Report*, Immigration, V. & P. Leg. Council N.S.W. (1842), p. 464.

working so well that there was no need for them to be kept in Sydney. The registry office remained open as a central depot from which the immigrants — men, women and children as well as girls — could be dispersed.

Like the Immigration Committee, which made its report in the same year, Mrs Chisholm believed that more immigrants would be needed in the following year. But this prophesied demand for labour failed in 1843 because the depression became much worse than anyone anticipated. However, Mrs Chisholm's suggestions concerning the types and numbers of immigrants she thought were needed are most interesting; they give a vivid picture, both of the immigrants, and of her understanding of them. It will be seen from her descriptions that the big demand was for country labour.

Single women she classified as firstly those fit to be country servants — stout, strong girls, accustomed and willing to work. Of these she wanted six hundred to be sent during the next year. Secondly, 'light, handy girls, who are willing to learn'; thirdly, those whom she frankly called the 'do-nothings', for she did not know any one useful thing they could do.

She divided the men into similar classes and declared that the first type — those accustomed to work — would always find employment whether they were married or single. Nevertheless, she considered that 'no man ought to think of emigrating to this Colony who has more than three children except some of them are above nine years of age'. Every colonist seems to have been of the same opinion. The 'do-nothing' class of men she called the 'Black-riband Gentry' because 'as soon as they land in Sydney, they go to a draper's shop, and purchase two yards and a quarter of black riband; this is put round their necks — sometimes a spy-glass suspended, this is, however, rare, a dressing-case key with a silver top, is the favourite of these fashionables'. Unfortunately, because of laxity in policing the regulations, the class was a numerous one. Mrs Chisholm could do little for them because, for the most part, they were quite unfitted to struggle for existence among the hardy colonials.

In placing the immigrants she remarked on the difficulties of finding tempers as well as characters to suit. She did not make many mistakes, but sometimes she could not match temperaments and the results were amusing. One mistress called a servant 'an idle, lazy, insolent girl', and another was so satisfied with the same girl's services that she wrote asking Mrs Chisholm to send

her another as housemaid, because she would rather trust to
Mrs Chisholm's selection than her own. She found the fine ladies
of Sydney 'a little spoilt by the assignment system' and apt to be
haughty in their bearing to those working for them.

Female Immigration was dedicated to the clergy of Australia,
and she gratefully recorded that 'in Sydney and the country' she
had been 'ably supported by the clergy of all denominations'.
Although a minority suspected her motives, the majority were
behind her to a man. It was a great victory. She made grateful
mention also of the press, which had given her so much help.

Without this publicity given by the press probably she would
not have received the generous public support which enabled
her to continue her work. In the very beginning she had to make
some payments from her own pocket, but these were soon refunded by public donations. She says 'I met with great Assistance
from the Country Committees [of the branch homes]. The
squatters and settlers were always willing to give me Conveyance for the People . . . At Public Inns the Females were sheltered
and I was provided myself without any Charge'.[3]

With this public support the remarkable record of her first
year's work was achieved. During that one year she estimated
that she had been 'the instrument either directly or indirectly
of serving upwards of 2,000 persons'.[4] Among the 1,400 women,
seventy-six prostitutes had been reclaimed and only seven of
all the women had, in the euphemistic Victorian phrase, 'lost
character'. The branch homes had been established and, she
concludes proudly, 'The amount of subscriptions received is
£156, the expenditure £154; cash in hand £2; subscriptions due
£41; debts none'.[5] It was well that she had begun her work in
this year 1842, and that her country depots were well organized;
next year the depression was severe, and the system of dispersion
she had evolved was taxed by large numbers of unemployed.

[3] *Report*, Colonization from Ireland, H. of L. (1847), xxiii. 409.
[4] *Female Immigration*, p. 2, see Appendix A.
[5] *Memoirs*, pp. 82-3.

3

Colonizing Practice and Theory

THE DEPRESSION OF 1843-4

By 1843 the colony was in the grip of depression and drought. In 1839 sheep were sold for 35s. a head; in 1843 they went for 6d. 'and the station given in'. Horses costing £50 to £70 in 1839 were sold at £7 in 1843. In the preceding year a Bankruptcy Act had been passed which left debtors their freedom on condition that they handed in their estates, otherwise the gaols would have been full to overflowing.

The demand for city labour had practically ceased, and the unemployed sought desperately for work. As one Sydney man said, 'I have been round to every shop till I am tired; the people make a laugh at us, and say it is no use for us to call'. Sometimes they found casual labour for a few weeks but not often. Their families had to be fed and the rent paid; 'in some cases they had been selling every article of furniture and clothing they could part with, and lived on that'. One family was in such need that 'the children were eating potato parings, which they had found in the street'; the man was willing 'to take charge of two flocks of sheep; his wife was willing to act as hut-keeper, and they would go for whatever the employer might choose to give them, provided sufficient were allowed to find their children with food'.

There was still a demand for labour in the interior, but most of the Sydney unemployed were dubious about their chances of finding it. 'I would willingly go into the country', said Benjamin Sutherland, who was an upholsterer by trade, 'if I were offered an engagement but to go on chance two or three hundred miles, without finding work, would be worse than remaining in Sydney.' Those men who had children found it impossible to go 'unless some means of conveyance were found for them'. And those who ventured inland and could find no work returned to the city with ill-luck stories which discouraged others. The practice of

42

many country station owners of paying their hands by orders drawn upon Sydney rather than in cash helped to increase the poverty-stricken crowds in the city.

The majority of the unemployed were hard-working people. Henry Bremer, a blacksmith, described their feelings when he said sadly, 'We wished to maintain ourselves in a little respect, as we had done all our lives'.[1] They could not understand the reasons for their distress, and remembered the days of the boom with puzzled bewilderment.

It was the fall of prices and depression in England, combined with the drought in New South Wales, which broke the boom. But those who lived through the 'bad times' blamed the distress upon lesser factors. They criticised the home government for sending out city-bred immigrants who disliked going to the country, and men with large families of young children. They deplored the sudden flood of immigrants which had arrived in Sydney as the result of the demand for labour during the boom.[2] And they castigated the high price of land.

In August 1843 the government had attempted to give some relief by putting the unemployed on to public works, but by November, when long insolvency lists were appearing every day in the newspapers, conditions were so bad that a petition signed by 'upwards of four thousand of the inhabitants of Sydney' was presented to the Legislative Council. In response to this a Select Committee on Distressed Labourers met to try to find some solution to the problem of the unemployed. By then, in Sydney alone, there were 1,243 workless with 2,505 dependants — 3,748 in all out of a total population of 29,973.[3]

The committee interviewed a number of representative unemployed, whose evidence has already been quoted. Mrs Chisholm was also a witness.[4]

She considered that there were three classes of distressed: those already employed by the government and the city council at relief work; those who were supported by friends and the

---

[1]The details in the above paragraphs are based on evidence given before the Select Committee on Distressed Labourers. See *Report, Distressed Labourers, V. & P.* Leg. Council N.S.W. (1845), pp. 726-9, 744, 743.

[2]*Report*, Distressed Labourers, *V. & P.* Leg. Council N.S.W. (1843), p. 730.

[3]*Ibid.* p. 729.

[4]The members of the committee were : Dr Lang (president), Mr Cowper, Dr Nicholson, W. C. Wentworth, the Colonial Secretary, Mr Robinson and the Colonial Treasurer.

credit of shopkeepers; and the unemployed who were completely destitute.

She found it comparatively easy to find employment for the single girls and men; the young married couples with only a few children also were easy to place, but those who had numbers of young children were more difficult. There were some trades, too, which were not much needed. Shoemakers and tailors, for instance, were well represented among the workless.

She had given the problem of unemployed families much thought while she had been working with the immigrants, and was ready with a scheme which she considered would not only relieve the immediate distress, but give permanent prosperity to a number of families. This was that they should be distributed up country in small parties, and settled on land with long clearing leases of ten to fifteen years. No rent was to be paid in money, or in kind. She had interested Captain Towns[5] in her scheme, and he had offered her four thousand acres at Shell Harbour in the Wollongong district for the settlement of fifty families.

Mrs Chisholm described to the committee how her 'first arrangement would be to select from the fifty families, one man who was a good judge of land, and one of the women, as the women would require to know what kind of a place they were going to — whether the children would be comfortable and whether the native dogs would bite, or run away with them'. She would also need two or three good bush hands from Hyde Park Barracks 'and these she would set upon the land to clear half an acre in order that the people might see what could be done in a given time. I then intend that one allotment shall be set apart as a family allotment, which must be first cleared and cultivated to provide a supply of food for the whole community, and then the land must be divided and apportioned to the different families. I have a schoolmaster who will go with the party, and I expect to get land for him free from rent; the parents of the children have consented to pay, in labour and produce, for the education of their children.' She declared confidently that the unemployment could be relieved for the expense of £1,000 if it were done at once, and not made more difficult by delay.

But the Legislative Council had a plan of its own. This was to grant two sums of £500 each, as they were needed, to remove

[5]Captain Robert Towns, a wealthy landowner interested in immigration. He was later a pioneer in the South Sea trade, and the first to introduce cotton-growing in Queensland; Townsville is named after him.

the distressed to the country; Moreton Bay was the district chosen for them, and the government was to provide steamer passages as well as rations and lodgings until the unemployed found work for themselves.

Mrs Chisholm was asked her opinion of this scheme. She said 'I would not at present send them [to Moreton Bay]; my object is to get a large number to settle with advantage to themselves'. She thought the government plan would 'prove an expensive one' — it was a temporary measure which would not permanently establish the unemployed. Her own scheme was 'not a plan of today . . . the distress will be removed, and those persons who are now suffering in Sydney will, within three years, become employers of labour'.

These were fatal words; the land-owning members of the committee at once stiffened. Mr Cowper spoke for them: 'I am afraid we should find that these people becoming employers of labour would do us a mischief'. She denied this, and pointed out what valuable labourers the children of such settlers would prove. But besides fearing to create new land-owners the committee considered that her plan would involve the government in the expense of supporting the settlers for at least a year until they were established. It therefore preferred its own scheme by which families might be employed soon after they were taken into the country.

Almost a year later, Merewether declared that only £120 of the proposed £1,000 had been spent. Originally it had been estimated that the cost of removal would be £1 per head. If the cost was as estimated the conclusion is that only about one hundred and twenty immigrants were disposed of by the government. Merewether, a very cautious witness, declared that at the time the £1,000 was voted he had thought the numbers of unemployed were over-stated. But his chief explanation of the small numbers who had been given government assistance was that there was 'an indisposition even on the part of persons who were really in distress to remove to the country without a certain prospect of employment'. He reported that of those sent away 'some found employment, and some set up in business on their own account, all were disposed of'.[6]

Mrs Chisholm was not daunted by the lack of encouragement the committee had given her. She had Captain Towns'

---

[6] *Report*, Distressed Labourers, V. & P. Leg. Council N.S.W. (1844), ii. 612.

promised help, and after giving her evidence she went at once to the proprietors of the Wollongong steamer. They agreed to transport fifty families as well as 'their few articles of furniture . . . at a moderate rate', and to land them at Shell Harbour. The next day she reported this transaction to the committee and then, that same evening (15 November), set off herself for Shell Harbour. With the help of three men who accompanied her she had half an acre cleared in readiness for her settlers, before returning to the city.

Three weeks later the *Herald* reported that 'twenty-three families who are to be located on land near Wollongong on clearing leases, left Sydney by the steamer last night accompanied by Mrs Chisholm through whose exertions this arrangement has been made'.[7] Her optimistic fifty families had dwindled to twenty-three. Perhaps some had become faint-hearted at the thought of this new experiment — they wanted to work and save their earnings before investing in land of their own. Others — city-bred immigrants — may have feared to go inland. But a year later when she reported the results of the experiment she admitted there had been some failures, and added significantly that the plan 'had succeeded remarkably well' considering 'the many difficulties thrown in my way'.[8] Mrs Chisholm was unlikely to make a chance choice of words when she gave such evidence, and it seems possible that in some way the squatting interests had attempted to discomfort her. If she had been given the support of the government, and her scheme had been carried out on a larger scale, it might have made an appreciable difference to the general situation, but twenty-three families was a very small number compared with the estimated 3,748 in distress.

In 1844 another Committee on Distressed Labourers met before which Caroline Chisholm again gave evidence. On the surface, the position appeared to be worse than in 1843, for the fall in prices and bad conditions generally had hit the country so hard that many had thrown up their farms and crowded into Sydney. Yet, compared with the numbers distressed the year before, there were now only 2,034. At the committee's request, Mrs Chisholm had collected the figures herself. For several weeks notices appeared in the *Herald* asking the unemployed to register with her so that the numbers might be calculated. Her classifi-

[7] *S.M.H.*, 7 December 1843.
[8] *Report*, Distressed Labourers, V. & P. Leg. Council N.S.W. (1844), ii. 601-4.

cation was: married men, 489; wives, 481; children under eight, 981; single men, 83. Of the men, three were natives of the colony, 438 were immigrants of some years, 76 were new arrivals and 55 were old hands. They included two hundred and forty-four farm-labourers and fifty-nine carpenters. She remarked that there was now very little demand for shepherds in the interior, and there were very few women unemployed. This was chiefly due to her work.

The suggestions she made show that the Shell Harbour experiment had influenced the development of her ideas on communal farming. She thought 'that all those who have large families of young children, and who are good agricultural labourers should be provided for by allowing them a certain time on a cultivation licence . . .' She was able to say definitely that such families could be settled for £4 each. The government 'should open an extensive district of country and give, say five hundred cultivation licences, there must be roads made, and I would employ the men three days a week on wages and expend the four pounds in seeds and implements, etc'.

She knew this could not be done while the land purchase regulations were enforced, 'except a charitable error be discovered' in them. But the committee showed no inclination to discover such an error. The prospect of having to supply rations for these settlers deterred them, and once again the doubt was voiced: 'Is there not some danger that the children of those small landed proprietors will not become labourers?' Instead of settling the families on the land the committee again preferred to transport them to the country in order that 'depots of labourers and artisans would be formed in the interior'.[9]

There had been some failures among the settlers at Shell Harbour, but she had proved to her own satisfaction that 'the people *can* subsist on the land if they are industrious'. However, the difficulties 'thrown in her way' probably discouraged her from trying to extend the little settlement. Instead she determined to make journeys inland again with any unemployed families who would go with her. She offered to move one hundred and fifty families if half the expenses were borne by the government.[10] But the official mind refused to accept her offer until she had proved that she could successfully find employment for a party which she proposed taking to Goulburn. From information given by the branch homes, and her own knowledge of country

[9]*Ibid.* p. 600.   [10]*S.M.H.*, 25 October 1844.

conditions, she knew where hands were needed. Her optimistic certainty that work would be found gave many fresh hope, and she had little difficulty in gathering a large party together. At the end of October she set off once again with the drays into the heat and dust.

The government supplied her with carriage and 'a generous public' had donated coffee, a ham, tea and sugar, two cheeses, a case of portable soup, twenty pounds of biscuits, bread, and six bags of potatoes. Before the drays set off, flour, meat, more biscuits and a few blankets were included in the supplies. The *Herald* does not mention the numbers in the party, but they exceeded a hundred. The cavalcade arrived in Goulburn on 4 November, having left Sydney on 28 October. She was most successful in placing her people, and found no need to go on to Yass as she had intended. The *Herald* reported she had found positions for everyone who went with her. 'Some of those who could not get employment before she came up are speaking of putting themselves under her magic influence, for Mrs. Chisholm is everything.'[11]

By 16 November she was back at the Bent Street office, preparing to take another party south in a few days. The Goulburn venture had been a success, but there is no further mention of her offer to move the one hundred and fifty families inland. Probably this was because conditions were improving, and there was no need to move such a large number of unemployed.

Early in December she was on the road again with a party which increased to two hundred by accessions on the way. Some of the journey was made in very bad weather and the report from Picton gives an idea of her difficulties, and the way she surmounted them. Mrs Chisholm and her immigrants arrived in a heavy rain-storm. The township rallied round to help her, and she was immediately supplied with meat by Mr McAllister and flour by Mr John Martin. 'Notwithstanding the rain coming down in torrents, she proceeded on her journey but one woman having been confined at the George Inn on the evening of arrival, and an accident occurring with one of the teams at Razor Back, some portion of the party did not proceed from Picton until Sunday.' There was one cheering note in this tale of misfortune, for, says the report, 'our roads are free from bushrangers'. The people of Picton were annoyed because of the governor's refusal to allow any of the immigrants to be

[11]*Ibid.* 11 November 1844.

employed by them, as the township was too near Sydney. They had subscribed to their maintenance on the road and felt that the prohibition was unjust when they were in need of labour; but Gipps was attempting to disperse the immigrants as far inland as possible.

She took her party on to Yass and Gundagai, and places were found for all except 'a very few whom she hopes to settle on the road back'.[12] This is the last mention of any party of immigrants Mrs Chisholm took inland. Conditions must have been improving, and this is hinted at in a letter published in the *Herald* just before she set out on the journey to Goulburn. In this she remarks that the Bent Street office may be considered finally closed, 'as it is my intention to confine my exertions to the interior until those who wish for employment are provided for and then my work is done'.[13] She found it necessary to open her office again in November,[14] while preparing for the party she took to Yass and Gundagai, but it is not mentioned in 1845.

That she was able to find employment for the large parties she took to Goulburn, Yass and Gundagai proves that the depression was passing. In September 1843 when it was at its height, and three of the banks failed, an Act of Council had permitted the banks to lend against liens on livestock and wool. By taking advantage of this the pastoralists managed to give security for payment of loans. This provided a good deal of relief and helped the return to normal conditions.[15]

The ruinous price of sixpence a head for sheep was avoided when boiling down, begun as a cure for scab, became widely used. Tallow was sold at a steady 4s. to 5s. a cwt. on the English market. The papers of the time became full of references to it, and of advertisements for boiling-down 'establishments'. The practice was gradually discontinued as the demand for stock revived.

There was no further need for Mrs Chisholm to make arduous journeys inland with parties of unemployed. The first part of her work had really ended by the beginning of 1845.

MRS CHISHOLM AND DR LANG

Whatever the theory behind immigration may be, there are at least five important practical considerations: If the immigrants

[12]*Ibid.* 30 December 1844.   [13]*Ibid.* 25 October 1844.
[14]*Ibid.* 18 November 1844.
[15]See Brian Fitzpatrick, *British Empire in Australia* (Melbourne, 1949), pp. 76-7.

themselves are of poor quality and a balanced ratio between the sexes is not maintained difficulties must arise. If the finances of an immigration organization are unsound, or its passages too expensive, it will not last for long. And even the best types of immigrants will be adversely affected by bad conditions on board ship. Then, after they arrive in a new country, they should be given opportunities to find work. They should also be dispersed so that they are placed to the best economic advantage both of themselves and of older settlers. Lastly, their immediate assimilation into the new country will depend largely on whether they are settled singly or in family groups.

Mrs Chisholm had begun by helping the immigrant girls because they urgently needed her, not because she then had any particular theory of immigration with which she wanted to experiment. In this lay her chief strength. 'Unencumbered with colonizing theories',[1] she looked at the facts first, weighed the evidence, and then decided on the rights and wrongs of the case.

By the end of her first year's work, when she published *Female Immigration*, she was still concerned with reforming an old system which was not of her making. Then, as she worked with the immigrants, and settled them on the land, her ideas of a new and better system both of introducing and settling immigrants began to take shape.

The natural remedy for the evils she deplored in the colony was so clear to her that she never ceased to advocate the necessity for female immigration to reduce the disparity between the sexes. Synonymous with this was the need for the encouragement of family life. The championship of the family became her watchword. During the depression, the unfortunate situation of many immigrant families gave her the chance to experiment with a practical scheme of family colonization, and she began to think of ways in which family immigration, and family settlements, could be encouraged.

As she expounded her Shell Harbour scheme she stressed the fact that settlers on small farms should gain ownership of the land by deferred payments. She believed that the immigrants would do no good if they had everything given to them. They had to work for their land, and pay for it. This encouragement of independence was one of the fundamentals of the society she founded later to promote family colonization.

By the time the Shell Harbour settlement was made in 1843

[1]Therry, *Reminiscences*, p. 417.

she seems to have begun consciously to advocate settlement by
means of small farms. She, herself, was the daughter of an
English yeoman farmer. She understood the position of the
yeoman farmer in England, and thought that the system of small
holdings could be transplanted to Australia. It was the practical
demands of the situation — the distress of the unemployed
families — which made her try to establish small-holdings for
them, but beyond the need of the moment she saw the need of
the future. She was a friend of William Charles Wentworth and
the Macarthurs, leaders of the Australian squatters, but she made
no secret of the fact that she favoured closer settlement and
this implied the break-up of the great estates. In this attitude
she expressed her condemnation of the social injustice whereby
the squatter held many more acres than he needed, and excluded
the small farmer from making a living. She became an acknowledged champion of the middle and the working classes, and
denounced the continued existence of bachelor stations.[2]

Both of the Legislative Council Committees on Distressed
Labourers disliked her plans for small farms. If the cost of
rationing such settlements had not been sufficient excuse for
rejecting her schemes, other excuses would have been forthcoming. Caroline Chisholm understood this well but held her
peace, for she had no wish to antagonize the great landowners,
and she still hoped to be able to work with them. The question
of the squatters' rights and privileges was being debated hotly
throughout the colony. By increasing the numbers of pastoral
holdings, and then by formulating occupation and purchase
regulations, Governor Gipps had come to grips with the lords
of the land. At this time, however, Mrs Chisholm took no active
part in the controversy over the land question. It was not until
ten years later, when she was in Victoria, that she added her
voice to the cry of the people's party against the squatters.

One member of the committees heard her suggestions with
sympathy and approval. This was the Reverend Dr John Dunmore
Lang who was as interested as she in immigration and labour
problems. Lang had arrived in Sydney in 1822, a clever and
ambitious young man of twenty-three who thought the new
country promised more advancement than the old. Sir Thomas
Brisbane was then Governor of New South Wales, and the Lang
family knew him well, for both the Brisbanes and the Langs
came from the Scottish town of Largs. George Lang, John

[2]*Duncan's Weekly Register*, 30 August 1845.

Dunmore's elder brother, had gone to the colony first and his brother had asked him 'to make a moral survey of the country on his arrival'.

Even John Dunmore's missionary zeal was shocked by the convict society he found in Sydney and in his diary he exclaimed: 'O generation of vipers! Will they never be warned to flee from the wrath to come? I scorn to be the pensioner of thieves and adulterers! I shall stay here only till I get our Scots Kirk finished and till I can leave the place honourably.'

He was minister for the Scots National Church, and when he arrived in the colony the services were being held in the Court House. He had set his heart on building Scots Kirk. He thought Governor Brisbane should grant him a subsidy and his stormy career began with a violent quarrel with the governor. Brisbane was not to be moved, but such was the fire and drive of the young man that with the support of the Presbyterians he built Scots Church and then returned to England to complain about Brisbane.

Fortuitously the governor was recalled, and Lang returned in triumph after he had made an agreement with the home government that one-third of the expenses of maintenance of the Presbyterian Church were to be paid by the state, and he was to receive a salary of £300 a year. He was minister of the Scots Church, which had been built by his own courage and determination, until his death.

The Rev. Dr Lang was a militant Presbyterian who believed that anyone not conforming to the strictest precepts of the Scottish faith was well on the way to eternal damnation. Lang was an outstandingly able man but his intolerance, not only of religion but of all opinions other than his own, kept him continually in trouble. Before all else he was 'a fighter, unrelenting and vindictive in controversy'. He had no respect for the pomp and circumstance of authority and no fear of any man. Whatever he was interested in had his whole heart and he was always passionately convinced of the justice of his cause. He did a great deal to advance education and became a zealous advocate of immigration. But it had to be immigration which he considered was the right kind.

He had entered the field of the immigration theorists in 1830 when, in a letter to Lord Goderich, the Secretary of State, he pointed out how the distressed poor of England could be brought to Australia without expense. He suggested this could be done, firstly, by the sales of building allotments in Sydney, secondly by resuming and selling land which had been granted on certain conditions to the Church and School Corporation of New South Wales. These conditions had not been fulfilled. His letter to Goderich was published in Sydney, and as he had omitted to consult the holders of the land there was a furious outcry.

Determined to put his immigration ideas into practice, he brought out a hundred immigrants in the *Stirling Castle* in 1831. They, chiefly mechanics and agricultural labourers, were carefully chosen for their Protestant belief. Their passages were prepaid by a loan which was to be repaid within a given period after their arrival in the colony and he found this means of financing passages successful. Five years later he made use of the bounty system to bring out another three hundred immigrants. Among them were some suitable ministers for the Scots Church and several schoolmasters.

Lang was insistent that the immigrants should be carefully selected.[3] Those selected should be encouraged to migrate by liberal reductions in the cost of passages. Any passage money they paid should count towards buying land after they arrived, and the whole scheme should be financed by money from the sale of Crown Lands in the colony.

Lang's main emphasis, however, was on the selection of the immigrants — he believed that if good people were chosen very little else mattered. The aspect of the bounty system which aroused him to fury was the numbers of Irish Roman Catholics introduced by it. Because of the prevailing conditions in Ireland many more Irish than English or Scots immigrants arrived during the early 'forties and, to John Dunmore Lang, a true spiritual descendant of John Knox, the Roman Catholic religion was anathema. When he became one of the first members of the newly-established Legislative Council in 1843 he made the exclusion of the Irish Roman Catholic immigrants one of his chief aims.

It was this intolerance which set him apart from Caroline Chisholm. It was a difference in character as well as religion, for whereas her love of all mankind marked her as a Christian his deity was the angry jealous Jehovah of the Old Testament. Her tolerance made it possible for her to 'work for all and through all', and no matter what her private thoughts were concerning the muddling of officials she kept them to herself. In this way she eventually won public opinion to her side and was supported by the Government. The Rev. Dr Lang, on the other

[3]A. C. Child, 'John Dunmore Lang — Some Aspects of His Work and Character' (thesis, ML), pp. 70-1.

hand, had not the slightest patience with fools. It was impossible for him to work with anyone without friction, and woe betide those who were his opponents. Yet his interest in immigration was so close to that of Mrs Chisholm's that even though she was of the Roman Catholic faith, they were drawn together. He had, too, an even more clearly declared belief in free institutions than she had at this time. He supported the small farmer against the squatter, and trounced the *Sydney Morning Herald* for its support of the transportation of convicts.

Lang was chairman of the Committee on Distressed Labourers in 1843, and a member of the committee which sat in the following year, and had almost certainly met Mrs Chisholm before she gave her evidence. It was well known that she was a Catholic, and it was a complete reversal of all his fiercely held beliefs for him to realize both her quality and the disinterestedness of her work. But this he did, though only for the short time he was in close contact with her. Nothing else seems to explain his contradictory behaviour. It is a proof of her charm, as well as of her ability, that she was able to win him even for so short a time.

VOLUNTARY INFORMATION

Caroline Chisholm believed that if she could collect the actual facts concerning a large selection of immigrants who had become successful small farmers in Australia, the records would be of inestimable value as a guide and encouragement for those in England who wished to emigrate. She deplored the deceiving reports often made by the bounty agents who, in their efforts to collect larger numbers of immigrants, would publish puffs such as the one she quoted in *Female Immigration*:[1]

> A few Tailors will make a fortune.
> Clerks are in great demand.
> Dressmakers earn half-a-guinea a day.
> There is not a good Hairdresser in the Colony.
> Fifty Starch-makers would make a fortune.

Many an ignorant immigrant set sail with his mind 'filled with golden dreams of greatness',[2] and only awoke to the necessity for hard work after his arrival in the colony.

[1] p. 33.
[2] *Report*, Distressed Labourers, V. & P. Leg. Council N.S.W. (1843), p. 744.

She planned to travel through the colony and collect the voluntary statements of about three thousand settlers, but she calculated the expense of collecting this 'testimony of the people' at £300. This was beyond her means, and she interested as many as she could in the project in the hope that it would be financed for her. The press gave her its support, and 'the immigrants and the public generally were approving'.[3]

She hoped that the government might give her a grant to carry out the scheme, and it was with this in mind that she must have interested Dr Lang in the venture. On 30 November 1843 he moved in the Legislative Council that a select committee be appointed to take her plan into consideration, and he declared that he need not remind the house 'of the services which the Lady . . . had rendered to this country by her exertions in the cause of humanity'. Mrs Chisholm, he said, wished to submit her plan to a committee of the Legislative Council. 'A small outlay was required, and it was with a view to obtain the recommendation of the Government to sanction such an outlay that the motion was brought forward.'[4] Altogether the worthy doctor then appeared to have the very highest opinion of Mrs Chisholm.

William Charles Wentworth seconded the motion, but it was opposed on the grounds that an Immigration Committee had just sat, and its report was about to be discussed; therefore, any further action, especially during the depression, was not justified. The motion was defeated by seven votes to six.

She had no immediate opportunity to pursue the matter further. She was occupied with her little settlement at Shell Harbour, and next year she was taking large parties of unemployed inland. But the project was not abandoned. She asked Governor Gipps to make it known to Lord Stanley, the Secretary of State, and in his despatch dated 12 December 1843, Gipps at last acknowledged that 'during the course of the great Immigration into this Colony in 1841 and 1842 [Mrs Chisholm] rendered essential Services to the Government by her Exertions'. He explained her idea but with the dampening comment that he could not 'adopt all [her] views', and enclosed the list of questions asked, with some of the answers which were then in her possession.

Stanley requested Gipps to 'express to Mrs Chisholm the high sense which I entertain of the valuable and benevolent services which she has rendered to Emigrants in New South

---

[3]Caroline Chisholm to Smith, Elder & Co., 1 December 1843 (ML).
[4]Reported in *S.M.H.*, 30 November 1843.

Wales',[5] but he considered that the collection would be an unwarranted expense, and pointed out that some of the information was already obtainable. By this he meant information found in statistics, such as the rates of wages and current prices in the colony.

Nothing further was done in the matter until the depression lifted; then, early in 1845, she decided to collect the statements herself without government help. Her husband had returned to Australia at the beginning of that year,[6] and from this time onwards they worked together.

At the time of his retirement from the Army he was fifty years of age. His pension would probably have been £292 a year,[7] and besides this he must have received a substantial sum from his fellow officers. Because of the slow promotion it was then customary in the East India Company's Army for a senior officer to be given a purse to induce him to retire. The amount given varied, but a senior captain in an infantry regiment might receive something like £1,000.[8] Because there was no direct system of commission purchase in the company's army it attracted men who were not usually possessed of private means. Captain Chisholm probably had little or no other income besides his pension and the return from whatever investment he made of the possible £1,000. For the next ten years this was the financial basis on which he and his wife lived.

He was very interested in the 'Voluntary Statements', as they came to be called; indeed, his wife delayed beginning the undertaking because, as she says, 'I could not incur the responsibility of its expense, without the sanction and approval of my husband'.[9] He gave his whole-hearted approval, and together they journeyed through the countryside, travelling in a covered spring van from farm to farm and from station to station. Mrs Chisholm sometimes took down the statements of the settlers 'in their own dwellings, sometimes on the roadside, and sometimes in the ploughed field'.

[5]Stanley to Gipps, 31 May 1844 (*H.R.A.* xxiii. 619).

[6]He was replaced on the retired list of the Madras Army, 5 January 1845 (*East India Register and Army List,* 1846).

[7]He retired after twenty-eight years' service and therefore would have been entitled to the full pay of major — £292 a year. See *East India Register and Army List* (1846), p. xl.

[8]The amount of such a purse varied greatly. For a majority it might have been anything from £1,700 to £5,000; for a captaincy it was proportionately less. See *Report,* Purchase and Sale of Commissions in the Army, H. of L. (1857), xxvii. 47.

[9]Chisholm, *Prospectus,* pp. vi, iv, see n. 16.

She was so well known and people were so anxious to send news to their friends and relatives, that they invariably related their circumstances with the greatest readiness and cheerfulness.[10]

She collected the statements by 'placing in the hands of the individual a folio sheet of paper containing a column of printed questions, and a blank column for written answers'.[11] Each sheet was headed 'Voluntary information received from . . . parish of . . . county of . . . N.S.W. . . . 1845'. The answers to the questions gave the history of the settler before he arrived in the colony and his progress after his arrival. Not every question was answered, or intended to be answered, but the set questions gave the framework to each statement. The questions and answers occupied the first, second and third pages of each statement; the fourth was divided into three sections which were headed:

1. *Remarks by the Clergymen of the district.*
2. *Remarks by the Police Magistrate of the district.*
3. *Remarks by Mrs Chisholm.*

It was a tremendous undertaking. The colonists were only too ready to help and the directors of the Hunter River Steam Navigation Company gave Mrs Chisholm free passage to and from Moreton Bay.[12] During the year she and her husband were engaged in this work, they travelled over the length and breadth of New South Wales.

Without the assistance of a government grant the collection of the three thousand statements she had originally planned was impossible. *Sidney's Emigrants' Journal* declares that 'about six hundred biographies'[13] were finally collected, and other evidence confirms that six to seven hundred was about the final number.

The statements make fascinating reading.[14] Every one of consequence was 'attested by the relators, by some little family token or incident known to their relatives at home'.[15] Each statement is a compressed life history, an authentic record of comparative conditions in England and Australia. The conclusions of the settlers concerning the wisdom of emigrating are summed up in one vivid sentence by Ellen W. from London, who declared

[10]*Ibid.* quotation from 'a printed letter to the public'.
[11]*S.M.H.*, leader, 22 July 1845; *Duncan's Weekly Register*, 26 July 1845.
[12]*Duncan's Weekly Register*, 27 September 1845.
[13]*Sidney's Emigrants' Journal* (1850), p. 284.
[14]See Appendix B.
[15]*Emigration and Transportation*, p. 23.

that 'Old England is a fine place for the rich, but the Lord help the poor'. Australia, they all agreed, was the land of opportunity.

When the prospectus of the voluntary information was published the full title was given as *Voluntary Information from the People of New South Wales respecting the Social Condition of the Middle and Working Classes in that Colony.*[16] Mrs Chisholm forcefully expressed her hope that family immigration would increase, and urged that England should found 'a humane system of immigration', because then, instead of having to support one tenth of her population 'in pauperism and idleness . . . her *consumers* would become *producers* — her murmuring, idle poor would become contented subjects and useful members of society'. She deplored the 'monstrous disparity' between the sexes, and declared that if female immigration were encouraged, 'Civilization and religion will advance, until the spires of the Churches will guide the stranger from hamlet to hamlet, and the shepherds' huts become homes for happy men and virtuous women'. And she proved herself far in advance of her time by the observation that 'if the happiness of her own children does not induce England to adopt prompt measures to secure this blessing [more wives] to the Colony, the gradual destruction and extermination of the aborigines *demand* it from her justice!'

In commenting on the prospectus, *Duncan's Weekly Register* remarked that her object in publishing the statements was 'not confined to the introduction of small settlers and to breaking up the Bachelors' Stations'. Her work is addressed as well to 'gentlemen of moderate income in England . . . She is also desirous of attracting officers of the East India Company's service to a Colony combining salubrity of climate with the prospect of making a suitable provision for their children'.[17]

Another advertisement appeared in the *Register* two weeks later stating that the work was to be published 'by subscription in the early part of 1846 by Smith, Elder & Co., London, and dedicated by permission to His Excellency, Sir George Gipps'.[18] It is interesting that such a well-established firm had agreed to publish for her. It was to them that she had written in December 1843, immediately after the motion for a government grant had been defeated in the Legislative Assembly; and she had declared

---

[16]Announced in *Duncan's Weekly Register*, 30 August 1845. A copy of the *Prospectus* itself is available in the Mitchell Library, Sydney.
[17]*Duncan's Weekly Register*, 30 August 1845.
[18]*Ibid.* 13 September 1845.

then that it would be 'by the energies' of 'friends at home' that her plans would be carried into effect.

The price of the completed work was to be £2 8s. and it was to be published in eight parts at 6s. each 'to meet the convenience' of those 'who might only wish to purchase what related to their own district'. It seems, therefore, that the several districts of the colony were each to have a volume. But exactly how the statements were to be divided into 'districts' it is impossible to say. In spite of all her high hopes, the *Voluntary Information* was never published in its entirety.

RETURN TO ENGLAND

In her letter to Smith, Elder & Co. in December 1843 Mrs Chisholm had declared, 'I intend the information I wish to collect to support a system I intend proposing to the Home Government', and it seems certain that by the end of 1843 she had decided to return to England for this particular purpose. By the end of 1845 she and her husband had decided to sail for England early the next year.

While the collection of statements was being made, however, two other reasons for visiting England and the Emigration Commissioners had impressed themselves upon her. These were the cases of the emancipists' wives, and those of the children who had been left in the old country when their parents emigrated. From the settlers she heard many sad stories of abandoned children and lonely wives, and these determined her to do all in her power to reunite the separated families. She made lists of wives and children, and noted down all the facts which would help to identify them.

Numbers of children had been left behind because of unfortunate provisions in the bounty regulations. These stipulated that: 'The emigrants must consist principally of married couples, not above forty years of age at their last birthday; but for every child above fourteen an excess of one year will be allowed in the age of the parents if they are still hale and capable of labour. The Candidates most acceptable are young married couples without children.

'No family can be allowed a free passage which includes more than two children under seven or more than three under ten years of age. Nevertheless the Commissioners will under peculiar circumstances accept families with more than the prescribed number of children providing the passage of their children in excess be paid for at the rate of £7 each. The separation of parents from children under the age of eighteen will in no case be allowed'.[1]

Hard pressed parents had left children behind in order to comply with the regulations. Bitter as the parting was it was better to save a few than for an entire family to remain poverty-stricken in the homeland. The bounty regulations declared that the separation of parents from their children would not be allowed, but it was impossible to police the regulation, when the bounty agents knew nothing of the personal history of the emigrants, and were concerned only with filling their ships.

In February 1846 Mrs Chisholm, armed with a list of forsaken children, approached Governor Gipps.[2] He was impressed with her claims and communicated with the Colonial Secretary, Deas Thomson, on the matter. The latter eventually informed Mrs Chisholm that 'All the Government can do is to promote bounty on children who may have been left at home by parents who emigrated prior to 31 December 1841, and who were themselves eligible for bounty'.[3] She was also advised that 'detailed instructions will shortly be published by the Immigration Agent'. In order to give publicity to the matter, she quoted these statements in a letter to the editors of the *Sydney Morning Herald* published on 7 April. For the immigrants who had arrived after 31 December 1841 she could only hope that 'the same humane consideration on the part of His Excellency the Governor which led to the granting of the first, will also on due application, yield the same generous boon to the other'. She assured the public that 'no exertion on her part' would be wanting in attempting to return the children to their parents.

As to the emancipists' wives: during the heyday of the transportation system the home government had tried as far as possible to grant free passages to the wives and children of convicts as a reward for good conduct. In 1842 the practice was discontinued for reasons of economy.[4] Transportation to New South Wales had ceased in 1840, but there were still hundreds of convicts serving their sentences in the colony who had left

---

[1] Quoted in various Parliamentary Papers; see particularly *V. & P.* Leg. Council N.S.W. (1849), i. 532.

[2] Gipps to Gladstone, 9 July 1846 (*H.R.A.* xxv. 13).

[3] Quoted by her in a letter to *S.M.H.*, 7 April 1846. This was also published in the *Spectator*, 11 April 1846.

[4] Under-Secretary Stephen to S. M. Phillipps, 6 January 1847 (*H.R.A.* xxv. 401).

wives and families behind them in England. Mrs Chisholm had
made a list of the names of the women whose husbands were
eager for their wives to rejoin them, and collected money from
the men to help defray the cost of their passages.[5] She had
been living at Albert Park, Liverpool Road, but in January 1846
she moved to the Queen's Head Inn at the corner of York and
King Streets.[6] This made it easier for the families concerned
to see her and for the rest of the time she was in New South
Wales she was fully occupied dealing with those who wanted
her to communicate with their families and friends in the homeland.

The Chisholms had hoped to leave for England about 20
February, but it was not until 14 April that they sailed in the
Dublin barque.[7]

ACHIEVEMENT, 1838-46

During her eventful years in New South Wales, Mrs Chisholm
had seen many changes from the prosperity of the boom years
before 1841 to the misery of the depression and then to prosperity
again.

By the end of 1844 the 'bad times' were only a memory and
the conclusions of the Select Committee on Immigration which
met in 1845 show clearly that the colony was prosperous. In
giving evidence before it Mrs Chisholm remarked that wages
were rising, and that during the previous three months, on the
average, they had risen 15 per cent. Concerning the immigrants,
she had found that 24 per cent of them left the labour market
in four years and in six years became employers of labour themselves.

After considering her evidence and that of thirteen other
witnesses the committee advised that 12,500 immigrants should
be introduced annually. But the finances of New South Wales
were not sufficiently stable to permit this, and assisted immigration
was again suspended in 1846, not to be renewed until two
years later. Caroline Chisholm looked with satisfaction upon the
signs of prosperity, for even in the depth of the depression, she
had never doubted that the troubles of the colony were transitory;
but she was most dissatisfied by the way in which her suggestions
for reform of the immigration system were disregarded.

Assisted immigration had been renewed in June 1843 under

[5]Phillipps to Stephen, 15 January 1847 (*ibid*).
[6]*Spectator*, 7 February 1846.   [7]*S.M.H.*, 14 April 1846.

a modified bounty system, and it became entirely a government undertaking. It was not left to any bounty agent who might profiteer in shipping cargoes of immigrants. 'The old system of assisted emigration by private enterprise was merged into a system of contracts', for the Emigration Commissioners assumed the power to choose between the different shippers, and provided for 'strict supervision of arrangements for fitting out the ships and the conduct of the voyage'.[1]

New rules providing for stricter supervision of the ships and their equipment were issued in September 1843 and an effort was made to improve conditions on board ship. But the provision made for the protection of immigrant women and girls seems to have been no more satisfactory than before. Engagements were still allowed to be made on board ship — the practice Mrs Chisholm had deplored — and the old system of putting immigrant girls in the charge of married couples was to remain. It was to be regarded as 'sufficient protection' if the married couples admitted this responsibility in writing. They had to testify that the single women 'had behaved circumspectly during the voyage, and that their previous character had been good'.[2]

It was probably not faith in human nature but the lack of it which prevented any change in the laws. Governor Gipps expressed the average opinion when he pronounced that immorality 'will never be entirely got rid of, so long as single women are allowed to emigrate'. Yet, since women were urgently needed to correct the disproportion between the sexes, he was 'not disposed to alter in any way the regulations concerning them'.[3]

It was this defeatist attitude which Mrs Chisholm had constantly to fight against, and the evidence she gave before the Immigration Committee of 1845 shows that she had given the difficulties of female immigration further thought since publication of the first year's report of her home. She suggested that, instead of travelling under the nominal protection of strange families, immigrant girls should be sent out under the care of 'respectable ladies . . . such as the widows of clergymen and military officers'.[4] In some cases the ships could be filled with married families, and she declared she would have no single men sent out in the same ship with single women. When assisted

[1]Madgwick, *Immigration into Eastern Australia*, p. 189.
[2]*Ibid.*
[3]Memorandum on Immigration into the Colony of New South Wales (*H.R.A.* xxii. 47).
[4]*Report*, Immigration, V. & P. Leg. Council N.S.W. (1845), p. 639.

female immigration was first introduced in 1831 matrons had been appointed to care for the girls, but Mrs Chisholm wanted a much better type than those who had been supposed to supervise the government female emigrants. When she founded her own society she was to use family groups, not matrons, as the chief protection for her girls — a natural development from her idea of filling the ships with married families.

Because of the delay and difficulty sometimes experienced in filling a ship, she also suggested that emigrants should be sent out in smaller numbers, and that the ships be partly filled with merchandise. And she found fault with the provision of the regulations under which 'a number of persons are called upon to pay a sum in addition to that paid by Government for their passages'. This was the provision which caused some immigrants to abandon children.

Her other suggestions for reform of the old bounty system were not so flagrantly disregarded as those concerning protection for the women. To ensure a better choice of immigrant the new regulations provided that the Commissioners' certificates of character were to be abolished, and the fitness of the applicants was to be left entirely to the bounty agents (now under much stricter control by the Land Board), and the colonial authorities. The Commissioners also had the power to choose between the different shippers, and therefore, in some measure, they had the power to ensure that suitable immigrants were chosen.

As to the appointment of surgeons: the 1842 Immigration Committee had advised that it should be left to the Commissioners. This recommendation was adopted though there is no mention of the naval surgeons whom the committee had also recommended. But from this time onwards better men were chosen.

Unfortunately no better provision was yet established for the dispersal of the immigrants on their arrival; but the oversight was probably not so serious as it would have been if the immigrants had been introduced into the colony during the depression years. In prosperous times newcomers soon found employment.

R. B. Madgwick considers that the great majority of the immigrants introduced under the reformed system were satisfactory: 'Some of the women were badly chosen, and numbers of the men were not proficient at the occupations they professed. But in general they were a decided improvement on previous arrivals, and seemed to indicate greater care in the selection of applicants and better control during the voyage.'[5] In spite of this moderate improvement, however, Mrs Chisholm must have been sadly disappointed by the lack of any official regard for her ideas. Nevertheless, her actual achievement during the time she had been at work was magnificent.

In giving evidence before a committee of the House of Lords in England in 1847, she claimed to have settled eleven thousand in the six years she was at work in New South Wales.[6] This seems an amazing number for one person, and a woman at that, to have dealt with in such a short time. Yet, whenever her facts or figures were called in question, she was ready to back them with documentary proofs so complete that questioners were silenced.[7] No one doubted her figures in this case — the House of Lords Committee accepted them without question.

On further consideration her achievement will seem even more remarkable, for the great majority of those eleven thousand must have passed through her hands from the end of 1841 until the end of 1844 — the years of the worst distress. The total number of assisted immigrants for the years 1841 to 1844, when she was at work, was 31,076.[8] Her eleven thousand was roughly one-third of that number. The majority of the remaining two-thirds found a living for themselves, but a few of the 'do-nothing' type, badly chosen for colonial conditions, never found satisfactory employment.

During the years that she laboured for them, she had proved to the people of New South Wales, even if not to Governor Gipps, that female immigration need not be attended with immorality if the women were given proper protection. By proving this, she altered the attitude of the community to female immigration, and by fostering family life, she raised the social standard of the whole colony.

By the time she left for England, Mrs Chisholm had become a legend throughout the length and breadth of New South Wales. Indeed the trusting belief which some of the settlers had in her capabilities sometimes embarrassed her. She tells how one day on her travels she was accosted by a sturdy bushman.[9] 'Well, Mrs. Chisholm', said he, 'I have been waiting for your coming some time; here's this new-fashioned machine of mine somehow

---

[5] *Immigration into Eastern Australia*, p. 190.
[6] *Report*, Colonization from Ireland, H. of L. (1847), xxiii. 410.
[7] R. Harris, *What has Mrs. Caroline Chisholm Done for the Colony of New South Wales?* (Sydney, 1862), p. 5 (ML).
[8] Madgwick, *op. cit.* p. 222.   [9] *Memoirs*, p. 71.

won't work.' Mrs Chisholm looked over the thing carefully, manipulated parts of it hopefully, but had to acknowledge herself beaten. The bushman was astonished and indignant. He declared loudly that he had been told she could do anything, and here she was 'no cleverer than other people!' This remark put her on her mettle, and when she rode back to Sydney she spent some time in learning the intricacies of the machine. Three months later she returned in triumph to the bushman, and showed him exactly how it could be made to work.

Before she left the colony, a committee was formed in order to present a testimonial to her which would express the gratitude of the people. Dr Nicholson, who had always been one of her loyal friends and supporters, was the chairman. There were twenty-nine members, and among them were some of the best-known names in the colony. The amount of the individual subscription was limited to a guinea, and a formidable list of subscribers appeared in the columns of the press. Among them were names like those of Dr Lang, James and William Macarthur of Camden, Colonel Snodgrass and David Jones. These were the men who contributed a guinea each, the modestly chosen upper limit of the subscription. There were other names on the long list like those of Betsy McMahon and Ann Clark who contributed 2s. 6d. and 1s. 6d. Altogether there were about two hundred and fifty subscribers and two hundred guineas were raised.[10] With this money a piece of plate was bought and presented to her by a deputation consisting of Dr Nicholson, Clark Irving and several members of the committee a few days before she sailed for England. One is tempted to think that the actual money would have been far more use, but Mrs Chisholm was steadfast in her refusal to accept monetary reward and the committee was probably influenced by her attitude. In expressing her thanks, Mrs Chisholm declared that she hoped to attempt more than she had hitherto performed. It was a hope which was to be fulfilled.[11] Only a few years before she had arrived in the colony as an unknown visitor from India. She left in 1846 as one of the best-known and most beloved members of the community.

While she was being acclaimed on all sides as the benefactress of the colony, her last days in New South Wales were overshadowed by a revival of the old, bitter, religious enmity which had been such a stumbling block at the beginning of her work.

[10]*S.M.H.*, 20 February 1846 and 7 March 1846.
[11]*Spectator*, 6 and 18 April 1846.

This was made doubly hurtful because it was Dr Lang, whom she had every reason to regard as her friend and supporter, who raised the cry of 'No Popery!'

Dr Lang was also preparing to return to England where he hoped to further his immigration projects. During the years Mrs Chisholm had been at work in the colony he had evidently felt a sincere admiration for her. He knew her well — he had been a member (in one case chairman) of every Legislative Council committee before which she gave evidence, and it was he who had moved the resolution to appoint a committee to consider the collection of voluntary statements. Though he hated Catholics he acknowledged that her motives were disinterested; indeed, only a very short time before his attack on her, he had subscribed to her testimonial.

Considering all this, at first glance his action seems inexplicable. There is no documentary evidence to account for it — a remarkable fact, for I expected his voluminous private papers would bristle with references to Mrs Chisholm, but beyond one unimportant allusion there is no mention of her.[12] The explanation has to be sought in the character of the man. Bigotry may have been too much for him, and he may at this time have suddenly conceived the notion he held later that by promoting female immigration she hoped to encourage 'mixed marriages',[13] but I feel the explanation lies rather in wounded vanity than in intolerance. Lang had made immigration one of his chief interests, and before Caroline Chisholm came to the colony he was the only colonist to do so. He had done sterling work, but his rancorous hostility to all who opposed him had made him many enemies. On the other hand Mrs Chisholm's personal charm and tact had won her so many friends that the whole colony was singing her praises.

Lang was vain of his abilities; and here was this Mrs Chisholm, his rival in the immigration field, who had been in the colony for a much shorter time than he, being feted on all sides. Every fresh tribute to her irritated him, and the culmination came when the editor of the Roman Catholic *Chronicle*, who had no love for the fiery Presbyterian, criticized his immigration policy adversely. Moreover, the *Chronicle* editor praised the work of his rival. She was, as Lang later complained, considered 'an angel of light', whereas he 'was a perfect fiend of darkness'.[14]

[12]Possibly he was so enraged that he destroyed any private correspondence he may have had with her.

[13]J. D. Lang, *Popery in Australia and How to Check it Effectually* (Edinburgh, 1847), p. 21 (ML).   [14]*Ibid.* p. 30.

His hurt vanity fused with his loathing of Catholicism, over-threw all semblance of reason. With a rush of blood to the head he dashed off a bitterly anti-Catholic letter attacking Mrs Chisholm, and sent it to the *Sydney Morning Herald*. 'Of course, while my having anything either to say or do at home with emigration to this Colony is regarded with a sort of sacred horror by the Romish editor, *Mrs. Chisholm's* past and future connection with immigration is regarded by this personage with unqualified approbation. And why so? Why simply because Mrs. Chisholm is a Roman Catholic, a zealous and devoted Roman Catholic who, he imagines will as a matter of course render her influence and efforts in that way subservient in some way or other to the extension and prevalence of Romanism in this Colony and hemisphere.'[15]

He did not venture to say that Mrs Chisholm *would* do this. No, for 'individually, as member of the community' he was 'so little open to prejudice in this matter' (never did a man so misjudge his own character!) that he had subscribed to her testimonial 'in the hope that others, whom [his] opinion and example in such matters might influence would do so also'. He had the grace to remark upon her 'valuable services', and called her 'a truly benevolent lady', but he implied that she would encourage the immigration of Irish Roman Catholics which had been so large during the preceding years. He wanted, he said, to 'live and die amongst his own people' — not among Irish Catholics.

Mrs Chisholm was deeply hurt and in her answering letter[16] she gave her views on religious bigotry and religious tolerance with dignity and restraint. 'Conscious of my own weakness, anxious to do good to all men, am I not to be allowed to address my Maker after a weary day's work in the way that my conscience dictates? I dearly love justice and the praise of men may be pleasant to me; but a consciousness of my own integrity is more so for when I lose the approbation of my own mind, I forfeit one of the sweetest comforts that God permits a human being to enjoy. The Reverend Doctor expressed his wish to live and die among *his own people;* my idea of good neighbourhood is not so contracted. I have lived happily amongst pagans and heathens, Mahometans and Hindoos — they never molested me at my devotions, nor did I insult them at theirs; and am I not to enjoy the same privilege in New South Wales?' Then she attacked his proposal that all except Protestant immigrants should be

[15]*S.M.H.*, 14 March 1846.   [16]*Ibid.* 20 March 1846.

discouraged, and made the ringing declaration that 'any attempt to conduct emigration on a sectarian basis will most assuredly fail; the proposal is an insult to the Colony, and if introduced would only tend to create discord and strife'. She went on to mention the voluntary statements which she hoped would help her to establish 'a system of national colonization' — a subject which she wished to bring before the House of Commons within twelve months 'after her arrival in England'.

Dr Lang replied that nothing could have been further from his intentions 'than either to hurt the feelings or to depreciate the self-denying and praiseworthy exertions of Mrs Chisholm'. His perfunctory apology, however, only occupied a few paragraphs, and the rest of the typically bombastic letter is a diatribe against the Roman Catholics. He was compelled, he said, on public grounds to allude to Mrs Chisholm in the way he had, because he and she were the only two persons in New South Wales who took an effective interest in immigration, and both were on the eve of returning to England to further their schemes.

Once again he declared his one object in the matter of immigration — 'to do my best to deliver this Colony and Hemisphere for all time coming, from the justly apprehended and intolerably degrading despotism of Rome. If I regarded the subject of immigration in any other light — if I regarded it merely as a means of augmenting our population and procuring the requisite supply of labour for our settlers and squatters — sooner than have anything to do with it — for any pecuniary consideration whatever, either here or at home, I would abandon my profession as a minister of religion and open a Registry Office for Servants in one of the back lanes of Sydney.' This, following his partial apology, was unpardonable, for it was an obvious reference to the Bent Street home.

The controversy between the two immigrant champions served to emphasise what they hoped to accomplish in England. Caroline Chisholm's chief aim was to establish a system of national colonization which was to serve all impartially. Dr Lang intended to do his best to overthrow the 'degrading despotism of Rome', and encourage Protestant emigration to Australia.

Mrs Chisholm never had any intention of obstructing her adversary's plans but Dr Lang, envenomed by the opposition she had expressed in her letter, intended to obstruct her wherever possible. As was to be made painfully evident he had not yet done his worst.

4

Mrs Chisholm and the Colonial Office

THE HUNGRY 'FORTIES

The Chisholms had left England in the year of the great Reform
Bill, when it seemed to many that at last misery and want would
be banished from the land. But the Reform Act of 1832 gave
the vote to the ten-pound householders, and marked the beginning
of that supremacy of the moneyed middle class which was to
become a characteristic of the Victorian age. The working class
soon found that the millenium had not yet arrived, and when
reforms came they were far from revolutionary.

The conditions of life for the majority of the population were
appalling. There might be misery and dirt in Sydney, but at least
there was the open bush beyond, and somewhere ahead a promised
land of prosperity. In the homeland the hopeless present led
only to a yet more hopeless future. The mushroom growth of
the great industrial towns was responsible for a large part of the
misery. There had been a migration within England as well as
from England to the colonies, for the rural population, static
for centuries, was now moving into the factory towns. During the
'thirties, chiefly because of the Poor Law Amendment Act passed
in 1834, young men and women were leaving the country districts.
The concentration of workers in the Midlands and the North
had already begun.

There were no building restrictions or town planning schemes.
The building acts which did exist applied only to part of London
and a few other towns, and they were concerned solely with
regulating the thickness of party walls between houses to prevent
the spread of fires. Street cleaning was haphazard; only parish
streets were supposed to be cleaned, and the rabbit warrens of
alleys and courts were left untouched. It was inevitable that such
conditions should bring forth disease, and from the 'thirties onwards cholera haunted the mean streets of the great towns and
terrified their teeming inhabitants. There was no escape to the

green countryside; the 'melancholy streets in a penitential garb of soot, steeped the souls of the people who were condemned to look at them out of windows in dire despondency'.[1] Few could find solace among books, for there was little education. During the 'forties some were taught reading, writing and a little arithmetic in the 'Ragged' schools and in Sunday Schools, but there was no national system of education in England until 1870. The lack of any state interest in education made it possible for such schools as the Dotheboys Hall of *Nicholas Nickleby* to flourish. Dickens had investigated the conditions in the notorious Yorkshire schools and, even if due allowance is made for his delight in anything grotesque, the conditions he described were little worse than those sometimes to be found.

For many, drunkenness was the only escape from an intolerable existence. The gin shops and beer houses were the clubs of the unfortunate; their rusty, creaking sign boards hung above the crowded streets and gave promise of oblivion. Moralists might rail against the beastly drinking habits of the majority of the population, but considering the conditions they endured, it is a wonder that any one of them was ever sober.

In Scotland the widespread enclosure movement had an even more marked effect than in England, for the farm lands were being converted inexorably into pasturage. There was no Poor Law, and the landlords were only too eager to make conditions intolerable so that the crofters, deprived of the meagre living they had wrung from the stony ground, were forced to emigrate.

But it was in Ireland, land of legendary unhappiness, that the sufferings were greatest. In 1815 the population was approximately six million; in 1845 it had risen to eight and a half million with 'no corresponding increase in the land under cultivation or the methods by which it was cultivated'.[2] Five-sixths of this population was housed in mud huts or cottages of a single room. The potato was the staple food; it was estimated that four million in Ireland, and two million in Great Britain lived almost wholly on potatoes.[3]

During the early 'forties thousands of Irish had to emigrate or die. Shiploads of them crossed the Irish Sea to England. By 1841 one-tenth of the population of Manchester and one-seventh of Liverpool's was Irish.[4] A stream of emigrants flowed to

[1]Charles Dickens, *Little Dorrit*, ch. 3.
[2]E. L. Woodward, *The Age of Reform* 1815-70 (Oxford, 1939), p. 316.
[3]*Ibid.* p. 338.
[4]J. L. and B. Hammond, *The Age of the Chartists* (1930), p. 23.

Canada and the United States; another reached Australia. After 1846, the year of the disastrous famine which followed the failure of the potato crop, the streams became torrents which poured from the stricken country.

In England, as in Australia, the Irish were unpopular because their lower standard of living kept wages down. Wherever they settled the unfortunate people were the cause of trouble and bitterness.

When Caroline Chisholm returned to England the city people — numbers of whom were to become her emigrants — were still huddled in dirty, airless, disease-stricken dwellings, and in spite of harsh discouragements there were many inmates of the workhouses.

EMIGRATION

One remedy was often suggested as a cure for poverty and unemployment. Emigration abroad seemed the gateway to a new world. Many looked hopefully to Canada, the United States and Australia, and thousands crossed the oceans.

For several reasons North America was much more popular with emigrants than Australia. Australia was further away and in a different hemisphere. The antipodes were regarded as an almost incredible part of the world where there were topsy-turvy seasons, and all manner of strange flora and fauna. The Australian settlements, too, were only a little over fifty years old, and during the early years of the convict era, free immigrants were not wanted. Then, during the 'thirties when immigrants were wanted, the high price of land had discouraged them. On the other hand, settlement in Canada and the United States was well established. They were closer to the homeland than Australia and many emigrants could afford to pay the cheaper passage across the Atlantic and keep their independence. In the United States, too, there was a religious and political freedom which was attractive to emigrants like the discontented Irish. The rebellions in Canada and the unsettled times which followed there helped to increase the emigration to Australia during the early 'forties, but when assisted emigration to New South Wales had to be suspended for two years because of the lack of funds, many intending emigrants lost interest in the antipodes.

More was known of North America than of Australia, but the current superstitions concerning American conditions were remarkable. 'Some thought of [it] as a wild land infested with hostile Indians, poisonous snakes and tarantulas, and plagued with forest fires and racking fevers. To others it was a land of perfect equality, free from any of the miseries that perplexed the Old World.'[1]

The ignorance and superstition which clouded the general knowledge of Australia were much worse. Even Mrs Chisholm had found it difficult to persuade many of the immigrants to leave Sydney and work in the country. They had heard so many horrifying tales of the bush that they sincerely believed they could not survive its terrors. As late as the beginning of 1850 a resident of Sydney scornfully described the 'weak and fantastic minds' of the immigrants, who 'conjure up a thousand Hobgoblins in the shape of Blacks, Snakes, flying foxes, Squirls, Mad Bulls and other dreaded Animals as equally ridiculous'.[2] Caroline Chisholm hoped to help combat this ignorance by the publication of her voluntary statements, and also by her personal influence. Dr Lang hoped, too, to disperse some of the superstitions so firmly believed by many intending emigrants. They were each to accomplish a good deal of their objective.

Before these two champions of immigration returned to England, potential settlers learned of Australia almost entirely from the highly coloured reports of the bounty agents. These reports were deplored by the Land and Emigration Commissioners,[3] but the general ignorance was encouraged by the indifference of the government towards colonial affairs. It was an indifference, however, which had been enlivened several years before this time by the evidence given before the Select Committee on Transportation of 1837-38. Earl Grey and Sir George Grey, with both of whom Mrs Chisholm was to talk, were members of the committee, and the 'laborious enquiry' it made into all the conditions in New South Wales must have given them a much fuller knowledge of Australia. The Committee's findings had far-reaching effects because it concluded that 'the continuance of Transportation to the Australian colonies would be inconsistent with the policy of encouraging emigration there, for Transportation has a tendency to counteract the moral benefits of emigration, while on the other hand, emigration tends to deprive Transportation of its terrors'.[4]

[1]Hansen, *The Atlantic Migration*, p. 147.
[2]*Household Words*, i (1850), 23. ('A Bundle of Emigrants' Letters').
[3]Land and Emigration Commissioners to Stephen, 14 September 1840 (*H.R.A.* xxi. 28).
[4]*Report*. Transportation, H. of L. (1838). xxxvi. 35.

It condemned transportation and advised that it should be abolished — advice which was followed by the cessation of transportation to New South Wales. From then onwards, emigration had to be given every encouragement, and it was likely that both Mrs Chisholm and Dr Lang would be given a sympathetic hearing by the Colonial Office.

But official circles still believed that independence was the inevitable destiny of the colonies; and the rebellions in Canda had strengthened this belief. Lord Durham had been sent to investigate the Canadian troubles, and his famous report can well be considered the Magna Carta of the empire. He advocated the introduction of responsible government in Canada. This recommendation was not immediately put into effect, and there was a dangerous delay until Lord Elgin became Governor-General. When he took office in 1847 the provinces of Upper and Lower Canada were united; he introduced a system of responsible government in accordance with Durham's report, and the discontent died down. At the time the significance of Durham's report was not understood and it was thought that Canada was going the way of her rebellious neighbour.

The Colonial Office was politically unimportant. The various Secretaries of State for the Colonies who held office during the 'thirties were 'either well-intentioned nonentities, or men of first-class ability who took this minor office as a step towards higher place'.[5] It was the small permanent staff which really ruled the empire. In particular, it was the head of this permanent staff, the permanent Under-Secretary for the Colonies, who was all-powerful. The great Sir James Stephen held the office from 1836 until 1848, and it was he who advised successive Secretaries of State. His opinion of the future of the colonies did not differ from that held by nearly everyone else. He thought that in time Canada and Australia would break away, but he hoped that the break would be friendly; as for the smaller colonies he regarded them as 'wretched burdens which in an evil hour we assumed and have no right to lay down'.[6] He did not realize the significance of the Durham Report. When Elgin became Governor-General of Canada, Stephen gloomily noted in his diary that the appointment was not unlikely to be the last one ever made.[7]

[5] Woodward, *The Age of Reform*, p. 351, quoting Walpole, *Life of Lord John Russell*, p. 39.
[6] *Ibid.* p. 352.
[7] W. P. Morrell, *Colonial Policy of Peel and Russell* (Oxford, 1930), p. 44.

MRS CHISHOLM IN DOWNING STREET

Caroline Chisholm did not believe that the empire was inevitably doomed to disintegration. There is nothing in her actions or writings to indicate that she ever considered such a possibility. She was always far too busied with the urgent present to worry about something which might never come to pass. Moreover, unlike the stormy Dr Lang, she was no rebel against established authority. She was a woman with a job to do — an exacting and difficult job which needed all her energy.

On their arrival the Chisholm family were met by Archibald Boyd who seems to have been a good friend to Mrs Chisholm. He advised her to take 'a house convenient to the steamers and railroads where country people could see us without much expense',[1] and by the end of October the family were established at 29 Prince Street, Jubilee Place, off Commercial Road. By choosing to live in this crowded district of the East End she made some sacrifice of her family's comfort in order to help prospective emigrants.

Commercial Road lies behind the great docks of London, and the three little Chisholm boys, fresh from the sunlit spaces of the colony, must have been thrilled and awe-struck by the 'roar and rattle' of the city streets. They gazed at the 'steeples, towers, belfries, shining vanes, and masts of ships . . . Gables, housetops, garret-windows, wilderness upon wilderness. Smoke and noise enough for all the world at once'.[2] This was the London of Charles Dickens. In a few years' time he was to meet the Chisholm family, and look with a maliciously observant eye upon the busy household.

Mrs Chisholm's mother was probably soon established as a part of the household and the children must have been left largely in their grandmother's care. Their mother was soon beset by importunate callers and had to deal with a vast correspondence.

Her fame had gone before her. Nearly all these first inquirers, she remarks, 'mention having seen or received letters from friends

---

[1]Caroline Chisholm in a letter to a Sydney friend dated 29 October 1846 and printed in *S.M.H.*, 5 April 1847. Archibald Boyd was one of the leading squatters in New South Wales. After being defeated in the Legislative Council election in 1844 he went to England where he was active in advancing the squatters' claim, and was one of those who made formal protest against Gipps' Occupation and Purchase Regulations (*H.R.A.* xxiv. 642, 575).

[2]Dickens, *Martin Chuzzlewit*, chs. 30, 9.

in Australia who desire them to apply to me'. She soon found that her decision to live in the East End had been wise, for, she says, 'several people who have been to see me have had a penny by steam, or a three-penny rail, and walked the rest, twelve or twenty miles'.[3] Not only did some tramp miles to see her, but she was soon deluged with enquiries concerning emigration, and the scarlet-coated postman became glad to unburden himself of his load at Mrs Chisholm's door. These letters 'occupied nearly the whole of [her] time and the best part of Captain Chisholm's to answer'.[4] They also involved expense; in one week Captain Chisholm paid out £1 4s. 3d. for postage. With some anxiety she realized that within three months she would need extra aid for this alone.

Before making any attempt to establish a system of national colonization she decided to ask the help of the Colonial Office for her two lesser projects: the finding of the lost children, and the reunion of the wives of ticket-of-leave men and emancipists with their husbands. Nevertheless, she thought constantly of ways in which emigration might be encouraged, and in a letter to a Sydney friend[5] she suggested that an immigration society might be established in Sydney independent of, but co-operating with, the government. She believed she could work with such a society from England by establishing smaller village societies there. These smaller societies would choose suitable emigrants.

It was late in the autumn before she made her way to the Colonial Office which was then housed in a 'commonplace brick house' standing 'at the top of Downing Street where the steps to-day go down to St. James' Park'.[6] It was an old house built in Charles II's reign, entirely unsuited for public business, and so dilapidated that its occupants philosophically accepted the possibility of the building falling about their ears.[7]

Earl Grey had recently become Secretary of State, the first occupant of this office who 'combined a knowledge of his subject with a recognized authority in Cabinet'.[8] Moreover, 'at a time when many leading men believed that the colonies would secede, he opposed this idea'. He thought that England's overseas possessions

[3]*S.M.H.*, 5 April 1847.
[4]*Ibid.*   [5]*Ibid.*
[6]E. Trevor Williams, 'The Colonial Office in the 'Thirties', *Historical Studies*, May 1943, p. 141; Douglas Woodruff, 'Expansion and Emigration', in G. M. Young (ed.), *Early Victorian England* (Oxford, 1943), p. 355.
[7]Williams, *op. cit.* p. 141.
[8]Woodward, *The Age of Reform*, p. 351.

were valuable economically to her, and that by 'diffusing the blessings of Christianity and civilization' England conferred a great boon on many of her colonies.[9] Grey's advent was a most auspicious moment in the history of the Colonial Office, and it was fortunate for Mrs Chisholm that she began her work in England when he was unwearied by office, and ready to listen to suggestions for reform. Sir James Stephen was still the Permanent Under-Secretary.[10]

The Colonial Office was accustomed to meeting men from New South Wales who were possessed of power and influence. The energetic members of the the Macarthur family never failed to pay it a visit whenever they happened to be in England. And Dr Lang must have been well-remembered by weary officials after the visits he had made several years before. But this female missionary was a novelty. Caroline Chisholm was then a mature woman, in conscious possession of her great abilities. Russet-haired, tall, and of generous proportions, Eneas Mackenzie describes her at this time as 'stately in her bearing, frank, easy, and lady-like in her manners; her mouth expresses the firmness and decision of her character; her eyes are grey, penetrating in their glance; and her countenance beaming with kindness, which at once causes confidence in her intentions; a certain calmness and earnestness rests on her features which is aroused to powerful expression as the subject of her discourse is that of advice, affection or contempt; her voice is musical, without the slightest provincialism; she speaks with fluency and appropriateness of phraseology, and as occasion calls forth can be affecting, sarcastic or witty'.[11]

The Colonial Office was impressed and, though Mrs Chisholm had 'neither rank nor influence' and 'an income scarcely amounting to a competency',[12] she seems to have had little difficulty in making contact with the rulers of the empire. To Earl Grey, Sir George Grey (the Home Secretary) and the Land and Emigration Commissioners, she advocated her cause with all her persuasiveness. She had carefully arranged the documents which proved the justice of her claims, and official doubts were soon answered. One fact which must have pleased her hearers was that the

[9] H. L. Hall, *The Colonial Office* (1937), pp. 54-5.
[10] He ceased work in his office in 1847, the latter half of which year he was on sick leave (Williams, *op. cit.* p. 153). He was succeeded as Permanent Under-Secretary by Herman Merivale.
[11] *Memoirs*, pp. 143-4.
[12] *Illustrated London News*, 14 April 1877.

lonely husbands had given sufficient money to defray part of the
cost of their wives' passages.[13] She came away with 'a strong hope
that with much trouble I may be able to obtain the boon of a
free passage for their wives and families'.[14] She knew officials too
well to believe that her request would be easily granted.

At this time she suggested to Earl Grey that five hundred single
women should be sent out to relieve 'the forlorn state of the
Australian bachelors'. Grey listened to her with 'much interest
and humanity',[15] and promised that if she wrote to him on the
subject, her letter would receive full consideration. As Mrs Chisholm
urged him to action, Grey must often have been reminded of the
evidence which had been put before the Transporation Committee
of 1838. The information she gave him bore out that evidence,
and he was convinced that her claims were just.

In the two weeks after she first wrote telling her Sydney friend
of her progress Mrs Chisholm was twice in Downing Street for
interviews with the Emigration Commissioners.[16] The voluntary
statements which she had spent so much time and labour in
collecting caused 'much amusement and satisfaction'. But she
was beginning to feel the negative attitude of the official mind
towards colonial matters. In spite of interest in the statements
she was offered no assistance to help finance their publication,
and this worried her, because her own means 'only allowed [her]
to print on a very limited scale'.[17] Although Grey was favourable
to her proposals, the Colonial Office refused to be hustled into
anything which might remotely be considered hasty action.

But the procrastinating officials did not know her mettle.
Between her interviews, she had managed to move her family
to more convenient lodgings in King Street, Covent Garden,[18]
within walking distance of Whitehall; she knew the Colonial
Office would have to be constantly besieged if she was to do any
good. By the time the move was made autumn had drawn into
the long northern winter which she had not experienced for
fourteen years. During the whole of that winter, 'when the snow
lay ankle-deep . . . and walking was no pleasant task . . . backwards
and forwards, again and again, day after day, she passed with her
neatly-tied evidence, between her lodgings . . . and Downing
Street, Park Street and Whitehall'.[19]

[13]*H.R.A.* xxv. 401.
[14]Letter in *S.M.H.*, 5 April 1847.
[15]*Ibid.*   [16]*Ibid.*   [17]*Ibid.*
[18]Harris, *What has Mrs. Chisholm Done for N.S.W.?* p. 5.
[19]*Ibid.* p. 5.

The headquarters of the Land and Emigration Commissioners were in Park Street — the third house on the right. Mrs Chisholm could soon have found her way through the office blindfolded. She worried the commissioners to exasperation, but at last won her point. Both Grey and Stephen were convinced of the wisdom of sending out the convicts' wives. Stephen regretted that the practice of giving such wives free passages had been discontinued. As he truly said, 'it was the single measure habitually taken by this country for mitigating the great moral evils incident to the creation in the Southern Hemisphere of Societies composed exclusively of male convicts'.[20]

With the two most powerful men in the Colonial Office favourable to her proposal it was only a matter of time and patience before she won her battle. An ally rallied to her when Sir George Gipps returned from New South Wales. Sir James Stephen remarked that Mrs Chisholm had already brought the subject of the emancipists' wives before Sir George Grey; Gipps suggested to Stephen that he should also see Mrs Chisholm's list of about thirty women, the wives of ticket-of-leavers in New South Wales. By 1 March 1847 Downing Street intimated that if Earl Grey were given this list he would communicate on the subject with Sir George Gipps.[21] But Gipps had died suddenly the day before this official note was written, and Mrs Chisholm had lost a stalwart friend. She struggled on and eventually it was decided to send the wives and families by a ship which was taking female convicts to Van Diemen's Land; the government gave them a free passage to Van Diemen's Land, and the money which the husbands had entrusted to Mrs Chisholm was used to pay their passages from there.[22] Mrs Chisholm also agreed to defray the cost of the rations.[23] Altogether it was a good bargain for the government.

By the end of March she could write thankfully that she had embarked 'several convict families on board the *Asia* to join their husbands'. Captain Chisholm had had to meet the women and take a boat for them from London to Woolwich, and the

---

[20]Stephen to Phillipps, 6 January 1847 (*H.R.A.* xxv. 399).

[21]Stephen to Phillipps, 1 March 1847 (*ibid.* p. 402).

[22]Phillipps to Stephen, 15 January 1847 (*ibid.* p. 401).

[23]In a despatch dated 21 March 1850 (ML) Grey remarks to FitzRoy that Mrs Chisholm had done no more about defraying the cost of the rations, but he 'had not thought it necessary to renew the application to Mrs. Chisholm for that small expenditure . . . no further proceedings need be taken on the subject'.

expense of this was met by the Chisholms themselves. Some of
the women were so poor that clothes had to be begged for them;[24]
but at length the thirty wives were all embarked.

Mrs Chisholm continued to agitate for the forsaken wives and
families who were still in the homeland. On 22 June 1847 she wrote
that she 'had just left the Home Office and had obtained a passage
per *Waverley* for forty-nine souls'.[25] She had no doubt that other
ships would soon follow.

Many of the other free passages promised her were granted
during the next two years. In September 1848 Earl Grey wrote
to Governor FitzRoy in New South Wales censuring him for
granting free passages for all and sundry who applied for them.
FitzRoy, Grey thought, had gone beyond his instructions; the
grant of free passages should be a reward for good conduct, "It
was never intended to grant that boon to all who might apply
for it, and who had merely avoided gross misconduct'.[26] The
practice of sending out the convicts' wives and families continued until twelve years after New South Wales ceased to be a
penal colony. In October 1852 Governor FitzRoy was notified
that, as convicts were no longer to be sent to the colony, their
families could no longer be sent out at the public expense.[27]

As she had won her battle for the emancipists' wives, Caroline
Chisholm turned her attention to the abandoned children. Before
she left New South Wales she had extracted a half-hearted
promise that the home government would 'promote bounty on
children who may have been left at home by parents who emigrated prior to 31 December 1841 and who were themselves
eligible for bounty'.[28] Gipps was so favourable to her scheme
for reuniting the children with their parents that he had caused
an enquiry to be made in the colony concerning the numbers
of them still in England.[29] By 9 July applications had been
made for passages for thirty-seven males and thirty-two females.[30]
The Colonial Office, as always, was certain that there would be
many difficulties to prevent the project being carried through
successfully, and found its gloomy prognostications partly fulfilled.

The official correspondence concerning the abandoned children

---

[24]*S.M.H.*, 9 August 1847, extract from letter 30 March 1847.
[25]*Ibid.* 9 November 1847.
[26]Grey to FitzRoy, 13 September 1848 (ML).
[27]Grey to FitzRoy, 30 October 1852 (ML).
[28]Quoted by her in a letter to *S.M.H.*, 7 April 1846.
[29]Gipps to Gladstone, 9 July 1846 (ML).   [30]*Ibid.*

is often unconsciously amusing, for the Land and Emigration Commissioners, though reluctant, were badgered and blandished into decisive action. In the first place the commissioners were sanguine. Speaking of a notice which Gipps had had posted in New South Wales, they remarked that 'the persons who can claim the benefit of this notice cannot amount to any inconvenient number'; therefore they would be 'happy to do their best to procure passages'.[31] Less than a month later, when more investigation had been made, and a plan of action had been worked out, the Emigration Commissioners were not so happy. The parents of the children were to apply to the local authorities and deposit £5 for each child, to ensure that it would be withdrawn from the care of public charity. If the parents' applications were granted, the children were to be sent to the Emigration Commissioners with their names, ages and residences, and the names and addresses of the references. The board was then to inquire into the cases, and to guarantee the allowance of bounties according to the current rates.[32] After all that was done, the children were to be produced before the Emigration Agent in good mental and bodily health; every male under fourteen and every female under twenty was to be placed in charge of a married couple; and every male over eighteen and female over fifteen was to bring a testimonial of good character from the clergyman and a 'respectable inhabitant' in the place of residence. On board ship a matron and schoolmaster were to be provided.[33]

The commissioners then became alarmed at their temerity, and in justice to them it would seem as if their misgivings were well founded. They pointed out that applications had been made by 102 people for 147 children, and 110 of these children were under fourteen years of age. Therefore, as well as the matron, married couples had to sail with the children to care for them, and these married couples had to be given a bounty. This was an added expense to the government. If this had been their only complaint they would have deserved very little sympathy, but the biggest difficulty was that of the 147 children whose passages had been applied for, no less than 142 were scattered over the eighteen counties of Ireland. There was very little shipping from Irish ports to New South Wales, and the children would have to be collected in Ireland, shipped from Dublin to Plymouth, and

[31]Elliott and Wood to Stephen, 12 January 1847 (ML).
[32]Elliott and Rogers to Stephen, 2 February 1847 (ML).
[33]Chisholm to Hawes, 28 February 1847 (*H.R.A.* xxv. 407).

sent from there. As the commissioners pointed out, they knew
from bitter experience that there was bound to be a heavy
mortality when dealing with such numbers of young children,
and the risk would only be increased by the roundabout journey.
Nevertheless, in spite of the difficulty, they remarked ruefully
that the disappointment would be too great if the scheme were
abandoned because 'we are embarrassed by the hopes that have
been raised amongst the parents in the colony and their relatives
in this country'.[34]

Mrs Chisholm was asked for her opinion of the scheme, and
this gave her the opportunity to attack the bounty regulations
once again. She denounced the old provision which considered
the protection of strange married couples to be sufficient for
young girls. She pointed out, too, that the rule declaring that
parents were not to be separated from their children was effectually cancelled by the proviso that the 'candidates most acceptable
are young couples who have no children'. The latter she considered
to be the most invidious provision of all. But she was very pleased
with the arrangements which had been made for these children,
and especially commended the 'wise provision' of the matron and
schoolmaster.[35]

The Emigration Commissioners were hurt by her criticisms.
They remarked that though the 'nominal protection of . . . any
married couple . . . was probably worth very little indeed', it
would not be 'practicable or expedient to have a matron with
every ship for young females who had not relatives on board'.[36]
As to her chief complaint — the unfortunate results of the regulation which aimed at the exclusion of families with too many
young children — they declared that 'the whole emigration to
Australia is far too limited to cause the rejection of an extraordinary number of families on this particular ground'. The
difficulty, they implied, was to get families to emigrate to Australia
at all.

The commissioners insisted that the discrimination against
young children on board ship was good, for wherever there
were young children there were liable to be epidemics and a
high mortality on the voyage. In this last protest they were
justified, for the mortality among young children on long voyages
was heart-rending. Nevertheless this could certainly have been

[34]Elliott and Rogers to Stephen, 2 February 1857 (ML).
[35]Chisholm to Hawes, 28 February 1847 (*H.R.A.* xxv. 409).
[36]Elliott and Rogers to Stephen, 12 March 1847 (*ibid.*).

reduced by better conditions and fewer immigrants on board the ship. Mrs Chisholm later showed how this could be done by improving conditions on her own ships.

Altogether, the commissioners regarded the revised bounty regulations as well tried and practicable, though they admitted that there were faults. They had given Mrs Chisholm some concessions, but were not to be moved any further.

Meanwhile, the plans went ahead for shipping the children to New South Wales. In spite of all her efforts, the venture cannot be regarded as a success. In most cases the children had been separated from their parents when they were very young, and the parting had taken place so many years before that it was difficult to persuade them to uproot themselves and sail for a strange country. In many instances the guardians who had taken charge of them when they were abandoned by their parents refused to part with them. The result was that of the 147 children whose passages had been applied for, only seventy-five eventually arrived in Australia.[37] They were shipped in the *Sir Edward Parry* which, as the Emigration Commissioners complained, was chartered for them at great expense.[38] The ship arrived at Sydney in February 1848. Two of the children were from Scotland, three from England and seventy from Ireland,[39] and this was the occasion for the editor of the Melbourne *Argus*, at all other times one of Mrs Chisholm's friends, to remark, 'What else was to be expected from Mrs Chisholm's agency?' which was unkind, and certainly ill-deserved, for she had had no hand in sending out the children's parents. She must have been disappointed at the result of all her struggles, but she had little time to spare for regrets.

The suggestion which she had made to Earl Grey when she first met him, that five hundred single female emigrants should be sent out to relieve 'the forlorn state of the Australian bachelors'[40] also failed. Grey had asked her to write to him on the subject, and when she did so[41] her request received close consideration. In her letter she stressed the 'frightful disparity between the sexes' in the colony and mentioned the evils which resulted from it. She considered that the distress in England,

[37] *Argus* (Melbourne), 15 February 1848.
[38] Land and Emigration Commissioners to H. Merivale, January-April 1848 (ML).
[39] *Argus*, 15 February 1848.
[40] Letter quoted *S.M.H.*, 5 April 1847.
[41] Caroline Chisholm to Earl Grey, 25 January 1847 (see Appendix C).

and particularly in Ireland, could be relieved by sending emigrants to Australia, and preferably female emigrants. Therefore, she asked that free passages should be given to emigrant girls of good character. The Land and Emigration Commissioners expressed their disapproval strongly because of the difficulty of preventing immorality on board the emigrant ships. Grey was favourable to the scheme, but was at length convinced by the arguments that it was impracticable.[42]

By the end of 1847, after a little more than a year at work, she had sent the emancipists' wives and families to Australia, and a number of forsaken children had embarked on the voyage to their parents. Two of the tasks she had set herself to do in England were achieved. The greatest, the establishment of a system of national colonization, still lay ahead. Meanwhile, her time was fully occupied, for besides her other activities in this year she wrote a pamphlet letter to Earl Grey, a series of articles for *Jerrold's Weekly Newspaper*, and gave evidence before two House of Lords committees.

The pamphlet letter to Earl Grey was entitled *Emigration and Transportation Relatively Considered*. The question of transportation was then a burning one, for though convicts had ceased to be sent to New South Wales in 1840, there were still many there 'out on their tickets' and with the cessation of transportation to the older colony, the whole flow had been diverted to Van Diemen's Land. The home government had attempted some reform of the penal system by introducing the 'Pentonville' system of probation, and at this time Earl Grey hoped that New South Wales and the Port Phillip District might be persuaded to take some of these 'superior' criminals. His hopes were rudely shattered, because the colonists refused to have anything to do with the 'Pentonvillains'. The controversy was at its height when Mrs Chisholm's pamphlet was published. It was written as part of her campaign to arouse interest in Australia and emigration. Assisted emigration to the colony had been suspended again in 1846 because of the exhaustion of the land fund, and she hoped by her arguments to encourage the home government to renew the system.

Against the background of unhappiness and want in England she painted a bright picture of wealth and abundance in Australia. 'Is it not a lamentable thought that deaths should daily result from starvation among British subjects, while in this valuable

[42]Madgwick, *Immigration into Eastern Australia*, p. 192.

Colony good wheat is rotting on the ground for the want of hands
to gather it in; — that tens of thousands of fine sheep, drove after
drove, thousand upon thousand of fat cattle are annually
slaughtered there and "boiled down" in order to be rendered
into tallow for the European market, while the vast refuse is
cast into the fields to be devoured by dogs and pigs, and yet
no effort is made by England to provide for her struggling people
by a humane system of colonization?' There is a strangely modern
ring about this passage.

As to the way in which emigration was to be financed she
pointed out that if the land in Australia could not be sold, naturally
there were no funds. But (and here she hit out at the squatters)
when the land was needed for large capitalists it was sold readily
enough, 'nor did the sales cease until the Colonial Banks rocked
like cradles and the Insolvency Court was open'. She argued
that if the price of land was too high, naturally there would be
no fund for immigration. This is the first public attack she made
on the Wakefield system. Like many of her contemporaries she
blamed the systematic colonizers for all the ills of the colony.
It was difficult for those living at the time to realise the fundamental
causes of speculation and depression in New South Wales. To
the colonists the price of land did not seem too high until overseas
prices fell and pulled those in the colony down with them. Mrs
Chisholm did not like the Wakefield system, and she liked it
less and less as the years passed; she accused it of much for which
it was not responsible.

But even if she disliked what she thought were the results of
Wakefield's ideas, her own suggestions in this pamphlet are often
a reflection of his. To England she stressed the need to 'provide
for her struggling population' and the value of Australia as an
outlet for capital investment. Of every hundred emigrants sent
to the antipodes ninety-nine remained, whereas if a hundred
were sent to Canada (and she remarked upon the vast numbers
moving across the Atlantic) only thirty-five remained and sixty-
five went to the United States. In this way she thought the
homeland lost money on the transaction. She proved with exact
painstaking figures that the poor of England, then profitless
consumers, would become producers of capital in Australia —
'the consumers must become producers before any good can
be done'.

Wakefield considered the advantages resulting to England
from colonies were the extension of markets for surplus produce,

the relief from excessive numbers, and the enlargement of the field for employing capital.[43] His teachings permeated the thoughts of all those interested in colonies, and she was probably unconscious of echoing his ideas. Labour was so badly needed in the colony, that if emigration was not encouraged, she decided transportation would have to be resumed. She considered the advantages and disadvantages of this course and decided against it. She testified to the 'sterling worth and exemplary conduct . . . of the emancipists of New South Wales . . . but transportation had doomed thousands and tens of thousands to the demoralizing state of bachelorism'; therefore she could not countenance it.

Eighteen of the voluntary statements formed an appendix to the pamphlet. In this same year a number of the statements were published in a booklet under the title *Comfort for the Poor! Meat Three Times a Day!! Voluntary Information from the People of New South Wales collected in that Colony in 1845-46*.[44] This publication must have been made at her own expense; no more is heard of her hope to publish the statements in several volumes, for government assistance was not forthcoming and she could not afford the venture herself.

Emigration and Transportation is better written than her first pamphlet, *Female Immigration*. This is partly because she had a clear case for argument, whereas in the earlier work she had to tell the complicated story of how she had begun her work. But the later pamphlet is more mature; she marshals her arguments clearly and states them forcefully. She discusses poverty in England, the dearth of labour in Australia and the way in which the one can be used to help the other. Then she passes on to consider and reject transportation. The conclusion she made as to the relative value of assisted emigration to Canada and Australia was a telling one, for in that age, as she said, 'mercenary pursuit was the prevailing passion of man'. The pamphlet was very valuable propaganda for Australia; it helped to arouse the interest of the people, and to give them true information as to colonial conditions.

The two House of Lords committees before which she gave evidence were the Committee on the Execution of the Criminal Law, and the Committee on Colonization from Ireland. Before both, she was the only woman witness. To the first committee she gave evidence concerning her experience with the emancipists

[43]R. C. Mills, *The Colonization of Australia*, p. 93.
[44]British Museum, Catalogue of Printed Books.

and ticket-of-leavers in New South Wales. She stressed the fact that whereas the immigrants were often homesick, the ex-convicts never wanted to return.[45] To the second committee she told the story of her work in New South Wales, and at the end of her evidence she again suggested how emigration to the colony could be encouraged by the formation of an emigration society.

The Committee on Colonization from Ireland advised concerning the distribution of immigrants in New South Wales. Members considered that 'the same system which is adopted in North America might advantageously be introduced into Australia, and an official agency established for the Distribution of Labour in the Interior to collect Information respecting Employers in want of Labour and thus to assist the Emigrants in procuring Employment without Delay'.[46] The committee acknowledged that this advice was the result of the evidence given by Mrs Chisholm.

The New South Wales government followed part of the advice, and five years later there were Government Immigration Depots at Parramatta, Maitland, Moreton Bay, Newcastle, Twofold Bay, Port Macquarie and Bathurst.[47] These depots fulfilled the same purpose as those she had established. Whether or not the government actually used some of her old depots, she had at last achieved her hope that the immigrants would be properly dispersed.

At this time, the colony for which she had done so much tried to give her more material assistance. Dr Nicholson was chairman of a committee which recommended to Governor FitzRoy that a grant should be given to Mrs Chisholm from the public funds.[48] When Dr Nicholson made this suggestion it was not certain if the general rules of the public service would permit this being done. But the question never arose because Mrs Chisholm, determined that her work should continue on its philanthropic basis, declined the offered assistance.[49] This seems to have been one occasion when her ideals got the better of her common sense. If the world in general was not convinced of her disinterested motives by that time it never would have been, and she badly needed the financial help which the grant would have given her.

[45]*Report*, Execution of the Criminal Law, H. of L. (1847), xxiv. 386.
[46]*Report*, Colonization from Ireland, H. of L. (1847), xxiii. 14.
[47]'A Return setting forth the several places at which Depots for the accommodation of Immigrants are at present maintained, with the number and description of Immigrants forwarded to each Depot during the years 1854-5,' *V. & P.* Leg. Council N.S.W. (1855), ii. 412.
[48]FitzRoy to Grey, 22 September 1847 (*H.R.A.* xxv. 760).
[49]Grey to FitzRoy, 8 March 1848 (*H.R.A.* xxvi. 260).

But she may have felt that in England there was even more need to prove her disinterested motives than there had been in New South Wales.

During the years she spent in the homeland, there was an exaggerated fear of Catholicism. In the early 'forties, the Oxford Movement was in full swing and its leader, J. H. Newman, had become a Roman Catholic convert in 1845. The numbers of Roman Catholics were increased by the steady influx of Irish immigrants, and the Protestants began to develop a 'Popish Plot' psychology. The growing numbers and influence of the Roman Catholics aroused Dr Lang to a fury; while Caroline Chisholm was trying to win the favour of the Colonial Office he was trying to do all he could to hinder her work. He became what she called 'an insulting affliction' and because of his attacks she was surprised that she was able to accomplish so much. Fortunately she had friends who testified to her disinterested motives, but Dr Lang's machinations annoyed her extremely. There is an unusual note of asperity in the letter where she complains that 'it is really unfair to attack me here as he has done knowing that, as a lady, I could not reply'.[50] Presently his accusations were to become so outrageous that she threw Victorian scruples to the winds and joined open battle with him. For the time being his activities filled her with apprehension, but they also engaged her close attention because, besides his vitriolic hatred of Popery, he had an emigration scheme of his own which he wished to establish. She was interested in his struggles with the Colonial Office, and in some of the difficulties his emigrants encountered; though he would have been enraged by the thought, Dr Lang's misadventures were a valuable object lesson to his rival.

THE MILITANT DR LANG

Like Mrs Chisholm, Dr Lang was a voluntary agent and in no sense an official representative of the New South Wales government. This should be remembered, because later he let it be thought that he had official status. He had been rejected as the official representative of New South Wales, and the Hon. Francis Scott had become the accredited representative of that colony. Andrew Cunninghame represented the Port Phillip District in England.[1]

[50]*Port Phillip Patriot*, 9 August 1847; letter from Caroline Chisholm, 13 March 1847.
[1]*Morning Chronicle*, 29 November 1849, letter from Caroline Chisholm, 'The Threatened Rebellion in Australia'.

Dr Lang had to have financial backing to put his Protestant emigration schemes into operation, and soon after he arrived in England in 1846 Archibald Boyd advised him to ask the Union Bank to advance him £100,000. This money was to pay for the emigration of ten thousand Highlanders to the Port Phillip District. He hoped the money would be advanced 'on the security of land to be selected in the south western district'. The Union Bank, however, refused to make such a loan unless it was guaranteed by the government. But the latter would have nothing to do with the scheme; nor would Lang consider such a course of action, for he thought the loan would be used to send Irish Catholic emigrants to the colony. He declared that 'Mrs Chisholm and the Bishops' were 'agitating in this direction', but he had written to Earl Grey 'recommending that the Government should not pledge itself in any way for emigration but leave it to private efforts'.[2] As was to be expected the government was only too glad to accept such advice.

At this time Andrew Cunninghame, Archibald Boyd and the Hon. Francis Scott were attempting to negotiate an emigration loan so that assisted emigration could be resumed, and the crying need for labour in the colony assuaged.[3] Lang's intervention prevented the success of the negotiations, and Cunninghame, who had gone to London especially to see Earl Grey, was discomfited. As the apostle of Protestant emigration unctuously remarks: 'Mr. Cunninghame either did not foresee or did not care for the sure and certain result of such a measure in the present condition of the South of Ireland, but having other and higher interests at stake I interfered, although in a way that would create additional difficulties for myself, to save the colony from a serious inundation of Irish Popery.'[4]

Mrs Chisholm had certainly suggested to Earl Grey that the distress in England, and particularly in Ireland, might be partly relieved by sending out female emigrants who would reduce the disparity between the sexes in Australia. But in so doing she was not concerned with the religious question, and in reporting the results of Lang's intervention the *Port Phillip Patriot* became furious because of his 'traitorous conduct' in hindering the efforts of Andrew Cunninghame, the colony's accredited reresentative. As the *Patriot* vehemently declared, the colonists did not greatly

[2]*Port Phillip Chronicle*, 15 July 1847, quoting a letter from J. D. Lang.
[3]*Ibid*. 4 October 1847.
[4]*Ibid*. 15 July 1847.

care of what religion the immigrants were so long as the demand for labour was supplied.[5]

Dr Lang, however, was never discouraged by the fulminations of his opponents, and though he had failed to secure a loan for the emigration of the Highlanders, he continued his vigorous campaign. In 1847 he published three pamphlets. The first two were most informative concerning Australian conditions. One was *Phillipsland; or the Country hitherto designated Port Phillip; its Present Conditions and Prospects, as a highly eligible Field for Emigration.* The other was *Cooksland, in North Eastern Australia; the future Cotton-field of Great Britain; its Characteristics and Capabilities for European Colonization, with a Disquisition on the Origin, Manners and Customs of the Aborigines.* In these pamphlets the worthy doctor had taken it upon himself to rename the Port Phillip and Moreton Bay districts without consulting their inhabitants, and the inhabitants were properly indignant at this cavalier treatment.[6]

The third pamphlet, *Popery in Australia and How to Check it Effectually,*[7] is marked by unreasoning bigotry, and Mrs Chisholm was attacked violently. Dr Lang praised her work among the immigrants in New South Wales, and described how he had tried to help her; therefore, towards her personally, he could not be 'actuated by any uncharitable or unworthy feelings'. But, he went on, 'Mrs. Chisholm is a Roman Catholic, of no common caste, a perfect devotee of the Papacy. In all her efforts on behalf of emigration she is completely identified with the Romish priesthood of New South Wales . . . her whole and sole object is to Romanize that Great Colony and by means of a second and, if possible, still greater land-flood of Irish Popery under the guise of a great scheme of National Emigration, to present it in one time to God, the Virgin Mary and the Pope, purified, or at least in the fair way of speedily becoming so, from the foul and pestilential heresy of Protestantism!' This opinion, he declared, was held by some of the most influential colonists of New South Wales.

In a footnote he pointed out the dangers of the large number of 'mixed marriages', which, he was satisfied, were 'part of the machinery for the extension of Popery in the Colony'. He insinuated that, as Mrs Chisholm hoped to revive the practice

[5]*Ibid.*   [6]*S.M.H.*, 19 April 1848.
[7]This is described as *An Address to Evangelical and Influential Protestants of all Denominations in Great Britain and Ireland* (Edinburgh, 1847).

of sending out numbers of female emigrants, she hoped to promote as many of these marriages as possible.

Lang was a vigorous pamphleteer, and no more damaging attack could have been devised. But, if he did his best, or worst, to destroy her work, he did a great deal to popularize and encourage emigration to Australia. Besides publishing the two pamphlets, *Phillipsland* and *Cooksland*, he lectured from one end of the country to the other and, as these lectures did not seem to arouse all the interest he wished, he began to write a series of weekly articles in the *British Banner*.[8] These began in March 1848 and did not cease until he left England in November 1849.

He had set his heart on colonizing the Moreton Bay district and establishing there a cotton-growing industry, but the Land and Emigration Commissioners refused to allow his Moreton Bay emigrants to be included 'as a portion of the whole number of Government immigrants',[9] and so he began trying to form his own joint stock company.

It was essential to his scheme 'that land should be issued free to immigrants in proportion to the amount of passage money to be paid'.[10] The principle was later adopted both in Queensland and New Zealand, but at this time the home government refused to accept it. Lang spent hours writing to the Colonial Office and expostulating with the various officials. Grey himself[11] was wary of becoming involved with Lang. He had known him some years before when Lang had given evidence to the Committee on Transportation, and he must have had lively memories of the pertinacious Presbyterian. It was, therefore, Benjamin Hawes, the Parliamentary Under-Secretary, whom Lang interviewed, and Lang later declared he had 'received an intimation' that his request for land would be granted. But both Grey and Hawes later denied that any such intimation had been made. Grey said Lang had been 'repeatedly warned' that any emigrants sent out on such an understanding would not be entitled to grants of land. The correspondence between Lang and Hawes bears this out, yet Lang hurried on the departure of the first ship which

---

[8]The *British Banner* had a circulation among the more extreme Protestants.

[9]Child, 'Studies in the Life and Letters of J. D. Lang', *Journal*, Royal Australian Historical Society, xxii (1936-7), 77.

[10]Child, 'Dr. J. D. Lang — Some Aspects of His Life and Work' (ML), p. 83.

[11]Grey to FitzRoy, 15 December 1849 (ML).

was to sail before the company was formed.[12] With characteristic impetuosity and optimism he had the audacity to assume that Hawes' verbal consent was sufficient authority; and he wrote to Governor FitzRoy implying that the necessary authority for the land grant had been given him.[13] This high-handed conduct was to cause stormy recriminations.

The Port Phillip and Clarence River Colonization Company was never legally established, but between September 1848 and November 1849 six emigrant ships were sent by Lang to Australia with 1,424 emigrants.[14] In his own estimation he considered that his emigrants had succeeded 'to a reasonable extent' in providing 'a sufficient check and antidote to the rampant Popery and Puseyism of the country'.[15]

His emigrants were sturdy, hard-working Scotsmen and Scotswomen of the labouring class. Their emigration did a great service to Australia, and he rendered this service almost entirely by his own exertions. The home government gave him no assistance; the 'gentlemen of England' gave him 'literally and absolutely nothing'; the colonists gave him no more than £100.[16] His passage home cost him £210; he does not state the exact amount payable for the chartering of the six ships, but one alone cost £2,000.[17] He sold a small property of his own in the west of Scotland and raised £700, and seems to have given unstintedly of his own resources. Free passages were given to the ministers and schoolmasters he sent out, and he expected that these passages would later be repaid by the colonists. There were also other sums for which he had given drafts on the colony in the expectation that the money would later be repaid.[18] But because of the muddle over his land grants the New South Wales Legislative Council passed a vote of censure on him, and he was forced to foot the bill for his emigration scheme from his own estate.[19] Lang had many faults, but parsimony was not among them; he was willing to impoverish himself in the interests of his adopted country.

The quality of his emigrants was unimpeachable, but the scheme for financing their introduction into the colony broke down, and there was some justified criticism of conditions on board his ships. He remarked of the discomforts of the voyage

[12]*British Banner*, 12 July 1848.
[13]Grey to FitzRoy, 15 December 1849 (ML).
[14]Child, 'Studies in the Life and Letters of J. D. Lang', p. 72.
[15]*British Banner*, 21 November 1849.   [16]*Ibid.*
[17]*Ibid.* This ship was the *Clifton.*   [18]*Ibid.*
[19]Child, 'Studies in the Life and Letters of J. D. Lang', p. 82.

that, 'if a little privation . . . will prove materially conducive to the subsequent comfortable settlement of a family for life, it ought surely to be cheerfully undergone'.[20] Mrs Chisholm never dismissed the discomforts of the long Australian passage in such an easy fashion. She watched most carefully for all unfavourable criticisms which were made of his scheme, and noted them so that they would be of help to her when her own society was established.[21]

The worst fault in the handling of his emigrants was the poor reception given them on their arrival in the colony. This fault was directly caused by his arrogant assumption that the home government would agree to the emigrants being given grants of land in proportion to the amount of passage money paid. The Colonial Office flatly denied that any such agreement had been made, and the acrimonious quarrel which ensued brought both Mrs Chisholm and Dr Lang into the public limelight.

FitzRoy refused to grant the land without the necessary authority and 'in consequence many of the emigrants [were] put about'.[22] The New South Wales government granted them food and water, but nothing else, and Lang had not made proper provision for their shelter on arrival. There was, as a result, a great deal of adverse criticism of his scheme in the colony. Lang's only answer to the complaints about the land grants was that the lack of land was of no account — the emigrants who paid their passages 'had full value in that passage for all they paid; the land was entirely in addition'.[23] Nevertheless, after the emigrants in the first two ships were denied their grants, he discontinued the engagements for land, and prepared to return to the colony to try to straighten out the matter there.

He was quite unchastened by the rebuke he had received. Dr Lang never had any compunction in attacking the greatest in the land if he thought they deserved attack, and while preparing to leave England he found time to make ready a 'blistering plaster' for Earl Grey. Not only the Secretary of State, but Mrs Chisholm, felt the withering power of his invective in this famous letter. All his other denunciations of the Colonial Office are meek and mild compared with the philippic which was written on board

[20]*British Banner*, 12 July 1848.
[21]The late E. Dwyer Gray possessed an old book of her newspaper cuttings. Most of these refer to Dr Lang's activities and are carefully underlined and annotated by Mrs Chisholm.
[22]*British Banner*, August 1849 (exact date missing from cutting).
[23]*Ibid.* 31 October 1849.

the *Clifton* while she lay off Gravesend, and published in the
British Banner on 21 November 1849.

He begins by describing his reasons for returning to England,
and the success he had achieved as a promoter of Protestant
emigration. Then, having dispensed with the preliminaries, he
proceeds to castigate the Colonial Office for its neglect and
discouragement of his schemes. This he contrasts with 'the
officious encouragement and assistance' given to Irish female
emigration. The emigration of Irish orphan girls from the Irish
workhouses to Australia had started in the spring of 1848.[24]
It was paid for out of the colonial funds, and the Australian
colonies gladly welcomed the emigrants. But Dr Lang furiously
attacked Earl Grey for allowing such an emigration to take place,
for he thought it a measure 'simply to supply Roman Catholic
wives for the English and Scottish Protestants of the humbler
classes in Australia'. These 'mixed marriages' were, of course,
engineered by 'an artful female Jesuit, the able but concealed
agent of the Romish priesthood in Australia, who had thus adroitly
managed to attach both your lordships . . . to her apron string'.
Lord Clarendon, the Lord-Lieutenant of Ireland, is included
with Earl Grey as being Mrs Chisholm's dupe.

But Earl Grey was his chief quarry. He spoke of 'the haughty
and contemptuous disregard both of the feelings and wishes of
British Colonists and Colonial Legislatures' shown by Grey's
administration. As an instance he cited Grey's attempt to resume
transportation to New South Wales. This was a telling blow,
because feeling was running high over the 'Pentonvillains', and
Grey was deservedly criticised for his action in the matter. If
the resumption of transportation was proceeded with, Lang
prophesied rebellion in the colony, and declared that 'your
Lordship has, for three years past, been knocking at the gate
of futurity for the President of the United States of Australia . . .
For these three years of gross mis-government' which Grey had
permitted throughout the colonies, Lang considered he deserved
'both dismissal and impeachment'. Thereupon he signed himself
Earl Grey's 'very humble and most obedient servant' and turned
his back upon England.

[24]During the two years (1848-9) that this Irish Orphan Scheme was
in operation, twenty ships with 4,775 Irish girls were sent to the colonies.
Sixty-one girls went to the Cape of Good Hope, the rest all landed in
New South Wales and South Australia. The scheme was discontinued
because the girls were too young and inexperienced for housework
(Madgwick, *Immigration into Eastern Australia*, p. 24).

This remarkable epistle, published after the ship sailed, caused a sensation which must have been most gratifying to its writer. Grey was at once moved to write a reply which, in the form of a despatch to Sir Charles FitzRoy, was given wide publicity. It was dignified and marked by commendable restraint. To the accusation of discourtesy made against his department he remarked that he had never seen Lang himself, but he was assured by the 'gentlemen of his department' that there had been no discourtesy. He also pointed out that Dr Lang had made no complaints to him while in England, but only now when he was leaving and his accusations could not be effectively answered. Lastly, he described Lang's conduct concerning the land grants, and declared his letter was 'calculated to create an entirely erroneous impression'. In this Grey was undoubtedly right. The storm of angry passions aroused by the letter helped to obscure some of the doctor's manifest sins of omission and commission. *Lloyd's Weekly Newspaper*[25] made excited comment and considered that as Lang was the representative of the people of New South Wales, he would not have spoken lightly. After making a depressing survey of conditions in the various colonies, the paper decided that Earl Grey had mismanaged colonial affairs and something had better be done about it. The assumption that Lang was the representative of New South Wales was the type of 'erroneous impression' which Grey had feared. Lang was *not* the representative of New South Wales — the Hon. Francis Scott was the agent for the colony; but in the letter to Earl Grey, Lang described himself as 'a representative of the people of New South Wales' — a description which was calculated to mislead. In a later letter he remarked 'I came not as anybody's delegate, but of my own choice and at my own charges'.[26] But by the time this admission was made it was already firmly fixed in the minds of a great number of people that he *was* the representative of New South Wales and that Grey had spurned him.

Not everyone was deceived; the *Morning Chronicle* and the *Spectator* smiled 'at the deliberate intention which he imputes to a certain busy matron' of promoting 'mixed marriages' in Australia.[27] Mrs Chisholm had kept a discreet silence when he had attacked her alone, but now the unfortunate Irish orphans had suffered. She rushed to their defence, and wrote a stinging reply to his letter which did a great deal to expose his mendacity.

[25] 25 November 1849.   [26]*Ibid*. 21 November 1849.
[27]*Morning Chronicle*, 19 November 1849.

Her reply was printed in the *Morning Chronicle* and she headed it boldly 'The Threatened Rebellion in Australia' — a title which commanded attention. She refuted his contention that the Irish had preponderated among the emigrants to Australia, and quoted Australian assisted immigration figures for 1848 which proved that the proportion was: English and Welsh 4,483; Scots, 1,483; Irish, 1,778.[28] 'With regard to religious persuasions . . . of the emigrants landed in the districts of Port Phillip and Sydney . . . 6,558 were Protestants and 1,317 Catholics.'[29] The Irish orphans, she said, 'the theme of vituperation, the objects of ire, are the hapless victims of famine, the remnants of youth rescued from a gnawing death . . . When this is borne in mind, some will be filled with indignation, some with astonishment, and some with deep regret, that a man undoubtedly of talent, and a clergyman, should not be the first to advocate the cause of the most helpless of the human race — young female orphan children.'[30]

This man too, she pointed out, was *not* the accredited representative of New South Wales, and she quoted colonial newspapers to prove her point. If he had met with discourtesy from the officials of the Colonial Office she inferred that it was his own fault, for she had 'even to thank the very messengers and door-keepers for their civility'. She had 'set her heart upon the reunion of families', and had Lang 'joined [her] in these labours' she would have worked with him 'most heartily'. She pointed out how dangerous his letter was, for if intending emigrants thought rebellion was imminent in Australia they would naturally turn instead to America.

Mrs Chisholm had facts to back all her arguments, but there had been some excuse for Lang's assumption that an undue proportion of the assisted emigrants were Irish. Assisted emigration to Australia was resumed in August 1847. In that year there was great difficulty in securing English and Scottish emigrants because of the demand for labour for railway construction. Consequently the emigrants on board the first four ships were almost entirely Irish.[31] Thereupon Dr Lang, with his incorrigible impetuosity assumed, as he wished to assume, that an unwarranted preference

[28]*V. & P.* Leg. Council N.S.W. (1849), ii. 883.
[29]*Morning Chronicle*, 29 November 1849, letter from Caroline Chisholm. She quoted these figures from the report of the Government Emigration Agent at Sydney for 1848. See *V. & P.* Leg. Council N.S.W. (1849), ii. 883.
[30]*Ibid.*   [31]Madgwick, *op. cit.* p. 196.

was being given to Irish emigrants. As Mrs Chisholm's figures
showed, the position was reversed by 1848 in favour of the
English and Scots.

Her letter helped to correct some of the misconceptions which
had arisen from Lang's abuse of Grey, and the Colonial Office,
smarting from his attack, must have been a little mollified by her
tribute. Earl Grey deserved some censure for his administration
of the Australian colonies, but certainly not 'dismissal and
impeachment'. He did not cease to be Secretary of State until
1852, and therefore it is fairer to consider his administration later.[32]

But rash and ill-considered as Dr Lang's attack on the Colonial
Office was, it was of value in that it shook the complacency of
the government and had done much to make Australia known.
Mrs Chisholm was able to appeal to an even larger public, and
when her own emigration society was established she was able
to avoid some of his mistakes.

[32]See pp. 155-7.

Family Colonization

THE LAND-TICKET SYSTEM

Colonization by family groups had been tried in a haphazard fashion many times, for often an immigrant family could work a farm without any outside labour. But before Caroline Chisholm founded her society there was no organized emigration by such family units.

At the Select Committee on Immigration in 1845 she had hinted at the plan she had in mind. This was the land-ticket system by which every emigrant was to be issued with a ticket worth five shillings. The tickets were 'to be received as cash in payment for land at the Government sales. When a man is the holder of twenty tickets he is to receive . . . interest at seven per cent payable in land tickets for twelve months; at the end of this period if ten tickets are added to the twenty, interest to be allowed at six per cent for six months but not for a longer period except more tickets are purchased, the value of the tickets will remain stationary'.[1]

This was the scheme she expounded before she left Sydney. By the time she tried to win support for it in England eleven years later she advised that the tickets should cost ten shillings each; more tickets of the same value could be purchased. The emigrant was also to be issued with land remission orders worth five shillings each, and each bearing interest at 4 per cent. He could save to collect the number of tickets sufficient to pay his passage, and then be given land on his arrival in the colony.[2]

Mrs Chisholm mentioned the plan before the House of Lords Committee on Colonization from Ireland, and admitted that it had been adversely criticized in Sydney on the ground that it might be abused by speculators. In 1855 the same criticism was made in the columns of the *Argus*. Mrs Chisholm answered by suggesting that the tickets 'could be cashed only when they had

[1]*S.M.H.*, 10 January 1844.   [2]*Argus*, 30 June 1855.

the Government Emigration Agent's signature showing the emigrants had embarked'.[3] She also pointed out the points from which they could embark could perhaps be limited to about nine English, Irish and Scottish ports.

The main objection to it was not the possible speculation in the tickets, however, but the squatters' fear that the new immigrants would at once become established as landowners.

Before she left Sydney, said Mrs Chisholm, 'several gentlemen of that city expressed themselves as favourable to the plan, but thought the period was not propitious for carrying it into effect'. In England, she 'submitted it to a gentleman who possesses a national repute for his knowledge of finance'.[4] Her unknown adviser liked the land-ticket scheme, but warned her that 'certain interests will oppose it' — a warning which proved to be justified. They discussed the plan with several influential bankers and business men who enthusiastically approved it. A letter was drafted 'in which an audience was solicited to lay my land-ticket system before Her Majesty's Government'. All was going well when her first friend received a letter from 'a powerful person' (whom she knew as well as he did), requesting him to 'exert his influence to prevent the bankers and merchants from memorialising the Government in favour of Mrs Chisholm's land-ticket system'. Thereupon, Mrs Chisholm 'relieved her friend of his unpleasant position' and nothing more was attempted.

The plan would not have lowered the price of land. Mrs Chisholm remarked that it made no difference to its working if this was '£20 or £5 an acre'. Indeed, speculation in the tickets might have raised the price and increased the aggregate amount held by the squatters. But the wealthy landowners could not see this; the landholders in the colony and those in England who had interests in Australia were suspicious of any plan which seemed to encourage closer settlement. Moreover the demand for labour in the colony was then so great that a scheme which might involve the establishment of fairly new immigrants as capitalists and landowners was bound to be frowned upon. The landed interests feared her plan would not keep the immigrants as labourers long enough.

THE PLAN OF A LOAN SOCIETY

Though she had failed to have the land-ticket scheme adopted, she was still determined to establish a 'national' system of coloniza-

[3] *Ibid.* 26 July 1855.   [4] *Ibid.* 30 June 1855.

tion. Government-assisted emigration to Australia had been
renewed in August 1847, but her hopes that sweeping reforms
would be introduced had not been realized. As the land fund
was exhausted, it was to be financed by debentures issued in the
colony, and the immigrants were to be divided equally between
New South Wales and the Port Phillip District. Three months
later, it was announced that New South Wales was permitted
to create 'a funded debt to a moderate amount to finance immigration'.[1] The home government took charge of the selection of the
emigrants; the Colonial Board which had previously examined
them on their entry into the colony was abolished, and the Land
and Emigration Commissioners in England were given the final
responsibility of choice.[2] The sole duty of the shipowners was to
find and fit out the ships; they were not permitted to select the
emigrants as they had been under the bounty system.

Though a better selection of emigrants was provided for, there
was no better protection for single women than there had been
under the revised bounty system. They were still entrusted to
the care of married couples. The commissioners soon found,
however, that it was difficult to find suitable married couples
for this purpose, therefore numbers were sent out in the care
of matrons.[3] The Irish orphans, whose emigration infuriated Dr
Lang, were sent out in this way. Earl Grey was anxious to promote
female emigration. He was insistent that the disproportion between
the sexes was the main cause of the depravity in colonial society,[4]
and he did all he could to correct it. His insistence upon this was
so marked that very probably he was acting under Caroline
Chisholm's influence.

From the time Mrs Chisholm returned to England she had

[1]Madgwick, *Immigration into Eastern Australia*, p. 195.

[2]If they wished, the colonists could nominate immigrants. 'Persons pur-
chasing land before leaving England had been able, since 1843, to
nominate emigrants in the proportion of about three emigrants for each
£100 expended, and in 1848 this concession was extended to purchases in
the Colonies.' The Land and Emigration Commissioners were also em-
powered to give passages 'at reduced rates to persons nominated and paid
for by their friends in Australia. In these cases £8 was charged for each
adult below thirty years of age, if of suitable class, and £10 for other
persons' (T. A. Coghlan, *Labour and Industry in Australia, 1788-1901*
(Oxford, 1918) i. 365-6).

[3]Madgwick, *op. cit.* p. 196. A year later, however, the reform which Mrs
Chisholm had always demanded was made when it was decided that
immigrant girls should not be engaged on board ship but should be taken
at once to the Immigration Barracks. See V. & P. Leg. Council N.S.W.
(1849), ii. 890.

[4]Madgwick, *op. cit.* p. 196.

been an unofficial emigration authority. Settlers in New South Wales had written to their relatives, and had told them of her arrival. She had also been seeking out the fathers, mothers, brothers and sisters of the colonists who had given her their 'statements' before she left the colony. This made her known to many families and individuals who were interested in emigrating. She was so deluged under 'a mass of letters'[5] that she had to engage a writer to do some of the clerical work. From the beginning of her stay in England until July 1847, she received no less than 4,071 applications from intending emigrants to New South Wales,[6] and to the best of her ability she gave advice to all who asked her help. The fact that many of those who sought her aid had relatives in the colony impressed her forcibly. During the months she and her husband had spent collecting the voluntary statements, and during the long voyage to England, she had had some leisure in which to consider emigration problems. With her belief in the family as the nucleus of society, added to the pleas of all those longing to rejoin their dear ones, it was natural for her to evolve a scheme of emigration with the family unit as its main feature. At some time during the busy first year in England she formulated her plan. Her hopes for her land-ticket system had been dashed, the new government Emigration Regulations disappointed her, but she was not discouraged; she began at once to advocate her new scheme.

She pointed out to the House of Lords Select Committee on Colonization that sums of money were sent by settlers so that relatives in England could eventually pay their passage to Australia. In many cases this money never reached the rightful recipients; in others it was frittered away and not put to its intended purpose. Usually only small amounts of £5 or £10 were sent, and it took years to pay the passage money. If an emigration society were formed, contributions to passage money could be made out of its funds which would be made up of these small savings. The society should be a voluntary one, independent of the government, but co-operating with it. Such a society would be able to help many to emigrate who, without its assistance, would not be able to leave England. Men over forty were excluded by the emigration rules at that time but such men, if they had families of older children, were very valuable immigrants. She

[5]Her letters in *S.M.H.*, 5 April 1847, dated 29 October 1846, 16 November 1846, 30 November 1846.
[6]*Report*, Colonization from Ireland, H. of L. (1847), xxiii. 424.

suggested that the land purchase regulations should be reconsidered, and small farms made available for the poor man to buy as soon as he had saved his money. She knew only too well how unpopular this suggestion would be with the landed interests. Soon she was to defy them, but at this time she did not press her point.

She calculated that the passage of one adult to New South Wales would cost £15, and equal the passages of two children. Thus a subscription of £100 to the society would give a passage to six adults and two children, or to two adults and ten children. This was the first clear statement of the principles upon which the Family Colonization Loan Society was to be established.

In 1845, speaking of the faulty choice of bounty immigrants, she had declared that 'too many mechanics were amongst them, and persons who were rather above common labour and yet had not sufficient capital to work for themselves; *it is the poor peasantry that are wanted in this Colony*'.[7] It was two years since she had given that opinion, and during those years she had become acquainted with English conditions. She had discovered the great numbers of those who had small savings but 'not sufficient capital to work for themselves'. Many of them had helpful relatives in New South Wales, and she was convinced that they would become most valuable colonists. It was the squatters who demanded the 'poor peasantry', and she was fast coming to have little patience with their demands.

The House of Lords committee did not comment on her suggestion. Evidently she could expect no more government help for this plan than had been given for the land-ticket scheme. The influence of the Australian squatters was powerful.

Shortly after she gave her evidence before the House of Lords Committee her old friend Dr Murphy, now the Roman Catholic Bishop of Adelaide, visited the Chisholms. He found them 'as busy as the most fully employed government officials',[8] getting up an emigration committee among the merchants of London. Caroline Chisholm knew she must have the support of such men if her society was to be a success, for in the early stages of the venture it was essential to have financial backing.

Mrs Chisholm and her husband worked from dawn to dark answering letters and receiving callers. Sometimes as many as

[7]*Report*, Immigration, V. & P. Leg. Council N.S.W. (1845), ii. 639.
[8]*Argus*, 27 August 1847, quotation of a letter in the *Adelaide Observer*.

three hundred letters were received during one day,[9] and for
several years they received an average of two hundred and forty a
day.[10] The devoted Captain Chisholm laboured with this gigantic
correspondence.[11]

Her visit to Scotland, which was also mentioned by Dr Murphy,
was in the nature of a lecturing tour to publicize the society, and
to give information of Australia to those who wished to emigrate.
The pamphlet, *Emigration and Transportation Relatively Considered*, had made her aims known to many of those who were
interested in emigration problems. But the majority of the population of the British Isles was still illiterate. Like Dr Lang, she had
to seek out possible emigrants, and tell them of the need for
labour in the swiftly developing colonial society. The dispossessed
crofters of Scotland listened eagerly. As Dr Lang so often asserted,
these men, born farmers and fiercely independent, were first-class
colonizing material.

In the next few years she must have visited every corner of
the British Isles. Sometimes a casual note in an Australian newspaper, such as the report of Dr Murphy's letter, gives an indication
of the way in which she proselytized for the emigration cause.
The reports of her lecturing are unanimous in praising her persuasiveness. The *Illustrated London News* declared that she
spoke as she wrote, 'with vigour, humour and pathos'.[12]

Towards the end of 1848 she had perfected her plan, and 'by
personal communication and by letter, had taken the opinion
of considerable bodies of the working classes upon it'.[13] With
characteristic thoroughness she worked out every detail of the
scheme before she approached the man whom she wished to
sponsor her society — Lord Ashley, the most famous philanthropist
of the age. She approached 'other influential parties'[14] as well,
among whom were Sidney Herbert, later the friend and champion
of Florence Nightingale, and Vernon Smith, M.P. for Northampton,
the city she had known so well as a child.

In spite of her thorough preparation another year passed before
the plan was publicized, but at last, by the end of 1849, the dream
became reality. At the beginning of the next year news of the
proposed scheme had reached Australia, and the *South Australian*

---

[9]Caroline Chisholm to Earl Grey, 25 January 1847 (see Appendix C).
[10]*S.M.H.*, 2 February 1924, an article by the late E. Dwyer Gray.
[11]*Argus*, 31 August 1853, from the London *Daily News*, June 1853.
[12]17 April 1852.
[13]*Argus*, 22 July 1850, quoting her letter to Lord Ashley dated August
1849.   [14]*Ibid.*

Register, the *Sydney Morning Herald*, and the Melbourne *Argus*
gave long notices of it.[15] Her emigration society was to be called
the Family Colonization Loan Society and, though later modifi-
cations were made in its organization, the general scheme did not
alter after the first plan was made. The 'immediate object was to
relieve the distressed and to help the poorer class of people to
emigrate', and wherever possible the reunion of families was to
be encouraged. Her ultimate aim was to raise the moral standard
of the people, and she hoped to further this by giving her people
the opportunity of paying their own passages.[16]

There was to be a Central Committee in London consisting of
Lord Ashley, M.P. (President); Sidney Herbert, M.P.; Vernon
Smith, M.P.; John Tidd Pratt, Esq.; F. G. P. Neison, Esq.; and
W. Monsell, M.P. Pratt and Neison, the only non-members of
parliament, were both prominent lawyers. As well as this Central
Committee there seems to have been an Emigration Committee
which administered the actual emigration. Captain and Mrs Chisholm were certainly the leaders of this committee, and there may
have been one or two other members, but there is no explicit mention of them. Branch, or local, committees were to be established in
different localities to forward prospective emigrants to the Central
Committee in London. In Australia, agents for the society were
to be appointed in Sydney, Melbourne and Adelaide. These men
had to know the conditions of the colony and where particular
types of labour were needed. It was hoped that these three
Australian colonies would co-operate to form branch committees
similar to the proposed English ones, and these Australian branch
committees would then assist the society's agents.

So much for the organization of the society. As its name
implies, it was intended to be a loan society, and by voluntary
contribution Mrs Chisholm hoped to form a fund of from £100
to £1,000 for its support. After this was done the next step was
'for persons desirous of emigrating to form themselves into groups
of not less than three, and not more than twenty families, all
willing to go to the same Colony. Each intending emigrant on
enrolling to pay £1 and 2s. a quarter until despatched. Then each
family in each group must muster its funds and raise the utmost

[15]*South Australian Register*, 23 February 1850; *S.M.H.*, 3 April 1850;
Argus, 22 July 1850.
[16]See *S.M.H.*, 3 April 1850; Chisholm, *The A.B.C. of Colonization*
(London, 1850), p. 24; *Report*, The Present System of Immigration, *V. & P.*
Leg. Council Vic. (1852-3), ii (2), 901.

sum it can towards the required passage money'. For instance, five families among them might contribute £80. 'To the £80 raised by the joint exertions of the five families the Loan Society adds £80, making a gross sum of £160.' After that the Central Committee of the Society would proceed 'to take joint and several security from members of the five families who were of age and then to pick out the parties who shall have their passage money paid out of this sum of £160'. Having made their choice of perhaps thirteen individuals, chiefly for their wage-earning capacity, the Central Committee would then despatch them to the colony where they would be found employment by the society's agent. This agent was to hold the notes of hand of the members of the families 'and duly collect from them such portion of their wages as they can spare towards the loan due to the Society and to their own families'. If the thirteen individuals earned altogether £200 a year, and each paid the agent £7 10s. 9¼d. (total £98), then the families left in England could add £10 to this. The accumulated sum of £108 would then be used in sending out more adults. The process was to continue until all members of the group had been helped to emigrate, and in two or three years the loan would be repaid.[17] A reserve fund was to be established to bear any losses such as the death or default of an emigrant, and as the last instalment towards the passage money adults paid 5s. and children 2s. to this fund.

In connection with the Family Colonization Loan Society, Caroline Chisholm proposed to establish a system of remitting money from Australia to England. When she had worked in New South Wales Australian banks had charged as much as £15 to remit £50, and £50 was not a sum easily saved by struggling farmers. She had argued the problem out with Governor Gipps, and he had 'communicated with the banks through the Colonial Secretary'.[18]

The banks had then agreed to remit small sums if this could be done through Mrs Chisholm. A great deal of her time was involved, for she had to vouch for each depositor and go with him to the bank. After her society was established, she made arrangements with Messrs Coutts & Co. of the Strand to receive small remittances from Australia and pass them on to the society.[19]

One weakness in her scheme leaps to the eye — there was no

[17]*S.M.H.*, 3 April 1850.
[18]Caroline Chisholm, letter to *The Times*, 16 August 1852.
[19]*Ibid.*

proper security for the repayment of the loans. The *Sydney Morning Herald* said that the security 'would be first legal, secondly self-interest, thirdly the force of family and friendly opinion'.[20] These considerations certainly had weight, but it remained to be seen if human nature would repay the trust placed in it.

Meanwhile, the society was founded, and so, almost three and a half years after her return to England, she was able to begin what she considered a national system of colonization. But why was she able to found such a society when, only such a short time before, her land-ticket system had been rejected? The Family Colonization Loan Society aimed to send out emigrants who in a few years would take up holdings of their own. It was that very expectation which seems to have prevented the establishment of the land-ticket scheme. The squatters wanted cheap labour, and would have nothing to do with an emigration system which encouraged future small settlers.

The fact that the poverty and distress in the British Isles was becoming worse instead of better may have carried some weight. The dreadful results of the Irish famine were not fully manifest until a year or two after it occurred. Emigration was a safety-valve which could not be discouraged, no matter how much the squatters feared that their lands would be wrested from them. But the United States and Canada had been the popular choice of emigrants during the early 'forties, and it was only towards the end of the decade, when Mrs Chisholm's society was founded, that Australia was favoured. If it had not been for this increased interest in Australia, the squatters' counsels might have prevailed, the society might not have been founded, and many more emigrants might have crossed the Atlantic to North America.

A combination of causes had quickened interest in the antipodes, and one of these was a direct result of the squatters' activities. About this time Australia had completed the capture of the English woollen market and now supplied 80 per cent of the wool imported into England.[21] To manufacturers, also, the growing use of steamships[22] promised easier communication with the distant colony. Business men had good reason to learn some-

[20] *S.M.H.*, 3 April 1850.
[21] H. Burton, 'Historical Survey of Immigration and Immigration Policy', in F. W. Eggleston and P. D. Phillips (eds), *The Peopling of Australia* (Melbourne, 1933), p. 39; S. H. Roberts, *The Squatting Age in Australia* (Melbourne, 1935), pp. 50-9.
[22] *The Times*, 23 and 24 April and 31 May 1850.

thing of Australian resources. The change from indifference to interest is reflected in the columns of *The Times*. During the early 'forties Australia is rarely mentioned, but long descriptions of American conditions appear frequently. By 1848, however, letters from Australia were being published telling of the urgent need for labour in the colony.[23] Moreover, letters from English correspondents appeared remarking on the need for female immigrants in Australia, which could be supplied by the surplus girls in the English workhouses.[24] In this the hand of Mrs Chisholm is clearly seen. In 1848, 7,855 assisted emigrants embarked for New South Wales. This was the largest number since 1841.[25]

The foundation of Mrs Chisholm's society was helped forward by the increased commercial and popular interest in Australia, but it was fortuitous news from the colony which made the squatters' protest seem meaningless, and gave the final impetus to the acceptance of her scheme. This was the story of Sir Thomas Mitchell's explorations. Between November 1845 and January 1847 he had explored the Maranoa country at the back of the Darling Downs and discovered the sources of the Barcoo River. It was a good season, and the optimistic Sir Thomas gave a glowing account of the new land he had seen. His journal, published in London in 1848 under the title of *The Journal of an Expedition into Tropical Australia in search of a route from Sydney to the Gulf of Carpentaria*, made an immediate impression, and Mrs Chisholm quoted it to illustrate the value of Australian land.[26] Probably it was this news which galvanized Ashley and the 'other influential parties' into putting the scheme into operation after they had had it under consideration for 'upwards of a year'.[27]

The society was established, but before it could be a success Caroline Chisholm had to win public support. As she had depended on the people of New South Wales to support her Immigrants' Home, so she now depended on the people of England to support her Family Colonization Loan Society, and in 1850 she published a pamphlet, *The A.B.C. of Colonization*, in which she explained and advocated its principles.

From a literary viewpoint this is the best of her pamphlets.

[23]See particularly *The Times*, 20 and 24 May 1848 and 4 July 1849.
[24]*The Times*, 25 May 1848 and 6 June 1848.
[25]*The Times*, 4 April 1850.
[26]*The A.B.C. of Colonization*, p. 25. She also drew attention to the value of Mitchell's discoveries in her evidence before the House of Lords Select Committee on Colonization from Ireland, 1847.
[27]*Argus*, 22 July 1850.

Probably it owes a good deal of its forthright quality to the simplicity of the case argued. In her first pamphlet, *Female Immigration,* Mrs Chisholm had to tell a long and complicated story. In *Emigration and Transportation Relatively Considered,* as the title implies, she had a clear argument, and she argued it well in her persuasive, easy style. Nevertheless, she was still trying to persuade, whereas *The A.B.C. of Colonization* is not an attempt at persuasion — it is a denunciation of the government system of emigration. In comparison with the government system she then describes her own society, its aims and constitution. She considers its possible faults, and whether the government might be able to provide a better system, but decides that this seems impossible. The pamphlet finishes with a passionate appeal to all Englishmen to forget their differences, and unite in a common cause so that the misery in England might be relieved.

She wrote in righteous anger: 'I hold it derogatory to the high and moral feeling of Englishmen, that under the insignia of the Royal Arms of England, modest British matrons should be asked the question, "Whether any increase to the family is expected, and when?" . . . I consider it a gross outrage to humanity — a violent rending of the tenderest ties of nature, and injurious to morality, that heads of families above forty years of age and those who have a certain number of children under ten years of age, should be excluded from the advantages and rights of emigration — that under other rules children beyond a certain number should be taxed £7 each on account of passage money — that again single men past the age of thirty-five should not be considered eligible and that the "candidates most acceptable are young married couples without children".'

And at last she had attacked the squatters: 'It must be borne in mind, that the Board of Commissioners are but the agents of the squatting interest, or men of capital in the Australian Colonies, and that they are often necessitated to enforce rules which their best feelings must shrink from. Neither the Government, nor the parishes can give us a sound and satisfactory system of Colonization; they may give us convict emigration; exile emigration; pauper emigration or Government emigration, but they cannot give us a wholesome system of national colonization.' These were strong words; she had travelled a long way in the ten years since, as a diffident young woman in Sydney, she had feared to take 'a public step'.

The reunion of families was to be one of the paramount aims

of her society, and the group system was to be its keystone. The group system should help to achieve her design 'to raise the character and moral standard of the people . . . Parents and husbands would feel, not with shame, but with honest pride, the position they stood in — that a benevolent public was ready to co-operate with them, and thought them worthy to be entrusted with the means to transport themselves and their children to a land where they hoped soon to be enabled, by their industry and frugality, to repay the advances made to them.'

She hoped the friendships made between the emigrants would help to found 'bush partnerships' in Australia. The group system, she also thought, would help to make it very difficult for an emigrant to default in paying his loan. 'There is a code of honour, a sort of manly pride, amongst the industrious and working classes, that carries more weight at times than a court of law . . . a person guilty of [default] could hardly exist or remain in a district of the Australian Colonies. He would be known — he would be scouted and avoided — the stigma would attach to his very children — it would follow him wherever he went.' This was sound psychology, but she admitted that the repayment of the loan had been called the 'forlorn hope'. It remained to be seen if her faith was justified.

This pamphlet is a landmark in Caroline Chisholm's life and work. She was at last convinced that the government would not attempt to introduce the emigration system she desired, because the government was influenced by the squatters. She had hoped her society would be 'independent of but co-operating with the Government', but she had been forced to realize that the government would not give direct co-operation. Henceforth, therefore, she worked alone.

She had founded her society in defiance of the landed interests and with no prospect of official support; she had now to work furiously for its success. *The A.B.C. of Colonization* gave some publicity to her scheme, but a good deal more was needed, and it was at this critical moment that Charles Dickens gave her powerful aid.

CHARLES DICKENS

By the middle of the century the name of Dickens was known in every home in England. After a harsh childhood he had become a House of Commons reporter, and during the early 'thirties he must have heard most of the parliamentary debates. The knowledge which he gained of the abuses of the time as he listened to these debates, as well as the experiences of his childhood, had a profound influence on his work as a novelist.

In *Pickwick Papers* he had touched on the conditions in the debtors' prisons, but these were incidental to the joyous doings of the Pickwickians. It was not until *Oliver Twist* appeared in a serial beginning in January 1837, that he consciously began his career as a social reformer.[1] In this book, he attacked the New Poor Law, and drew attention to the evil conditions which prevailed in the miserable back streets of London. *Nicholas Nickleby* followed with its exposure of the Yorkshire schools.

With *Martin Chuzzlewit,* written after his visit to the United States in 1842, an interest in emigration begins to appear in his work. For some reason *Chuzzlewit* in its monthly issue did not sell well, and Dickens cast about him for a means of improving the sale, with the result that Martin hurriedly decided to go to America.[2] But though Martin's emigration was a sudden impulse on his author's part, Dickens seems to have been interested in the subject for some time previously. During those years it would have been remarkable if a man of his character had not considered the problem of unemployment, and also considered emigration as its solution.

From the point of view of the relationship between Caroline Chisholm and Dickens, *David Copperfield,* which began publication in 1849, has some interesting features. At its conclusion both the Peggottys and the Micawbers emigrate to Australia where the unquenchable Mr Micawber incredibly becomes a successful magistrate. When Martin Chuzzlewit emigrated to America he had followed what was then the fashionable path of emigrants. But in the five years since Martin crossed the Atlantic the focus of interest had shifted to Australia. A great deal of this change in public interest was due to the work of Mrs Chisholm, and by the time *David Copperfield* was being written Dickens had met her, and knew the details of the Family Colonization Loan Society.

The money which enabled the Micawbers to emigrate was supplied by David's aunt. There was no emigration or charitable society involved, but 'Mr Micawber's insistence on the exact way in which he would pay back the loan is rather reminiscent

[1]George Gissing, *The Immortal Dickens* (1925), p. 64.
[2]*Ibid.* p. 115.

of the Chisholm Family Loans'.[3] Though it is pure conjecture to think Dickens might have been influenced by the rules of her society, it would seem that her work had so interested him in Australia that the Micawbers and Peggottys were sent there.[4]

Apart from his books Dickens was practically interested in emigration. He was very friendly with the philanthropist, Miss Burdett-Coutts, heiress to the banking fortune of Coutts & Co. In 1846, when Miss Coutts established a charitable home at Shepherd's Bush to rescue fallen women, 'by testing their fitness for emigration',[5] he gave her great help and encouragement. 'He thought that if such a home were run in conjunction with an emigration scheme financed by Government, the girls, after re-education, would make excellent wives for colonists.'[6]

Mrs Chisholm and he had much in common. He approved of emigration societies and regretted the reluctance of public men of all parties to give the needful help to emigration.[7] To him, as to Mrs Chisholm, emigration seemed the proper outlet for the surplus population. He did not approve of Chartism or political movements as a means of redressing the grievances of the poor, for he had a 'horror of the mob'.[8] Caroline Chisholm distrusted Chartism because of the violent feeling it aroused, and she was very pleased when she was able to persuade a young Chartist carpenter, the first member of her society, that emigration was better for him than political meetings.[9] Dickens was a radical, but not a leader of radical thought;[10] and Caroline Chisholm, in spite of her flouting of the convention of the time, was no rebel against established custom.

There was one consideration which might have prevented his approval of Mrs Chisholm's society; this was the old religious stumbling block. At the time the society was founded anti-Catholic feeling was even more intense than it had been during

[3]Mr Humphrey House, author of *The Dickens World* (Oxford, 1941), pointed this out to me.
[4]Mr House writes: 'I am entirely satisfied in my own mind that if it had not been for Mrs. Chisholm's work and propaganda it would not have been Australia.' Mr G. M. Young also agrees with this view.
[5]John Forster, *Life of Charles Dickens* (1874), ii. 456.
[6]Una Pope-Hennessy, *Charles Dickens, 1812-70* (1945), p. 239. For his letters to Miss Coutts concerning this project see C. Osborne (ed.), *Letters of Charles Dickens to the Baroness Burdett-Coutts* (1931), pp. 71-99.
[7]Forster, *op. cit.* ii. 235.   [8]House, *op. cit.* p. 179.
[9]*Household Words*, iv (1852), 529 ('Better Ties than Red Tape Ties'); Harris, *What has Mrs. Chisholm Done for N.S.W.?* pp. 5-6.
[10]House, *op. cit.* p. 42.

the earlier years of her stay in England. In 1850 the Pope set up territorial bishops in England, thus causing a misdirected popular outburst against the so-called 'Papal aggression'.[11] Dickens was no exception to the average intolerant Protestant of his day; indeed, having the hasty temper often associated with a generous nature, he was more than ordinarily liable to prejudice. He believed that 'the dissemination of Catholicity was the most horrible means of political and social degradation left in the world'.[12] This was a pronouncement worthy of Dr Lang himself. Yet, in spite of this prejudice, he was so convinced of Caroline Chisholm's honesty of purpose that he was prepared to launch what was almost a campaign in favour of her society.

In spite of her busy life, Mrs Chisholm, like everyone else, must have found time to read Dickens' books as they appeared in serial form. She was impressed by his pity for misfortune and his fictional work may well have opened her eyes to some of the abuses of the time and have quickened her own interest in reform. She had almost certainly heard of his encouragement of Miss Coutts' home at Shepherd's Bush, and she was anxious to meet the celebrated Mr Dickens, and to interest him in her own work.

Mrs Herbert, the wife of Sidney Herbert, arranged the introduction. On 24 February 1850 she wrote:[13]

Dear Mrs. Chisholm,
    I saw Mr. Dickens to-day, and he has commissioned me to say that if you will allow him, and unless he hears to the contrary from you, he will call upon you at 2 o'clock on Tuesday next, the 26th. I told him about your emigrants' letters and he seemed to think that the giving them publicity would be an important engine towards helping on our work, and he has so completely the confidence of the lower classes (who all read his books if they can read at all) that I think, if you can persuade him to bring them out in his new work it will be an immense step gained. He is so singularly clever and agreeable that I hope you will forgive me for having made this appointment without your direct sanction and for having also told him that I knew you wished to make his aquaintance.
        Believe me, dear Madam, very sincerely yours,
                                    Elizabeth Herbert

[11]G. M. Trevelyan, *English Social History* (1944), p. 517.
[12]Forster, *op. cit.* ii. 274.
[13]*Advocate* (Melbourne), 16 August 1902, p. 9, reprint of an article 'Dickens and His Models' from the *Month* (London).

Dickens, greatly impressed by his hostess, decided to give
her all the help he could, and to begin by publishing a number
of her emigrants' letters.

In the first number of *Household Words*,[14] which was published
in March 1850 while he was working hard at *David Copperfield*,
an article concerned with Mrs Chisholm's emigrants' letters is
prominent. In this periodical he made it 'a rigid rule . . . that
all contributions . . . should appear anonymously, no matter how
famous or distinguished their writer might have been'. As well
as making this rule he 'so re-wrote many of his contributor's
articles that it was often difficult to judge which were his and
which not'.[15]

There is no doubt about the first article, for there is definite
evidence that it was the joint work of Mrs Chisholm and Dickens.
The evidence is found in the copy of the *Household Words* record
of contributors, now in the possession of the Dickens Fellowship.[16]
The article is entitled 'A Bundle of Emigrants' Letters', and begins
with an enthusiastic description of Mrs Chisholm's work, and
the proposed work of the Family Colonization Loan Society.
This part was almost certainly written by Dickens, but the
extracts from the letters Mrs Chisholm had lent him formed the
bulk of the article. In one letter 'Mrs. C.' is actually mentioned.
Dickens himself thought the letters 'extremely good',[17] and they
give a vivid description of Australian conditions.

One letter from a man in Melbourne deserves quoting, for it
indicates the cost of foodstuffs before the gold rush caused an
inflationary rise in prices. The emigrant writes: 'Tea is 1/6 a
lb., but it can be bought for 1/- by the chest. Coffee is 9d. lb.
which can be bought for 5d. but you must roast yourselfe or
send it to the roasters but you can do it at home very well for
everybody has what is called a lamp over here which costs about
7 or 8 shillings and you can bake your bread or your dinners at
your own fireplace. Potatoes are rather dear they are 1d. lb. but
they are butifully fine onions the same price. Cabbages 1½d. and
2d. each fresh butter 1/6 lb. and salt do. ½d. lb. Mushrooms grow

[14]Forster described this periodical as a 'weekly miscellany of general
literature . . . . to help in the discussion of the more important social
questions of the time'.
[15]B. W. Matz, 'Writings Wrongly Attributed to Dickens', *Dickensian*,
xxi-xxii (1925-26), 128.
[16]*Ibid.* xxxv (1939), 203.
[17]R. C. Lehmann, *Charles Dickens as Editor, Letters to William Henry
Wills, Sub-Editor* (1912), p. 24. He so described them in a letter to Wills
dated 6 March 1850.

very plentiful and you may go and get a bushel some time before breakfast.'[18]

Less than two years later these prices had doubled. But the economic upheaval which followed the gold discoveries was undreamed of when Mrs Chisholm's emigrant wrote his letter.

Another article influenced by Caroline Chisholm appears a week later. This is 'An Australian Ploughman's Story'. 'Big Jem', the ploughman, was a convict or 'speaking colonially, "a prisoner" '.[19] He describes his difficulties in remitting money home, and he is reunited with his wife through the agency of the narrator of the story, an unmistakable reference to Mrs Chisholm. This article was probably written by her and then re-written by Dickens. She must have given the typically Australian description of the shepherd's hut; and the conclusions, too, is pure Chisholm, for the ploughman declares: 'It is virtuous wives who rule us most, and in a lonely land make the difference between happiness and misery.'[20]

Two months later six short 'Pictures of Life in Australia' appeared, given by someone who is addressed by the different characters as 'Mrs. C.'.

In August, *Household Words* was praising the Family Colonization Loan Society and Mrs Chisholm again, and the scheme was described in detail.[21] The society is not mentioned again until May of the next year, when an article 'Safety for Female Emigrants'[22] praises her work and gives the pledge 'voluntarily proposed and unanimously passed'[23] by the members at one of Mrs Chisholm's group meetings before her first ship sailed.

'We pledge ourselves as Christian fathers and heads of families to exercise a parental control and guardianship over all orphans and friendless females proceeding with the family groups. To protect them as our own children and allow them to share the same claims as our daughters.

'We further resolve to discourage gambling and not to take cards or dice with us or to enter into any pernicious amusements during the voyage. We likewise resolve, by parental advice and good example, to encourage and promote some well-advised system of self-improvement during the passage. As the system

---

[18]*Household Words*, i (1850), 21.
[19]*Ibid.* p. 39.   [20]*Ibid.* p. 43.
[21]*Ibid.* p. 514.   [22]*Ibid.* iii (1851), 228.
[23]Trelawney Saunders, *The Story of the Life of Mrs. Caroline Chisholm, the Emigrants' Friend, and her Adventures in Australia with the Rules of the Family Colonization Loan Society* (1852), p. 21 (ML).

of repayment proposed by this Society is one that if honourably kept will add to the credit of the working classes as a body, and be the means of encouraging the generous and good to assist our struggling countrymen, we hereby solemnly pledge our honour as men, and our character as Christians to repay the loan advanced to us, and to impress the sacredness of fulfilling this duty on each and all of the members constituting the group. We also promise to aid the colonial agents in the recovery of all loans, and to make known in whatever part of the colonies we may be, the means by which parties well-to-do there may assist their relations in this country through the medium of the Family Colonization Loan Society.

'We further pledge ourselves not to introduce as candidates for membership of the Society any men but those we know to be of good character and of good repute.

'We also determine not to accept of payment for any services we may render the Society on board ship, but endeavour individually and collectively to preserve the order of a well regulated family during our passage to Australia, and to organize and establish a system of protection that will enable our female relations to enter an emigrant ship with the same confidence of meeting with protection as respectable females can now enter our steamers, trains and mail coaches.'[24]

The society had made good progress. Not three months after the plan was made public, about 370 people had enrolled and formed family groups. They 'consisted of respectable families of the working class, a few young men, and some friendless young women'.[25] The whole number was able to contribute £1,200 towards their passages. Some were from London, and others came from the rural districts of England and Wales. The society had also received several applications from Irish and Scots.

Mrs Chisholm held family group meetings at her home on the evenings of the first and third Saturday in every month, the first being held on 13 April 1850.[26] At these meetings the emigrants talked together and made friends with each other. Captain and Mrs Chisholm gave them advice on what to take with them on the voyage, and letters from emigrants in Australia were read. As many members of the Central Committee as possible attended and other notables were invited. Dickens may have been one of them.

[24]*Ibid*. pp. 21-2.
[25]*The A.B.C. of Colonization*, pp. 3-4.   [26]*Ibid*. p. 13.

A tremendous amount of preliminary work had to be done
before the first shipload of emigrants could be despatched. The
mere arrangement of groups took time and argument before all
were satisfied, but Mrs Chisholm was no novice in arranging
groups — it was not 'an idea of the day'. In 1850 she said 'I have
been working it out on a miniature scale during the last two
years, by getting emigrant families to meet at my own residence,
making them acquainted with each other, and placing often under
their charge single females proceeding to the Colonies'.[27] She
and her husband worked indefatigably dealing with correspondence, answering enquiries and arranging introductions between
emigrants. The only help they had was from one clerk and one
old woman who opened the door to the countless callers.[28]

Enough money had to be collected to charter a ship, and £500
to £600[29] was raised between a few friends of the society. Mrs
Chisholm chose the *Slains Castle,* a barque of 503 tons, as her
first ship. The vessel was fitted out in the East India Dock,
Blackwall, and chartered to take emigrants to Port Phillip and
Port Adelaide.[30]

The family unit was also to be the basis of the disposition of
the emigrants on board ship. Mrs Chisholm had come to dis-
approve of the rigid segregation of sexes which was enforced
on government emigrant ships. She used families for the protection of friendless girls and boys, and considered that family
life should continue on ship as on land. She tried to keep the
families together with a cabin for each of them. There were no
'cabin' passengers, because there were no class distinctions. No
children above fourteen years of age were to sleep in the same
cabin as their parents, and orphan girls were to be placed in the
same cabin as the older girls of a family (seven girls in one
cabin). If this was done Mrs Chisholm was sure that such girls
would be well guarded, for 'parents will be careful to see that
they behave . . . so that they do not contaminate their own
daughters'. 'Aged females' were to be placed with the young
girls, for 'age should be mixed up with youth so as to give a
steadiness to the party'.[31] The 'friendless lads', too, were to be
placed with boys of a family.

[27]*Ibid.* p. 21.
[28]*Illustrated London News*, 28 February 1852.
[29]*Argus*, 31 August 1853, quoting an extract from the London *Daily
News*, June 1853.
[30]*Argus*, 7 February 1851.
[31]*The A.B.C. of Colonization*, p. 20; Trelawney Saunders, *op. cit.* pp. 21-2.

Matronly duties were performed by 'six females of an appropriate age selected by Mrs. Chisholm'. They were to see 'that all the young females are in their sleeping apartments at a proper hour, and are earnestly solicited never to retire to rest leaving any young girl on the poop or deck of the ship. They are also requested to visit the female cabins at least once a day in order to give such directions as may be necessary for the preservation of order, cleanliness and that propriety of demeanour so becoming in young females.'

A reliable surgeon was to keep an account of the issue of medical comforts with the names of the emigrants who received them. He was also to 'issue three times a week to children under seven years of age, 4 ozs. of rice, or 3 ozs. of sago in lieu of salt meat'. [32] Long before, when she had published the report of her first year's work in New South Wales, Mrs Chisholm had suggested that the surgeon, and not the captain, should have control of the issue of rations. Now, in her own emigration society, she was able to make this reform. Each emigrant on Mrs Chisholm's ships had to provide himself with: 'a knife and fork; table- and tea-spoons; metal plate; hook pot; drinking mug; water can; washing basin; two cabbage nets; one scrubbing brush; ½ gal. of sand; ½ bath-brick; 2 sheets of sandpaper; 2 coarse canvas aprons; a hammer; tacks; leather straps with buckle to secure beds neatly on deck when required to be aired; and 3 lbs. marine soap. All these items except the scrubbing brush, sand and bath-brick had to be provided on any private ship.'[33]

The rations issued were a little more varied than those given on government ships though about equal in food value. The weekly dietary scale for each adult was: 'Biscuit, 3 lbs.; beef, ½ lb.; pork, 1 lb.; preserved meat, 1 lb.; soup bouille, 1 lb.; fish, ¼ lb.; flour, 3½ lbs.; raisins, ½ lb.; preserved fruit, ¼ lb.; suet, 6 ozs.; peas, ⅔ pint; rice, ¾ lb.; preserved potatoes, ½ lb.; carrots, ½ lb.; tea, 1½ ozs.; coffee, 2 ozs.; sugar, ¾ lb.; treacle, ½ lb.; butter, ¼ lb.; cheese, ¼ lb.; oatmeal, 2 ozs.; lime juice, 1 gill; pickles, 1 gill; mustard, ½ oz.; salt, 2 ozs.; pepper, ½ oz.; water, 5 gals. 1 quart; water for each infant 1 gal. 3 quarts.'

Some of the rules made to help the emigrants on board ship are found in Appendix E.

[32] The quotations in this paragraph are from Trelawney Saunders, *op. cit.* pp. 21-2.

[33] *Ibid.* p. 23. See *Household Words*, v (1852), 364 ('What to take to Australia'). The government emigrant ships provided their passengers with bedding and cutlery which they could keep after their arrival in the colony. See *V. & P.* Leg. Council N.S.W. (1848), p. 168.

No wine, beer or spirits were to be sold on board the society's ships — a prohibition which was also supposed to be enforced on government ships — neither were ceremonies in connection with 'crossing the line' permitted.[34]

At last, after patient preparation and many difficulties, the *Slains Castle* was ready. Eneas Mackenzie describes the way the ship was fitted. On the lower deck 'all usual erections being removed there was a clear length of one hundred feet of deck. The cabins ranged on each side, were numbered and resembled a ward in Greenwich or Chelsea Hospital. Those intended for a man and his wife were of a certain size, while those for a party of females were larger. The bedsteads for a married couple consisted of broad stout laths, one-half of the length of which were placed to fit into the other, so that when not needed to sleep upon they could be slid back, and the bedstead became one-half the size. By this contrivance there was a couch formed for the day, and by a board sliding in a support for the back, while the room gained left a private cabin for the occupants. A washstand in a corner, and other trifling articles, completed the fittings. In some there was a small bedplace a little above for a young child . . . By a space being left at the bottom, and the frame-work not reaching the roof by several inches, a free and perfect circulation of air was allowed in each cabin besides there being a small window covered by a piece of coloured cotton; thus there were privacy, air and light . . . Down the centre of the deck between the cabins were tables for the meals and other purposes . . . above which were shelves for dishes'.

Mackenzie describes the sailing of the ship enthusiastically. On Saturday, 28 September 1850, 'there was all the usual bustle of confusion and hurry of embarkation on the decks of the *Slains Castle*. The flag that has "braved the battle and the breeze" boldly graced the bows; others gaily decorated the vessel, but that which most attracted attention was one symbolic of the spirit that guided the present enterprise and hung from the mizen. It was a present from a party of ladies to Mrs Chisholm of "true blue" colour having in gold-coloured type a monogram of Mrs Chisholm's name "C. C." linked together by the stout part of the letters, and surrounded by the letters F.C.L.S. — Family Colonization Loan Society.'

Mrs Chisholm herself, like a good general, marshalled her emigrants, warned, exhorted and guided them. Her eye was every-

[34]Trelawney Saunders, *op. cit.* pp. 21-2.

where. 'It was surprising to watch how any unexpected difficulty that arose was promptly removed, how every petty detail was regarded and controlled by this extraordinary woman. A family at the last moment found they could not go by this vessel — another, anxious and ready, filled their places. A family presented itself, the mother of whom but four days before had undergone the ordeal of maternity — Mrs. Chisholm in respect of her sex promised a passage in three weeks in another vessel, but was met by a refusal; she then declined the responsibility of receiving the anxious emigrant without a doctor's certificate; this was procured and the invalid carried on board. The searching eye of Mrs. Chisholm caught the face of a baby, and she detected incipient measles in the family. They were tenderly refused admission and carefully placed in a cab with money for their immediate requirements and promise of future attention and an early passage.'

So it went on until she had all her emigrants safely on board; then the ship was cast loose, drawn out into the river by the steam-tug, and went down to anchor at Gravesend. The next day — a Sunday — there were services on board given by a Church of England clergyman, a Methodist minister and two Roman Catholic priests. Among the one hundred and fifty emigrants were one hundred and twenty Anglicans, two Jewesses and the rest about equal numbers of Wesleyans and Roman Catholics. Eight hundred visitors thronged the ship as she lay at anchor. She sailed on the Tuesday, and Mrs Chisholm gave an inspiring farewell address to her emigrants in which she 'begged them not only to be the guardians of the females, but also of religious liberty of their fellow-voyagers'. She turned to go and 'a young Jewess clasped her in her arms, kissed her, and called her "her dear mother". Other females wept aloud. The old women hung about her praying for the "blessings of God be her portion"'. The cheering rose in a roar of sound, and at the last a voice called 'Three cheers for Mrs. Chisholm's children!'[35]

Overwhelmed by the crowd's great surge of feeling, Mrs Chisholm went over the side down into one of the waiting boats. This was a tremendous moment as she watched her first ship sail for the antipodes. The *Slains Castle* weighed anchor late in the afternoon. Perhaps Charles Dickens saw the sailing too, and remembered it in describing David Copperfield's farewell to the Peggottys and Micawbers, which he wrote a few weeks later. 'It

[35]Mackenzie, *Memoirs*, pp. 174-8.

was then calm, radiant sunset. She lay between us and the red light, and every taper line and spar was visible against the glow. A sight at once so beautiful, so mournful and so hopeful, as the glorious ship, lying still, on the flushed water, with all the life on board her crowded at the bulwarks, and there clustering for a moment, bare-headed and silent, I never saw.

'Silent, only for a moment. As the sails rose to the wind, and the ship began to move, there broke from all the boats three resounding cheers, which those on board took up, and echoed back, and which were echoed and re-echoed. My heart burst out when I heard the sound, and beheld the waving of the hats and handkerchiefs.'[36]

The emigrants on board went to Melbourne and Adelaide. By instalments they had paid £1,403. The society had lent them £865.[37] Nearly all had relatives or friends in the colonies and found useful employment soon after their arrival.

Before the second ship was despatched, however, it was decided that the appointment of a Colonial Agent could no longer be deferred. 'As the society had no funds at its disposal for paying an agent',[38] Captain Chisholm left for Australia at his own expense in March 1851. As Colonial Agent he worked gratuitously so that the slender funds of the young society would not be strained. The Chisholms were ready to make any sacrifice to advance the cause of emigration, but, as Mrs Chisholm wrote at the time, 'with our means . . . it would not be possible that this separation could continue for any great length of time'.[39] It seems miraculous that they managed to do so much on the small income given them by Captain Chisholm's pension and whatever investments they had been able to make. He sailed in the *King William* and arrived in Adelaide at the beginning of August 1851, where he established the Adelaide branch of the society. He went on to Melbourne in September.

A second ship, the *Blundell*, was despatched a few months after the *Slains Castle*. The emigrants in this ship contributed a total of £1,942 towards their passage, and were loaned £674.[40] Of the *Blundell* emigrants 'not one [was] un-engaged the second day after the arrival'.[41]

Before the third ship, the *Athenian*, set sail the news of the

[36]Dickens, *David Copperfield*, ch. 57.
[37]Mackenzie, *Memoirs*, p. 175.
[38]*Adelaide Observer*, 2 August 1851.
[39]*Ibid.* [40]Mackenzie, *Memoirs*, p. 183.
[41]*Ibid.* p. 184.

gold discoveries in Victoria reached England. This had a galvanic
effect on emigration to Australia. In a few months sailing ships
were arriving in Port Phillip crammed with 'diggers' of every
nationality. Not only was there a migration from abroad, but
there was a migration within the Australian colonies. From
every part of the continent the diggers converged on Victoria,[42]
and Melbourne was almost denuded of male inhabitants.

In England Caroline Chisholm heard the excited stories of the
'rush' with mixed feelings. For in spite of the benefits which the
gold discoveries were bound to bring to Australia, a colony
afflicted by gold fever was no place for her virtuous young
females. Nor was the lure of gold without an unsettling effect
on staid fathers of families. She was working to send out families
and single girls who would give stability to the population; the
immigrants which the gold brought were not the kind she
approved.

Nevertheless, one of the immediate effects of the gold discoveries was to give her society financial security. In February
1852 a number of city merchants interested in the Australian
trade decided that 'their best mode of obtaining value for a
large sum of money . . . was to expend it on the plan under the
personal direction of Mrs. Chisholm.'[43] Between them they raised
'upwards of £10,000' as a donation to the society's funds. By
thus encouraging emigration they hoped 'to supply the blank
in the Australian labour market caused by the gold discoveries'.[44]
This support ended Caroline Chisholm's worries concerning the
finances of the society.

Her dubious opinion of the gold immigrants is reflected in a
Household Words article in January 1852. This is entitled 'Three
Colonial Epochs',[45] and after tracing the phases of Australian
history praises Mrs Chisholm's work in Sydney, and describes
some of the evil effects of the gold discoveries. Her method of
family colonization is advocated as the only remedy for the 'curse
of gold'.

A most interesting article appeared a month later.[46] This tells
the story of how a family tried to emigrate through the Land

[42]During 1852 no less than 48,253 immigrants from other parts of
Australia arrived in Victoria. Another 30,934 came from abroad (T. A.
Coghlan, *op. cit.* ii. 609).

[43]*Illustrated London News*, 17 April 1852.

[44]*Argus*, 31 August 1853, quoting extract from London *Daily News*,
June 1853

[45]*Household Words*, iv (1852), 433.

[46]*Ibid.* p. 529 ('Better Ties than Red Tape Ties').

and Emigration Commissioners, but was unsuccessful. The troubles and delays encountered by 'Dick Delver' in his dealings with the government are well described. He was rejected because he was not an agricultural labourer, and because he had three small children. Also he admitted that he would work for wages, but 'not longer than he could help'. Fortunately he had heard of Mrs Chisholm's society, and went to visit her. An excellent description of the house is given, where 'a remarkably narrow passage' led 'into a small room fitted like a school, with benches and a tier of broad shelves in one corner, which he was told formed an exact copy of the berths or beds on board Mrs. Chisholm's ships'. It was in this room that the group meetings were held, and the Delver family's experiences at a meeting are told. But the most interesting detail given is concerned with Dick's education. Mrs Chisholm found that he was illiterate; so, while he waited for a ship, she had him taught. The teaching was done by another prospective emigrant who taught Dick how to write and 'to measure his work'. In this way he was prepared for the time when he would have to depend on his own labour in the Australian bush.

The Family Colonization Loan Society is mentioned again in July 1852,[47] when emigrants are advised what to take on the voyage to Australia. The provisions for emigrants on board Mrs Chisholm's ships are warmly praised.

This is the last article in Dickens' periodical which directly mentions Mrs Chisholm and the Family Colonization Loan Society. How much his publicity had influenced its success it is impossible to judge, but the discovery of gold made it unnecessary for him to continue his campaign in the society's favour, for the interest in Australia was more effectually aroused by this news than by anything else in the sixty-four years of the colony's history. This intense interest in the goldfields and in Australia is reflected in *Household Words,* and Dickens did a great service by describing the difficulties to be encountered on the diggings, as well as the fantastic fortunes to be made by the lucky few.[48] There are frequent general references to the colony in the periodical until its publication ends in 1859. They are then continued in its successor, *All the Year Round.*

[47]*Ibid.* v (1852), 364.
[48]See particularly *Household Words,* viii (1853), 153 ('Bad Luck at Bendigo').

6

Fulfilment

THE SOCIETY ESTABLISHED

While her husband organized the colonial agencies, Caroline Chisholm carried on her work in England alone. As the society gained popularity her labours became herculean. In 1852 she travelled throughout England, Scotland, and Ireland publicizing her aims, answering countless questions, and gathering in emigrants like a female Pied Piper. In particular she set the doubts of the women at rest, for it was their fears which often prevented families from emigrating.

In April 1852 she was in Birmingham and held a most successful meeting at the Provident Institution. As a result a committee was appointed to establish a branch of the society in Birmingham.[1] In spite of the success of the meeting the old doubt of her religion was voiced.[2] This was evidently a direct result of Dr Lang's activities, for reference was made to his articles in the British Banner. Later in the year[3] she was in Ireland and an elaborate soirée was held in her honour at the Imperial Hotel in Cork. 'The attendance . . . most numerous and respectable'[4] included a number of the professors from Queen's College. She held a meeting, too, in Dublin.[5]

A large meeting was held in Glasgow,[6] and from Scotland it was planned to send out six hundred boys, and as many girls from sixteen to twenty years of age. Emigration would be a reward of merit.[7] There is no direct evidence that this plan was put into practice but probably the boys and girls were put in

[1]*Birmingham Journal* and *Birmingham Mercury,* 10 April 1852.
[2]Aris, *Birmingham Gazette,* 10 April 1852.
[3]Exactly when or how often she visited Ireland I have been unable to discover.
[4]*Cork Examiner,* 1852 (ML).
[5]*Report,* The Present System of Immigration, V. & P. Leg. Council Vic. (1853), ii (2), 903.
[6]*Ibid.*
[7]*Argus,* 1 April 1852, quoting one of her letters.

the care of different families, and distributed throughout a number of the society's ships.

She visited North Wales, too, in this year 1852.[8] All her journeyings throughout England and Scotland were franked by the railways,[9] and possibly her crossing to Ireland was franked in the same way.

At some time during the next two years Mrs Chisholm travelled through Germany, France and Italy.[10] She received several letters from some of the thousands in Europe who were interested in emigration. During these years a full-scale migration was taking place from the continent; in 1849 the *British Banner* reported that '57,000 persons embarked from Bremen alone principally for the United States',[11] but as well as those who went to the United States, many went to Australia. Mrs Chisholm also made a pilgrimage to Rome, where 'Pio Nono', the reigning pope, presented her with a portrait bust of herself and some other gifts.[12]

In 1852 the Family Colonization Loan Society sent no less than six shiploads of emigrants to Australia. One of these ships was the *Athenian;* the others were the *Mariner,* which arrived in Australia in June; the *Scindian,* the *Nepaul,* and the *Chalmers,* which set sail from London within a few days of one another, and reached Port Phillip in October and November; lastly the *Ballengeich,* which arrived in Port Phillip in December. The ships were filled as fast as possible, because it was known that the gold discoveries would cause a rise in passenger rates.

The first three ships were engaged by a broker, and chartered by the committee while the broker put the stores on board. But when the fourth ship, the *Mariner,* was chartered, it was decided that the Central Committee should furnish the stores, which therefore remained the committee's property. Any surplus was to be sold for the benefit of the society when the vessel reached the colony.[13]

Before each ship sailed a public meeting was arranged, and the meeting held before the *Mariner* sailed in February 1852

[8]*Report,* The Present System of Immigration, V. & P. Leg. Council Vic. (1853), ii (2), 903.

[9]*Argus,* 2 September 1854.

[10]R. Harris, *What has Mrs. Chisholm Done for N.S.W.?* p. 13.

[11]*British Banner,* 21 November 1849.

[12]The bust passed into the possession of Colonel Henry John Chisholm, her third son, who was for many years Police Magistrate at Yass, New South Wales; it is now reproduced by permission of the latter's grandson.

[13]*Report,* The Present System of Immigration, V. & P. Leg. Council Vic. (1853), ii (2), 901.

was widely reported. It was held at the British Institution, Tabernacle-row, City Road, and 'more than 2,500 people were present — every corner, every rafter, that could be reached was crowded, and the great hall viewed from the platform presented an undulating sea of faces, all deeply intent on the business of the meeting'.[14] The hall was decorated with the flags of all nations, and hanging opposite the platform was Mrs Chisholm's own large blue flag emblazoned with the initials 'F.C.L.S.'. Above the initials were the words 'Advance Australia', and beneath it the words 'God Speed the Plough!' In the week the *Mariner* sailed about £4,000 was subscribed.[15]

Mrs Chisholm gave powerful support to the Colonial and International Postage Association which was advocating the reduction of colonial postage rates. High postage rates were something about which she felt most strongly.[16] The 'penny post' applied only to the British Isles, and the cost of ocean postage was often exorbitant. Letters coming from the colonies to England, or posted in England for the colonies, were chiefly transported by private ships, and the captains could charge anything they chose for the carriage of mail. The position improved after the Cunard Line, and then the P. & O. and the Royal Mail contracted with the government to carry mail,[17] but colonial postage rates were still very high. One irate *Times* correspondent in July 1853[18] complained that he had been charged 4s. 1d. for a letter from Sydney, notwithstanding the fact that there was already 10d. in colonial stamps on it. The post office explained patiently that this letter had weighed over the half-ounce, but the correspondent was not appeased.

The Colonial and International Postage Association formed a deputation to the Postmaster-General in March 1853 and as a result a concession was made,[19] but it was not until November 1854, after Caroline Chisholm had returned to Australia, that the rate of 6d. the half-ounce was fixed for postage to Australia.[20]

[14]*Illustrated London News*, 28 February 1852.

[15]*Ibid.*

[16]In October 1846 she wrote: 'A letter from Sydney to-day cost me 2s. 3d. and Captain Chisholm paid £1 4s. 3d. for postage last week' (*Argus*, 5 April 1847). When she returned to Australia she defined a gentleman as one who 'when he wrote to her enclosed a postage stamp' (*Argus*, 2 September 1854).

[17]Sir G. Evelyn Murray, *The Post Office* (1927), p. 58.

[18]*The Times*, 20 July 1853. The letter was a hundred days in transit to England, then the average time.

[19]*Ibid.* 7 March 1853.　　　　　[20]*Ibid.* 4 November 1856.

In 1853, too, Eneas Mackenzie reports that 'her latest efforts have been for the establishment of post-office orders between this country and the Colony',[21] and in May 1853 it was announced that money-orders from the colonies could be received and paid by the ordinary banks.[22]

During these gold years she was besieged by emigrants, and each day was more breathlessly busy than the one before. 'As early as nine in the morning we have seen the door of her house surrounded by a crowd of persons, the passage lined by anxious inquirers, and the stairs rendered impassable by desirous emigrants. The average number of letters she received was a hundred and forty per diem: these she glanced over, and gave instructions for their being answered, and also other commands to six clerks. After seeing and advising from thirty to forty persons, she would set out for Blackwall; there, on reaching the docks, go on shipboard, minutely survey the work completed, give directions to carpenters and shipfitters, inspect the provisions, have interviews with brokers, make arrangements with government officers, and attend to numbers of persons who had come to fix on their berths; after some time thus spent, return to town, and transact bank business. On arriving at her home the audiences were resumed until nine o'clock at night, seeing an additional forty to sixty people.'

She had arranged to have some of the young female emigrants living near her, and after all the other work of the day was done, 'at half-past nine at night she went forth to visit them individually, inquire respecting their conduct during the day, and see them settled in their lodgings for that night'.[23]

Eneas Mackenzie's description of her 'minute survey' of the way her ships were fitted out is noteworthy, for one of the most important aspects of Caroline Chisholm's work with the Family Colonization Loan Society was her insistence that the conditions on board the society's ships should be of the highest standard obtainable. Some attempt had been made to regulate conditions on the ships carrying emigrants to North America, and a Passenger Act had been passed in 1849 which provided that only one person should be carried for every two tons of the vessel. But this act did not apply to ships on the Australian run, and these were sometimes dangerously overcrowded. They were dark,

[21]Mackenzie, *Emigrants' Guide*, p. 25
[22]*The Times*, 9 May 1853.
[23]Mackenzie, *Emigrants' Guide*, pp. 27-8.

badly ventilated, and evil smelling, with high death rates.[24] Married couples were crowded together, and slept on open shelves, or bunks. Sanitary arrangements were poor, for the closets were few in number and sometimes badly placed where they could be smashed by rough seas.

When Mrs Chisholm set about chartering her own first vessel she was adamant upon the way in which it was to be fitted.[25] She was determined that there should be separate cabins for each family; the ventilation should be by a fixed apparatus instead of the old defective canvas pipe; the closets 'should be sufficient in number . . . and retired in situation',[26] berths were to be well lighted, even if the deck had to be cut for the purpose, and proper baths, wash-houses and water supply were to be provided. In her fourth ship, the *Mariner*, she 'arranged for the cleaning of the decks by paying three men £4 each to do it'.[27] The reforms she made were consistently praised, not only by Dickens in *Household Words*, but by the Australian and English press. It was only in the last years of the Family Colonization Loan Society's existence, when Caroline Chisholm had no longer active connection with it, that the New South Wales Immigration Agent criticized the society's ships unfavourably.

She was not alone in her denunciation of the ship-board abuses of the time. The press gave publicity to some of the appalling happenings on board passenger ships, and the case of the *Douglas* which took passengers to South Australia is typical. In this ship, largely because of mismanagement and the criminal negligence of the captain and surgeon, there was a cholera epidemic. Those who died were tumbled into the water while 'scarcely cold', and their personal effects were then auctioned. A passenger who kept a journal wrote: 'We have sixty more passengers than we ought to have; we are huddled and messed together worse than pigs'.[28]

[24]Figures such as those given for the *Ticonderoga* and the *Borneuf* indicate some of the horrifying results of overcrowding. Both these ships sailed for Port Phillip in the early 'fifties. Of the 900 aboard the *Ticonderoga* 100 died of fever before she reached Melbourne. In the *Borneuf*, 85 died out of 800 (Biddle's 'List of Ships', State Library of Victoria, Melbourne).

[25]*Argus*, 31 August 1853, quoting London *Daily News*, June 1853.

[26]R. Harris, *What has Mrs. Chisholm Done for N.S.W.?* p. 8; *Chambers' Edinburgh Journal*, xix (1853), 243.

[27]*Argus*, 1 July 1852.

[28]*South Australian Register*, 15 January 1850. This is one of the press cuttings underlined and annotated by Mrs Chisholm, formerly in the possession of the late E. Dwyer Gray.

The conditions on this ship were exceptionally bad and apart from overcrowding were chiefly due to drunkenness. The sale of beer or spirits on board passenger ships had been forbidden by the act of 1849, but the prohibition was often evaded. The happenings on the *Douglas* and a few other ships horrified Mrs Chisholm and others like her. By the example of the good conditions on board her own ships, and by public denunciation of the abuses,[29] she helped on the movement for reform. The result was the Passenger Act of 1852.

This act applied to all British passenger ships — not only to those which crossed the Atlantic. Unmarried male passengers of over fourteen years of age were to be berthed in the fore-part of the ship, in a compartment divided off from the space appropriated to other passengers by a substantial and well-secured bulk head. If not berthed in this way they were to be in separate rooms fitted with enclosed berths. Moreover, not more than two passengers, unless they were of the same family, were to be placed in the same berth, 'Nor in any case' were 'persons of different sexes above the age of fourteen years unless husband and wife to be placed in the same berth'.[30]

Rules were laid down to provide for proper light and ventilation, and for 'at least two privies with two additional privies for every hundred passengers on board' which 'shall be maintained in a serviceable condition throughout the voyage'. The dietary scale, too, was improved.

At the time, the provisions of this act were revolutionary, and those concerned with morality, proper light, ventilation and better conveniences may have been directly influenced by Mrs Chisholm's work. Nevertheless, the conditions on her ships were still better than those on government ships, and chiefly by their example she continued to advocate more reforms.

Some time after her first few ships sailed she became friendly with W. S. Lindsay, one of the foremost London shipowners.[31] Lindsay was a remarkable man. He had followed the classical tradition by running away to sea as a boy, and then had left the sea to found the shipbuilding firm of W. S. Lindsay & Co. As he had sailed in ships himself he knew what reforms were needed in ship-building. He built the *Caroline Chisholm* for the Family Colonization Loan Society, and in this ship incorporated all the

[29]When she was lecturing at Liverpool she denounced the ship-board abuses. This is one instance recorded by Harris, *op. cit.* p. 9.
[30]Passenger Act, 1852.
[31]*Dictionary of National Biography*, under 'W. S. Lindsay'.

reforms in accommodation and provisioning which his and Mrs Chisholm's ingenuity could devise. She was one of the largest iron vessels ever built on the Tyne. Her figurehead was 'a well executed bust of Mrs Chisholm . . . An immense concourse of spectators watched her launching'.[32]

The *Caroline Chisholm* sailed from England in September 1853 with emigrants for Melbourne and Sydney.[33] This ship embarked her passengers at Plymouth as well as at London, and an interesting little group among them was at least twelve Jewish girls,[34] put in Mrs Chisholm's care by the Jewish Ladies' Benevolent Loan and Visiting Society. This committee was anxious to assist Jewish families to emigrate to Australia and America, and had the utmost confidence in Caroline Chisholm's care of the young girls placed in her charge. Many of the leaders of Jewish society of London were among her ardent supporters.[35]

A great number of Caroline Chisholm's emigrants came from the country to the sea-port from which they embarked, and they found it difficult and expensive to find accommodation for the few days before they set sail. Mrs Chisholm tried to make arrangements to meet this difficulty.[36] At Southampton the municipal authorities agreed to let her emigrants stay at a second-class hotel where a bed and three plain meals were to be had for 3s. a day. A similar arrangement was made at Plymouth, and in October 1853 she had hopes of providing further accommodation at Gravesend. She tried to persuade shipowners — Lindsay must have been among them — to include hotel and railway fares in the charge for the passage; if this had been done the emigrants would have known exactly what they had to pay. She was still advocating this just before she left for Australia in 1854.

CAROLINE CHISHOLM IN ART AND LITERATURE

Mrs Chisholm's work made her one of the most famous women in England; there was 'scarcely a hamlet in the three kingdoms'[1] where her name was not known.

A very good description of her appeared in the *Illustrated*

[32]*Geelong Advertiser*, 20 July 1854, quoting *Newcastle Journal*, 4 March 1854.

[33]Passenger list in the State Library of Victoria, Melbourne.

[34]*Hebrew Observer*, 24 June 1853, p. 200. Information by courtesy of Rabbi Faulk, C.F.

[35]*The Times*, 10 August 1853, list of subscribers to her testimonial.

[36]*Argus*, 16 January 1854, quoting London *Daily News*, 25 October 1853.

[1]*Argus*, 2 September 1854.

Magazine of Art.[2] The writer (accompanied by a friend) visited
her 'just before the departure of the *Scindian* and the *Nepaul*'.
Outside the unpretentious house in Islington was 'an assembly of
humbly-clad, but clean-looking persons'. Inside the front door,
the writer found a narrow passage 'crowded with intending emigrants, each more eager than the other for an interview' with Mrs
Chisholm. 'After considerable jostling and squeezing we, at length,
contrived to send up our name by a venerable female attendant
who expressed a fervent wish that we "might see her missus that
night, but she was sure she didn't know when".' The visitors
were at length ushered up the narrow uncarpeted stairs into the
audience chamber on the first floor, where Mrs Chisholm was
seated behind a large sea-chest raised upon a couple of benches.
The chest was covered with writing materials and baggage-papers,
which she was distributing to the various emigrants whilst at the
same time answering every possible enquiry and endeavouring to
satisfy almost every impossible complaint. The room (but dimly
lighted by two or three candles hung in tin candlesticks against
the wall) was furnished with a model of the sleeping-berths
allotted to emigrants on board the society's ships. Attached to
the sides of these berths were sundry utensils required by those
indulging in a voyage to the antipodes such as tin plates, hook-
pots and water-cans. These were evidently constructed by someone
having severe notions of economy combined with a vast regard
for durability.

Mrs Chisholm herself was 'a sedate, matronly lady with eyes
well set under a capacious forehead — orbs that seem to look you
through whilst addressing you, and withal a fascinating manner
which at once seizes upon you and induces you to prolong your
stay'.

The description of the house in Islington tallies with that
found in one of the *Household Words* articles.[3] The personal
description bears out the likeness painted in the best-known
portrait of her. This was by an obscure painter, Angelo Collen
Hayter, and was exhibited in the Royal Academy of 1852. The
original portrait is lost, but the engraving of it depicts a gracious
lady with a sweet mouth, and large, brilliant eyes. The whole
face is alight with intelligence, and Hayter has captured some of
the force of her personality. She is wearing one of her black,

[2]The cutting is undated but the article must have been written in the
middle of 1852, for it was 'just before the departure of the *Scindian*'.
[3]'Better Ties than Red Tape Ties', *Household Words*, iv (1852). 529.

brocaded silk dresses, and holding in her hand a letter written
by a poor emigrant girl in the interior of New South Wales,
imploring Mrs Chisholm to send out a near relative of hers. It
was addressed, 'Mrs. Caroline Chisholm, the Emigrants' Friend,
England or elsewhere'. The London Post Office had no doubts
as to who was meant, and the letter 'was at once delivered to Mrs.
Chisholm'.[4]

Walter Savage Landor, a great friend of Charles Dickens, was
moved to write a poem *To Caroline Chisholm*,[5] burdened with
classical allusion, and of doubtful literary merit:[6]

> Chisholm! Of all the ages that have rolled
> Around this rolling globe what age hath seen
> Such arduous, such heaven-guided enterprise
> As this? Crime flies before thee, and the shores
> Of Austral Asia, lustrated by thee
> Collect no longer the putrescent weeds
> Of Europe, cast by Senates to infect
> The only unpolluted continent . . .

More attractive verses, 'A Carol on Caroline Chisholm', appeared
in *Punch* in August 1853.[7]

> Come on all you British females of wealth and high degree
> Bestowing all your charity on lands beyond the sea,
> I'll point you out a pattern which a better plan will teach
> Than that of sending Missioners to Timbuctoo to preach . . .
> Beyond the roaring ocean, beneath the soil we tread,
> You've English men and women well housed
>   and clothed and fed
> Who but for help and guidance to leave our crowded shores
> Would now be stealing, begging, or lie starving at our doors . . .
> Who led their expeditions and under whose command
> Through dangers and through hardships sought they
>   the promised land?
> A second Moses, surely, it was who did it all
> It was a second Moses in bonnet and in shawl.
> By means of one good lady were all these wonders wrought,
> By Caroline Chisholm's energy, benevolence and thought,

[4] *Illustrated London News*, 14 April 1877.
[5] While she was at work in New South Wales, Robert Lowe had written
a poem to her; in later years two others, one by Henry Kendall, were
to be dedicated to her.
[6] First published in the *Examiner*, 13 August 1853.
[7] *Punch*, xxv (20 August 1853), p. 71.

Instead of making here and there a convert of a Turk
She has made idle multitudes turn fruitfully to work.
The Reverend Ebenezer I'd not deny his dues,
For saving Patagonians, and Bosjesmen, and Zooloos;
But Mrs. Chisholm's mission is what I far prefer;
For saving British natives I'd give the palm to her.
And now that a subscription is opened and begun
In order to acknowledge the good that she has done
Among that sort of native — the most important tribe —
Come down like handsome people and handsomely subscribe.

The subscription referred to was opened towards the end of
1853 when it was learnt she was to return to Australia.

The *Punch* poem insistently stresses Caroline Chisholm's work
in comparison with a great deal of the then fashionable philan-
throphy, which was remarkable for a myopic concentration on 'the
black heathen'. This is noteworthy considering what is the most
interesting, though anonymous, portrait of her.[8]

Dickens finished *Bleak House* in September 1853. In the fourth
chapter the incredible menage of Mrs Jellyby is described. Apart
from the fact that Mrs Jellyby is sheer joy in herself, she becomes
a very interesting person, if Dickens' knowledge of Mrs Chisholm
is considered.

Dickens believed that charity should begin at home.[9] In *Bleak
House*, as well as describing the ridiculous ramifications of liti-
gation in the Court of Chancery, he ridicules the philanthropy
exemplified by Mrs Jellyby and her formidable friend Mrs Pardiggle. Mrs Jellyby is passionately devoted to the African natives
at the expense of her insignificant husband, and her numerous
progeny, who are shamefully neglected. Her philanthropic scheme
is to establish 'a hundred and fifty to two hundred healthy
families' on the left bank of the Niger where they will cultivate
coffee and educate the natives of 'Borrioboola-Gha'. The benighted
natives are to be given the inestimable benefits of Christian
civilization, for there is a strong missionary flavour in Mrs Jellyby's
scheme.

Humphrey House in *The Dickens World* points out that ten
years before *Bleak House* was written the African Civilization
Society and Niger Association had been formed 'to open up trade
on the Upper Niger, and to establish a model farm there as a

---

[8] See the *Advocate* (Melbourne), 16 August 1902, reprint of an article
from the *Month* (London) on 'Dickens and His Models'.
[9] See particularly House, *The Dickens World*, p. 97.

centre of beneficent Christian civilization'.[10] A colony was founded which failed in a year because of climatic difficulties and insufficent preparation.

The African Civilization Association would seem to have been the model for the description given of Mrs Jellyby's work, but there is one important point to be noted in Mrs Jellyby's scheme. Her idea was to establish *families* on the left bank of the Niger. The planting of families was not a part of the plan of the African Association, but colonization by family was the very essence of Mrs Chisholm's society.

The personal description of Mrs Jellyby, too, is interesting. Mrs Chisholm was described as 'handsome and stately'[11] and the possessor of fine eyes which 'seem to look you through whilst addressing you'.[12] In 1851 she was forty-three years old. Mrs Jellyby was 'a pretty, very diminutive, plump woman, of from forty to fifty with handsome eyes, though they had a curious habit of seeming to look a long way off'.[13] Both Mrs Jellyby and Mrs Chisholm received an extraordinary number of letters. Dickens himself recorded that Caroline Chisholm received eighty letters in one day,[14] and Mrs Jellyby's correspondence was so overwhelming that there were 'four envelopes in the gravy at once'.[15] Both were serene in the face of all difficulties. Serenity was a characteristic of Caroline Chisholm's which was often remarked upon, but Mrs Jellyby's serenity as her children endangered their lives and limbs was superhuman.

Dickens depicts Mrs Jellyby as a slattern, which Mrs Chisholm was not, and he also depicts the way her children and household were neglected while she worked for the African natives.

By the time *Bleak House* was written Caroline Chisholm had six children. Besides the four boys, the eldest of whom was sixteen, and four-year-old Caroline, there was now the year-old baby, Monica. Even though their mother always managed to spend a short part of the day with the children, she was working so hard that they could have seen little of her. Their grandmother cared for them, and probably managed nearly all the household affairs. Mrs Chisholm had six clerks to help her with

[10]House, *op. cit.* p. 87.
[11]*Sidney's Emigrants' Journal* (1850), p. 271, quoting a letter written by Sir George Gipps.
[12]*Illustrated Magazine of Art*, 1852.
[13]*Bleak House*, ch. 4.
[14]*Household Words*, iv (1851), 533.
[15]*Bleak House*, ch. 4.

the society's business, and one old woman to attend to the door. At about this time, too, she had three orphans and 'a poor destitute girl' as domestic help. In fact, as she said, she had turned her kitchen 'into a sort of colonial training school', and the trainees were sent out as servants to some of her colonial friends.[16] Though the ultimate results of such a scheme may have been excellent, the training process would not have ensured a well-ordered household. It was inevitable, too, with six healthy children, as well as the orphans, that there should have been some disorder. Nevertheless, it would be absurd to think the Chisholm household was anything like the Jellyby one. Even though her work, which she believed was divinely blessed, came before her children, Caroline Chisholm's whole character and capabilities would have made it impossible for her to neglect them. The retiring Mr Jellyby may be a reflection of the self-effacing Captain Chisholm, but Captain Chisholm worked indefatigably to advance his wife's schemes; Mr Jellyby merely endured Borrioboola-Gha.

All these points of comparison are incidentals which might be mere coincidences, except that Mrs Jellyby's plan involved the settlement of families. This is not an incidental but is 'in the very character of the philanthropic scheme itself'.[17] The mention of family settlement, plus the incidentals described, and the fact that Dickens knew Mrs Chisholm well, indicates that he used his knowledge of Mrs Chisholm in the portrait of Mrs Jellyby. Some of the inevitable disorder in the busy household at Islington caught his eye when he visited Mrs Chisholm,[18] and when he came to write *Bleak House* his pen made a characteristic magnification, both of the household and children.

Yet his description of Mrs Jellyby does not detract from his admiration of Caroline Chisholm and her work. The *Household Words* articles are contemporary with the serial publication of *Bleak House*.

Dickens made a distinction between the 'two classes of charitable people: those who did a little and made a great deal of noise; the others who did a great deal and made no noise at all'.[19] Mrs Jellyby and Mrs Pardiggle with their friends and hangers-on were of the first class, but Caroline Chisholm was undoubtedly of the second class. The *Punch* 'Carol on Caroline Chisholm'

[16]Caroline Chisholm to Benjamin Hawes, 13 January 1849, C.O. 201/424 (Public Record Office, London).
[17]Letter from Mr House to me.
[18]Charles Dickens to Miss Burdett-Coutts, 4 March 1850.
[19]*Bleak House*, ch. 8.

stresses the fact that she was the antithesis of the Jellyby-Pardiggle philanthropy. In his art Dickens had no scruples in using his knowledge of Mrs Chisholm to make his descriptions of 'rapacious benevolence' more ludicrous — when his imagination ran away with his pen he had no scruples of any kind. The description of Mrs Jellyby was a characteristic quirk of his exuberant humour — it marked no alteration in his good opinion of Caroline Chisholm.

CAPTAIN CHISHOLM AND THE COLONIAL AGENCIES

While Mrs Chisholm worked with such success in England, Captain Chisholm was establishing the colonial agencies of the society. He had arrived in Adelaide in August 1851, and the South Australian committee of the society was established soon afterwards.[1] Among the members were the heads of the different churches — including Mrs Chisholm's old friend the Rt Rev. Dr Murphy, now the Roman Catholic Bishop of Adelaide — several members of the Legislative Council, and Marshall MacDermott, manager of the Bank of Australasia. The formidable committee had the power to add to its numbers.

Before Captain Chisholm left England, Coutts & Co. had written to Marshall MacDermott suggesting that the Bank of Australasia should take charge of the remittances. 'The Society would pay you [the Bank of Australasia], in gross sums such moneys as may be collected by them from time to time the amount of which would have to be remitted to us by you monthly or otherwise, as may be most convenient to you.

'We beg to mention that you would have nothing to do with the accounts of the Society's agents, as they would send the detail of the collections direct to the Society.'[2]

Coutts & Co. had also communicated with the branches of the Bank of Australasia in Sydney, Melbourne and Hobart.[3] As soon as Captain Chisholm arrived, the remitting machinery was set in motion.

Captain Chisholm spent two months in Adelaide teaching and encouraging 'the labouring colonists' to take advantage of the power of remitting to England. In seven weeks he received £3,000 in gold dust or cash, and wrote confidently that he should

[1] *Argus*, 25 October 1851.
[2] *South Australian Register*, 2 August 1851, quoting a letter from Coutts & Co., 28 February 1851.
[3] *Adelaide Observer*, 9 August 1851, quoting a letter from Captain Chisholm.

be able to remit £15,000 in twelve months.[4] This proved, however, an over-optimistic estimate. The remittances were made not only by immigrants sent out by the society, but 'from various persons of the humbler class who desired to be joined by their relations'[5] and wished them to come out on board Caroline Chisholm's ships.

Any sum from 2s. upwards could be paid to the colonial agent, either weekly or monthly. The agent lodged an amount in the appropriate branch of the Bank of Australasia from where it was remitted to Coutts & Co. The agent then forwarded details to London whereupon the society wrote to the relatives concerned to tell them that the money was there for them in Coutts' Bank. If the relatives did not wish to emigrate, the money was returned to the donors unless they specified otherwise.[6]

Unfortunately not all the immigrants who had arrived in the *Slains Castle* and the *Blundell* were prompt in making repayment of their loans. In September 1851 Captain Chisholm wrote to Charles Sturt, the Colonial Secretary in Adelaide: 'I have the honour to enclose to you the articles of agreement entered into between the members of the Committee of the Family Colonization Loan Society in England, and certain emigrants sent by the Society to this Colony, which I have to beg you will do me the favour of laying before His Excellency the Lieutenant-Governor in order that the opinion of the Advocate-General as to the possibility of recovering the loans under these articles from defaulters, by legal proceeding in the law courts of the Colony may be obtained. I also beg to enclose a form of promissory note that has been suggested as being sufficient for all purposes.'[7]

In reply the Colonial Secretary forwarded the opinion of the Advocate-General,[8] that 'there is no obstacle to enforcing in this Colony contracts made in England, excepting that which may arise from the absence of parties, or of the witnesses. The agreement . . . leaves it so uncertain to whom the money is to be paid or belongs, that I should hardly recommend proceedings upon it, though they might be successful. The best mode, probably would be to obtain a promissory note, not witnessed, expressed to be payable to A.B. or bearer for value received'.

It is impossible to say whether this advice was taken. The fate or whereabouts of the society's records remains unknown. No

[4]*The Times*, 16 August 1852, quoting a letter from Caroline Chisholm. [5]*Ibid.* [6]*Argus*, 24 October 1851. [7]Despatches on Emigration, Family Colonization Society, ordered by the Legislative Council to be printed 12 October 1852, *V. & P.* Leg. Council S.A. (1852). [8]*Ibid.*.

legal action seems to have been taken; instead Captain Chisholm wrote a long letter to the *Adelaide Observer* on 9 August 1851 appealing to defaulting immigrants to repay their loans. This appeal to better nature was only partly successful, and there were always a number of defaulters.

Captain Chisholm also set up an enquiry bureau for settlers who were anxious to get in touch with relatives in the homeland.[9] A registry of enquirers for relatives was also kept at the society's headquarters in London, and a duplicate was kept at the Adelaide office. In this way settlers in Australia and relatives in England had a chance of tracing each other. Before he had been a month in Adelaide Captain Chisholm had received no less than 143 enquiries.[10]

By the end of October 1851 he had left for Melbourne and William C. Atchison was then appointed agent for the society in Adelaide, Captain Chisholm keeping in close touch with him. It was probably at Captain Chisholm's direction that the South Australian committee forwarded a memorial to the Lieutenant-Governor, Sir Henry Fox Young, proposing that a grant should be made to the society from the South Australian Land Fund. This memorial was signed by all the members of the South Australian committee and was forwarded to the Colonial Secretary on 14 February 1852.[11]

The committee emphasized that the Land Fund had been used to bring out government immigrants who had failed to stay in South Australia, but had set off hot foot for the Victorian goldfields, whereas the well-chosen immigrants brought out by the society were not likely to leave the colony.

The memorial was passed on to G. V. Butler, the Government Immigration Agent, for his opinion. Butler made his report to the Lieutenant-Governor and gave his reasons for refusing the society's request. As the first immigrants brought out by the society had only been in the colony a little over a year, at least another year would have to elapse before a proper judgment of their worth could be made; they were 'not of that description for which we desire to pay, they appear to be in the same scale of society with those who generally come out in private passenger vessels'; the type of immigrants which were sent out in the

[9]*Adelaide Observer*, 2 August 1851, quoting a letter from Caroline Chisholm in the London *Daily News*, 14 March 1851.
[10]*Ibid.* 23 August 1851.
[11]Despatches on Emigration, Family Colonization Society, *V. & P.* Leg. Council S.A. (1852), which include Butler's report.

government ships, and 'which the Commissioners have invariably been instructed to send out', were quite unable to pay two-thirds of their passage money — the amount which it was considered desirable Mrs Chisholm's immigrants should pay. The colonists, particularly the squatters, did not want the money from the land fund to subsidize the introduction of immigrants who were prosperous enough to become landowners themselves in a short time, and so leave the labour market. Finally, Butler declared that 'however respectable a Society may be, it is unusual and would be in my opinion under present circumstances inexpedient, to advance public money to an irresponsible body. The Commissioners are responsible to Parliament and the Government, but such would not be the case as regards Mrs. Chisholm's Society'.

Butler seems to have acted with honesty of purpose, and in the circumstances of the society as they were then, he was justified in refusing a grant from public funds. The venture was an experiment which could not be proved to have been successful for more than a year. The South Australian government had trouble enough coping with the situation caused by the Victorian gold discoveries. Moreover, it was only just ten years since the 'Wakefield' colony had begun to struggle to establish itself on a sound financial foundation. With the memory of the disastrous first years of settlement, the government was very chary of risking any money at all, no matter how worthy the object.

By March 1852, when the South Australian committee was refused the grant from the land fund, Captain Chisholm had been in Melbourne for over four months. He had set up his office at 110 Swanston Street, in the heart of the town. Melbourne was then the clearing house for the rush of diggers who were coming from every quarter of the earth. Nearly every able-bodied man had gone to the goldfields, and those who were left had to cope with a sudden and enormous increase in population. The 'diggers' from overseas demanded lodgings, tools and transport, and every man wanted everything done at once. The lack of labour and the demand for goods, coupled with the large amount of gold in circulation, caused prices to skyrocket. The emigrant whose letter was published in *Household Words* and who quoted the prices of foodstuffs in 1850, must have been aghast at the prices of the same commodities a year later. In January 1852 Georgiana McCrae complained that: 'firewood is exceedingly scarce at 35s. (or £2 for a fortnight's supply) and this was due to "the want of men to fell trees and to cart them into town".

Water cost "6s. the little barrel; bread 1s. 8d. the 2 lb. loaf; flour 4d. the lb.; washing 5s. the dozen; groceries . . . double the former prices; bacon 2s. 9d. the lb.; butter 2s. 6d. the lb.; cheese 2s. 9d.; eggs 3s. the dozen; milk 1s. the pint; potatoes 2d. the lb.; vegetables and fruit hardly to be had. Not that there is any lack, but for want of men to convey the fruit to market".'[12]

William Howitt, a conservative Englishman who was affronted by the lusty life of the mining population, saw no romance in the quest for gold and its results; 'my effects will cost me more in getting them up to the town from the ship than they did in bringing them hither from London'.[13] As to Melbourne itself: 'every single tree has been levelled to the ground; it is one hard-bare expanse, bare of all nature's attractions, a wilderness of wooden huts of Lilliputian dimensions; and everywhere around and amongst them, timber and rubbish, delightfully interspersed with pigs, geese, hens, goats, and dogs innumerable. The streets, so called, which all run in the true gridiron or rather hurdle style, are not roads but quagmires, through which bullock drays drag fresh materials, with enormous labour ploughing the muddy soil up to their very axles.'

Nevertheless, there *were* a few trees, for Howitt later remarks that he has 'scarcely seen a tree under which do not lie the remains of bottles which have been dashed against it as they have been emptied'. The drunkenness was 'something fearful', for the diggers came into town and unburdened themselves of their hard-won gold as quickly as possible.

The streets were no place for weaklings, for the diggers were 'very cavalier and independent in their speech and behaviour'. If they rode, they never walked their horses but galloped furiously. It was 'everyman's business to take care of himself', and as Howitt ruefully remarked, 'it is a wonderful place to take the conceit out of men who expect much deference'.[14]

Small wonder that in the midst of such excitement Captain Chisholm found great difficulty in enforcing the repayment of the loans made by the society. There are several references to this in the contemporary press, and the *Argus* in particular belaboured those who were so carried away by gold fever as to forget their obligations to Mrs Chisholm.[15]

---

[12]*Georgiana's Journal*, ed. Hugh McCrae (Sydney, 1934), p. 190.
[13]William Howitt, *Land, Labour and Gold* (1855) i. 15.
[14]*Ibid*. p. 36.
[15]*Argus*, 26 and 30 April 1852 (leader).

A Melbourne committee[16] had been established soon after Captain Chisholm's arrival, and like the Adelaide one it was representative of every shade of religious opinion. Dr Perry, the Anglican Bishop of Melbourne, was president, and among the members were the Very Rev. Dr Geoghegan (head of the Roman Catholic Church), D. C. McArthur (manager of the Bank of Australasia), John Pascoe Fawkner, M.L.C., John O'Shannassy, M.L.C., William Rutledge, M.L.C., and S. M. South, Esq., the society's solicitor. During 1852 the committee met regularly on the first Monday of every month at eight o'clock in the evening. Special meetings were called as often as necessary, notice being given three days beforehand.[17]

By May 1852, £3,873 17s. had been remitted to London for the emigration of 474 people to Victoria.[18] These immigrants had arrived in the *Slains Castle, Blundell* and *Athenian*, the loan to the three ships being £2,603.[19]

In spite of the large remittances that were made, the Melbourne committee appears to have been at its wit's end to devise some means whereby the immigrants could be made to pay the instalments on their loans. At a meeting held in August 1852,[20] Father Geoghegan suggested posting the names of the defaulters on the church doors of each district, but Rutledge thought this would be ineffective, and suggested that the clergy should berate them from the pulpit. Mr Dalgety suggested that after two years the names of the defaulters should be posted, and the amount recovered by process.[21] It was then agreed that an advertisement to this effect should be published in the Melbourne papers, but this I have been unable to trace. Perhaps the committee decided to give the defaulters one more chance, or perhaps on further consideration it was decided that the society could not successfully enforce its claims by legal proceedings.

Captain Chisholm gave evidence before a Legislative Council Select Committee on 'The Present System of Immigration' which made its report in January 1853. He considered that 'the distance of Australia from the Mother Country is very much against emigration to these colonies',[22] and that the English working classes

[16]*Ibid.* 19 April 1852. [17]*Ibid.* 8 July 1852.
[18]*Ibid.* 14 May 1852. [19]Mackenzie, *Memoirs,* p. 183.
[20]*Argus,* 3 August 1852.
[21]Dalgety was reported as being a member of the committee by the *Argus,* 3 August 1852. He was the founder of the firm which is still well known in Australia.
[22]*Report,* The Present System of Immigration, V. & P Leg. Council Vic. (1853), ii (2), 899.

knew much more of American than of Australian conditions.
He thought that if knowledge of Australia was increased abroad,
the labouring class would probably go to the colony in preference
to America. He had some grounds for this opinion, because in
the two days before he gave evidence he had received £207 from
'parties here . . . for the emigration of parents, brothers and sisters
and a son now in America'. However, the numbers of American
immigrants were not considerable. By the time the 1857 census
was made Americans represented less than 1 per cent of the
total population.[23] Many were experienced gold seekers who had
taken part in the Californian 'rush' of 1848, but such men, forever
searching for easy wealth, did not usually develop into valuable
citizens.

A further achievement of the Melbourne branch of the society
was the establishment of a proper depot for the reception of
immigrants. The matter was discussed at a committee meeting
in August 1852,[24] and it was agreed that a deputation should wait
upon Governor La Trobe to ask for land where a shelter could
be built. The members of this deputation were Bishop Perry,
Father Geoghegan, William Rutledge, F. G. Dalgety, James
Graham and Captain Chisholm. O'Shanassy and Rutledge, the
two members of the Legislative Council, were to ask the Council
for a grant of £500. Captain Chisholm was to write to the London
headquarters of the society and ask for an iron building to be
sent out which would accommodate two hundred people.

The deputation was favourably received and La Trobe agreed
that a temporary site for the building should be placed at the
disposal of the committee, and money be granted for the cost
of its erection.[25] It was intended that the shelter should be used
not only by the immigrants brought out by the Family Colonization Loan Society, but as 'a general reception place for all emigrants arriving from Europe . . . when not occupied by the
Society's immigrants'.[26] Captain Chisholm undertook to organize
it, but as he was overburdened with work, wished the government
to appoint someone to take permanent charge.

The deputation had waited upon Governor La Trobe in August;
by October the shelter had been built 'at the western extremity
of Lonsdale Street',[27] where the government had temporarily

---

[23]*Census of Victoria*, 1857. This is the first census made in which there
is a classification of the place of birth of the population.
[24]*Argus*, 3 August 1852.   [25]*Ibid*. 14 August 1852.
[26]*Ibid*.   [27]*Ibid*. 13 October 1852, 10 November 1852

set aside an acre of land. The shelter was a wooden structure —
the idea of the iron building which was to have been imported
from England seems to have been abandoned. It had accommodation for sixty, and was erected out of £500 which had been
'advanced by the Executive'; a £40 residue was returned to the
government.[28] The building was one large room, sixty feet by
twenty feet, in which the women and children were housed.
About twenty tents were erected beside it where the men and
boys could find shelter. It was intended that a 'small fee' should
be charged the immigrants to help meet the cost of the erection
of the shelter.[29] This intention, however, could not be carried
out, for Captain Chisholm reported that 'in absence of any aid
he found it impossible to draw out or enforce any code of regulations, nor could he exact any payment for the accommodation
afforded'.[30] His intention to establish the shelter and then find
someone to take charge of it had not been put into effect.

There was urgent need for immigrant shelters when no less
than 1,400 people arrived in Port Phillip in one day.[31] Even if the
majority of these were would-be diggers they had to be sheltered
somewhere before they took the track to Bendigo and Ballarat.
Besides the Family Colonization Loan Society's shelter, and the
Government Barracks in South Yarra, there were government
shelters at Prince's Bridge, and Batman's Hill. By March 1853,
the Wesleyan Immigrants' Home had also been erected, and
for this the government had given a grant of £1,000.[32] This
Wesleyan Home gave bed and bedding besides three meals a
day, at a cost of 4s. The shelters in existence, including that of
the Family Colonization Loan Society, provided accommodation
for 1,526 immigrants.[33]

At the same time as it was resolved to erect the society's
shelter the members of the committee, prompted by Captain
Chisholm, resolved that two members in rotation should visit all
ships which arrived with immigrants in Port Phillip[34] to hear
reports by the immigrants of their treatment on the voyage. This
decision was probably made in accordance with Mrs Chisholm's
wishes, for she was then agitating for the reform of conditions

[28]Report from the Government Immigration Agent Relative to Public
Institutions for General Immigrants, 8 March 1853, *V. & P.* Leg. Council
Vic. (1853-4), ii (1), 36.
[29]*Argus*, 10 November 1852.   [30]See n. 28.
[31]*Argus*, 13 October 1852.   [32]See n.28.
[33]*V. & P.* Leg. Council Vic. (1853-4), ii (1), 42.
[34]*Argus*, 3 August 1852.

on board ship. It is an indication of the interest which the society took in the welfare of all immigrants, and not only of its own. The remittance system, too, was not confined to those interested in the society, but could be used by any settlers who wished to remit money to relatives in England.[35]

By the beginning of November 1852, £8,731 had been remitted to England for the reunion of families; £2,987 had been loaned to immigrants, and of this £430 had been refunded.[36] Even though comparatively few loans had been repaid, Mrs Chisholm's immigrants were introduced at very reasonable cost, and the remittances enabled many to leave England who, without the society's help, might have continued to live in poverty.

In July Captain Chisholm had asked that his resignation as the Victorian agent of the society be accepted. He wished to go to New South Wales to establish a branch there, and also to arrange the appointment of a suitable agent in Brisbane.[37] This was the immediate, but not the only reason for offering his resignation. Since the merchants of the City of London had ensured the financial success of the society, he felt that there was no longer an urgent need for his wife and himself to continue their heavy labours on the immigrants' behalf. He did not wish to continue as a paid agent, for he hoped that 'others, who have more leisure and means, will continue the operations which we could not well do in justice to our children'.[38] Mrs Chisholm, too, at the time when he had left England for Australia, had pointed out that with their slender means, such a separation[39] 'could not continue for any great length of time', and she had planned to return to Australia much sooner than she actually did.[40] But both were carried onwards by the success of the society, and the knowledge that without them that success might not be maintained. Captain Chisholm therefore agreed to remain as the Victorian agent until another could be appointed.[41] A reliable man would have been very difficult to find in those turbulent days, and evidently his resignation was held over indefinitely.

Captain Chisholm does not seem to have visited Sydney or Brisbane; the foundation of the Sydney branch of the society was evidently directly instigated by the Central Committee in Lon-

[35]*Ibid.* 24 October 1851.
[36]*Ibid.* 10 November 1852.
[37]*Ibid.* 8 July 1852.　　　　　　[38]*Ibid.* 1 July 1852.
[39]*Adelaide Observer*, 2 August 1851.
[40]*Cork Examiner*, 1852; *The Times*, 16 August 1852.
[41]*Argus*, 1 July 1852.

don.[42] Charles Edward Robinson, who was appointed secretary, established his office at 32 Hunter Street, and by July 1852 the Sydney committee was 'engaged in preparing a scheme of operations by which through agencies scattered through the Colony, every assistance will be afforded to those wishing to avail themselves of the advantages held out by the Society'.[43]

To help forward this work subscription lists were opened at several banks, and the seven members of the committee alone contributed £170. Mrs Chisholm was always anxious to establish country agencies, and in the case of New South Wales the depots which she had established before she left for England could have been used.

At least two ships are known to have taken immigrants to Sydney in 1853, and there seem to have been at least four or five other ships whose names and dates of arrival are uncertain.[44]

Mrs Chisholm found great difficulty in excluding young men whose sole purpose in emigrating was to join the gold diggers. This is apparent from the numbers of men listed in some of the extant passenger lists of the society's ships. She was known to favour female immigrants, and on the first three ships the ratio between the single men and women was fairly even. But with the fourth ship, the *Nepaul,* there were fifty-seven families (among whom, of course, were some unattached girls), six single women, and one hundred and nineteen single men. In the *Scindian* the ratio was thirteen women to fifty-nine men; in the *Chalmers* it was fifteen women to eighty-six men; and in the *Ballengeich* it was twenty-five women to fifty-two men. In the *Caroline Chisholm,* which arrived in 1853, the ratio was still less favourable — thirteen women to seventy-eight men.

Mrs Chisholm could only hope that many of the young men who asked her help to set sail for the diggings would afterwards prepare homes for their parents in Australia. In many cases her hope was fulfilled, for the golden dreams did not always materialize, and the dreamers found that farming was a more satisfactory occupation than the feverish search for gold.

The New South Wales government was so favourably impressed

[42]Correspondence between the Local Board of the Family Colonization Loan Society and the Local Government, *V. & P.* Leg. Council N.S.W. (1852), ii. 67.

[43]*Ibid.*

[44]One of these ships was the *Caroline Chisholm;* the other was one among whose immigrants were forty to forty-five operative engineers (D. Mackenzie, *Caroline Chisholm, a Memoir,* p. 35).

by the society's work, that a sum of £10,000 was voted by the
Legislative Council in 1852 to be 'unreservedly entrusted to the
London Committee'.[45] There were great hopes that the Victorian
Legislative Council would vote a similar sum, and the Colonial
Secretary introduced the matter to the House in October 1853.[46]
But it was not until Mrs Chisholm returned to Australia that the
Victorian Legislative Council voted £5,000 towards a testimonial[47]
made to her.

RETURN TO AUSTRALIA

The London merchants interested in the Australian trade had
given Mrs Chisholm their backing when it was most needed
and Vernon Smith declared the society would have failed without
them;[1] but they certainly altered the purely philanthropic outlook of the London committee.

About June 1853 the Central Committee was reorganized,[2]
and Sidney Herbert replaced the Earl of Shaftesbury as chairman.
The committee members, Sidney Herbert, the Count de Strzelecki,
Stuart Alexander Donaldson and Frederick Robert Gore,[3] undertook to manage the disbursement of the £10,000 which had been
given by the New South Wales Legislative Council, as well as
the other finances.

The reorganization was made in preparation for Mrs Chisholm's
departure for Australia. This had been delayed by difficulties
chiefly caused by the gold rush. She had stayed in England 'in
hopes that many of those who are going to the "diggings" and
who may feel an interest in the emigration of their aged parents,
may consult me and that I may be of greater use to them by
remaining'.[4] She intended leaving in the early part of 1853,[5] but
it was not until 1854 that she sailed.

Some very significant alterations were made in the regulations
of the Family Colonization Loan Society in February 1854. The
revised regulations[6] provided that 'parties making application
to the Society for a loan will be required to open a Deposit
Account in the Society's Books and to pay such a sum as the

[45]*Empire* (Sydney), 25 July 1854; *Argus,* 8 October 1854.
[46]*Argus,* 26 October 1853.
[47]*Ibid.* 1 November 1854. See ch. vii.
[1]*The Times,* 10 August 1853.   [2]*Ibid.* 31 August 1853.
[3]*Empire,* supplement, 25 July 1854.
[4]*Cork Examiner,* 1852.
[5]*The Times,* 16 August 1852, letter from Caroline Chisholm.
[6]*Empire,* supplement, 25 July 1854.

Committee may consider equivalent to half of the passage money, either in one payment, or in sums of not less than 20s. at a time. They will have to furnish a list of the names, occupations, ages and other particulars of their family, with the probable time of their being able to complete the entire sum required on account of their passage-money'. Moreover, 'emigrants before embarking will be required to sign a note-of-hand, payable on demand for the amount lent by the Society'. This document was to be forwarded to the Government Immigration Agent in Sydney.[7] After signing it the emigrants received a letter from the London secretary of the society to the Government Immigration Agent, 'stating that they are to be allowed to repay the Loan by instalments within a period not exceeding two years from the date of their arrival in the Colony'. Nevertheless, the two years' grace was only allowed if the immigrants reported themselves to the Government Immigration Agent on arrival, and informed him of their 'place of abode and later of any service into which they entered'. If this condition was not complied with, the Immigration Agent was 'entitled to demand and sue for repayment of the amount'.

The revised regulations indicate the influence of the city merchants. The emphasis put upon the 'note-of-hand', and the business-like tone of the new rules, show the necessity for some legal guarantee of the repayment of loans. Philanthropy had to be allied to common-sense commercialism if the society was to survive.

At the same time as these revised rules were made, the London committee announced 'that it is not advisable that the Society should incur the responsibility of chartering ships'.[8] Instead, when a sufficient number of eligible emigrants were recruited, arrangements for their passages were to be made with one or more of the leading ship-brokers whose vessels were fitted on the principles approved by Mrs Chisholm. By this time the society's plan of fitting out ships was well known and widely adopted by private ship-owners. Moreover, the gold discoveries had given such an impetus to emigration, and the demand for ships was so great, that the society must have been hard pressed to charter ships for its exclusive use. These two reasons seem to have influenced the decision to cease chartering.[9]

[7]Presumably also to the agents of the society in Victoria and South Australia; the letter quoted in the *Empire* refers only to Sydney.
[8]*Empire*, 25 July 1854.
[9]*Chambers' Edinburgh Journal*, xix (1853), 243.

The decision was made at the right time. The Crimean War began in March 1854 and every ship available was commandeered to carry troops to the Crimea; shipping was soon completely disorganized, and the activities of the society seriously curtailed. Sidney Herbert, the new chairman of the Central Committee, was Secretary for War in the Palmerston government which took office at the beginning of 1855. Florence Nightingale was his formidable protégée, and he had little attention to give anything else while he remained at her beck and call.

These difficulties were encountered without the strong hand of Mrs Chisholm to guide the Central Committee. She had set sail for Australia in April 1854 in the *Ballarat* — 'a fine, fast ship but with little room',[10] and she had to pay £100 for her passage, which was then 'a higher sum than has ever been paid by a Lady for herself'.[11] She took a number of families and young girls with her.

Before she left England a large sum of money was subscribed as a testimonial to her. The subscription was begun in August 1853 when a meeting was held at the London Tavern. Vernon Smith presided, and Robert Lowe,[12] Raikes Currie, Sir Isaac Goldsmid, Samuel Sidney, Stuart Donaldson and J. G. Hubbard all spoke in eulogistic terms of her 'long, arduous and successful efforts'.[13] A committee was formed and between £800 and £900 was subscribed at the meeting. Florence Nightingale, then the superintendent of a charitable nursing home in London, contributed £5; Robert Southey and his son, £5 5s.; W. C. Wentworth, £25; Lady Noel Byron, £50; the Countess of Pembroke, £20; Messrs Coutts & Co., £25; Lady Anthony de Rothschild, £15; Baroness Lionel de Rothschild, £15; Messrs N. M. Rothschild & Sons, £25; Viscount Canning, £10; and Lord Lansdowne, £10. A glittering array of celebrities must have attended the meeting. The final amount is not known, nor is there any indication of how the money was used — whether she paid some of her own, or her family's expenses with it, or whether she made a contribution of it to the society's funds. She and her husband were still determined to accept no monetary reward for their labour, and it seems unlikely that they kept this money for their own use.

[10]*Illustrated London News*, 15 April 1854.
[11]Caroline Chisholm to Miss Burdett-Coutts, 14 March 1854, see Appendix D.
[12]Robert Lowe had left New South Wales in 1850 after eight strenuous years in the colony.
[13]*The Times*, 10 August 1853.

Her record of work in England had been as remarkable as that of her early years in New South Wales. When she returned in 1846 she had been known by name only to a few Whitehall officials, and to the relatives of those she had helped in the colony.

Yet she had achieved much of what she had set out to do. She had despatched the emancipists' wives and families to Australia, and she had induced the Colonial Office to reintroduce the system whereby such women were given free passages. The least successful of her efforts was the return of the forsaken children to their parents, but as far as possible this had been done. In spite of many difficulties her dearest wish — the establishment of a system of 'national colonization' — had been accomplished, though without the help of the home government. By September 1854, a few months after she left England, the Family Colonization Loan Society had sent out three thousand immigrants and two hundred and seventy others were on their way; the society was free from debt and had £15,000 in hand.[14] The remittance system had been a great success, and a total of £9,800 had been remitted from Australia to England.[15] No remittances appear to have been made after May 1854. The Colonial Money Order System, introduced in May 1853, may well have made it unnecessary for the society to continue them.

Besides her other achievements she had helped reform conditions on board ship. In 1855 the Victorian Collector of Customs (Hugh Childers) claimed that 'the system of emigration had been much improved by the alterations in the Passenger Act which were made by the influence of Mrs. Chisholm'.[16] The Passenger Act of 1855, besides providing for a much better dietary scale, laid it down that 'not more than one passenger, unless husband and wife or females or children under twelve years of age, shall be placed in or occupy the same berth'. It also provided that there should be a sufficient number of privies with 'at least two water closets under the poop or elsewhere on the upper deck . . . for the exclusive use of women and young children'.[17]

[14]*Argus*, 2 September 1854.

[15]The records in the possession of Coutts & Co., London, show that this amount was remitted between 22 July 1852 and 2 March 1854. The records of the Bank of Australasia, Melbourne, show the society's account open between 16 October 1851 and 29 May 1854, during which time £7,944 was remitted to London. Other remittances may have been made from Adelaide or Sydney but there is no record of such transactions.

[16]*Argus*, 4 April 1855.

[17]18 & 19 Victoria, c. 119: An Act to Amend the Law Relating to the Carriage of Passengers by Sea.

During these years she had made Australia known to thousands who otherwise might have had no interest in the colony as a country where immigrants were wanted and welcomed.

THE SOCIETY'S ACHIEVEMENT: GOVERNMENT AND PRIVATE EMIGRATION

The society continued in existence for some years after Mrs Chisholm returned to Australia. Its last years were mainly occupied in expending the gift of £10,000 from New South Wales. A select committee of the New South Wales Legislative Council reported in November 1855 on the use made of it, and the evidence before this committee, as well as the annual reports of H. H. Browne, the Government Immigration Agent, give a great deal of information.

Eight ships had arrived between September 1854 and July 1856, bringing 1,211 immigrants who were for the most part 'exceedingly good'.[1] The ships were not chartered; the committee had advertised for suitable vessels and then paid so much per head to the ships' brokers.[2] This was the method that the government had used when engaging bounty ships.

The immigrants consisted 'principally of cabinet makers and the higher class of tradesmen and also gardeners, footmen, butlers, milliners, dressmakers and needle-women'. Browne remarked on the fact that they were 'exceedingly well dressed in frock coats and black beaver hats'.[3] None had any difficulty in finding employment, but the extra precautions taken by the reorganized London Committee to secure repayment of loans appear to have been fruitless. In May 1855 Browne reported that 'the amounts collected are too trifling to mention',[4] and by the end of that year only £58 10s. had been repaid. He thought there was 'little hope of realising much more';[5] it was very easy to evade payment because the settlement of the colony was so scattered. The country branch committees which the Sydney committee had intended establishing had either lapsed or never been in existence.

Browne was evidently a capable man, but he had a preference

[1]*Report*, Immigration, V. & P. Leg. Council N.S.W. (1854), ii. 980.
[2]*Ibid.* p. 1070. Evidence of Stuart Donaldson concerning the *Hanover*. This was the procedure adopted with the first ship and it was probably followed with the others.
[3]*Report*, Family Colonization Loan Society, V. & P. Leg. Council N.S.W. (1855), ii. 519.
[4]*Report, ibid.* Immigration Agent, 10 May 1855, ii. 544.
[5]*Report, ibid.* Immigration Agent, 10 July 1856, ii. 436.

for government immigration,[6] as opposed to private immigration such as that conducted by the Family Colonization Loan Society. His criticisms of the society's ships must be considered in the light of this. The complaints made both by him, and by some of the immigrants, are indicative of the change in the society's policy and administration after Mrs Chisholm's departure from England.

Browne objected strongly to the small cabins with which the ships were fitted; in five out of the six ships 'the heat has been so intense that the passengers have been obliged to cut large holes through the bulk-head, near the upper deck to give them ventilation'.[7] He considered the open, curtained berths in government ships much more satisfactory. In particular, the conditions on board the first ship, the *Hanover,* were not good, and the immigrants made a formal complaint after their arrival in the colony; no wash-house had been placed on deck, as the society had guaranteed, and an outbreak of measles had occurred because a child with the illness had been passed by the government medical officer who inspected the passengers in London. This last mishap was not the fault of the London Committee, but they must be held responsible for the overcrowding. Overcrowding was not specifically reported on the other ships, but in general, Browne 'could not speak favourably'[8] of their cleanliness. As to the protection of the immigrant girls he pessimistically reported that 'very few of them . . . ever [did] well in the Colony', because they were not properly controlled during the voyage.[9]

The terms under which the society appointed its surgeons, too, caused him to complain. Most of them were good, but in one case, though the surgeon 'kept tolerably sober while on board, it was six weeks before he could be found sufficiently sober to sign the receipt for his gratuity'. In comparison with the £20 given by the society, the surgeons on government ships began their services with 10s. a head, and advanced to 16s. according to the number of voyages they made. In addition, they received £40 for the passage home. This poor payment given to the society's surgeons was, of course, a shortcoming inherent in its constitution as a voluntary body. It could not afford to give the salary paid by the government. In conclusion, Browne recommended

[6]For instance, he disapproved of the 'general feeling among immigrants that they would rather be at liberty in a private ship than confined in a Government one'. *Report,* Colonization Loan Society, *ibid.* (1855), ii. 520.
[7]*Ibid.*
[8]*Report,* Family Colonization Loan Society, *ibid.* (1855), ii. 519.
[9]*Report,* Immigration, *ibid.* (1854), ii. 1056.

that the society's ships should be fitted out in the same way as the government ones, and its surgeons should be such that they 'would be qualified by the Commissioner's regulations to take charge of the ship'.

Yet, in spite of these criticisms, and the fact that it was impossible to call in the loans, he considered that the immigrants were introduced much more economically than those brought out by the government,[10] and that the £10,000 given by the Legislative Council to the society had been well spent.

Even if due allowance is made for Browne's bias against private immigration, there would seem to have been some cause for criticism of the London committee. The difficulties under which the committee was working did not absolve it from the guarantee of good conditions which Caroline Chisholm had always given her immigrants. Captain Chisholm's fear that the society might become commercialized was not unfounded. One recommendation of the committee is striking — 'that a preference shall be given to young married couples with *few or no children* or to single persons of both sexes between the ages of 18 and 30; and that care shall be taken that, at the least, as many females shall be sent out as males'.[11]

This is an echo of the Government Emigration Regulation, that 'the candidates most acceptable are young couples who have no children', and it was against this regulation that Mrs Chisholm had repeatedly protested.[12]

The general conclusion is that a good deal of the philanthropic spirit with which Mrs Chisholm had infused it was lost. Samuel Cogdon succeeded her as secretary in London, but there is no evidence of his activity or inactivity. In Sydney, Browne, the Government Immigration Agent, had to attend to the society's affairs as well as his other duties, and it was unlikely that the immigrants would be as well cared for as they had been during the first years of the society's existence.

By the time Browne made his report for the year 1855 eight

[10]*Report, ibid.* Immigration Agent, 10 July 1856, (1856-7), ii. 436. The society's immigrants cost £9 7s. 0¾d. [*sic*] for each statutory adult. At about the same date each Government statutory adult cost £20 (see Coghlan, *Labour and Industry in Australia,* ii. 593). A 'statute adult' was considered to be 'one person of the age of fourteen and upwards or two persons between one and fourteen years of age'. (*The Times,* 8 October 1847.)

[11]*Report,* Family Colonization Loan Society, V. & P. Leg. Council N.S.W. (1855), ii. 524.

[12]See particularly Caroline Chisholm to Benjamin Hawes, 28 February 1847, *H.R.A.* xxv. 407.

ships had arrived.[13] Possibly two or three ships arrived after this
date, as there was still £2,901 13s. 9d. left out of the £10,000
when the cost of five shiploads had been deducted. As the loans
were not repaid, Browne considered that the operations of the
society would inevitably cease as soon as the £10,000 was
exhausted.[14] After 1856 there is no further mention of the society's
activities, and the office at 29 Bucklersbury, London, does not
appear in the post office directory after 1857. The obvious conclusion is that it faded out of existence towards the end of the 'fifties.

It is doubtful exactly how many emigrants left England under
the society's auspices. In September 1854, after Mrs Chisholm
had arrived in Victoria, it was stated she 'had sent out 3,000
immigrants and 270 were on their way'.[15] The 1,211 taken to
New South Wales up till July 1856[16] must be added, and 4,481
is then the number of Mrs Chisholm's immigrants who arrived
in Australia. If two or three more ships were paid for by the
£10,000 given by New South Wales the number was probably
increased to close on 5,000.[17] In February 1867, after she returned
to England for the last time, Caroline Chisholm stated that her
scheme had 'provided . . . for upwards of 20,000 persons'.[18] This
figure is a leap from the conservative estimate of 5,000 and, as
there is no other press report to be compared with that given by
the *Empire,* it may be a mistake. When Mrs Chisholm returned
to Australia in 1854 the society had £15,000 in hand — £10,000
of which was the New South Wales gift. Doubtless the remaining
£5,000 was used to send emigrants to Victoria, and perhaps South
Australia but, as ships were not then being chartered in the
society's name, it is impossible to trace them. Voluntary subscriptions may also have increased the society's funds after its
foundress left England. Therefore, 20,000 is not an impossible,
though it is an improbable, number.

Between 1852 and 1861 approximately 554,000 immigrants
arrived in Australia; during the same period the population increased from 437,665 to 1,168,149.[19] That such a small population

[13]V. & P. Leg. Council N.S.W. (1855), ii. 521; (1856-7), ii. 449.
[14]Report from Immigration Agent, 10 May 1855, V. & P. Leg. Council
N.S.W. (1855), ii. 544.
[15]*Argus,* 2 September 1854.
[16]V. & P. Leg. Council N.S.W. (1855), ii. 521; (1856-7), ii. 449.
[17]That is, taking 151 as the possible number in each ship, this number
is the average of the eight known ships.
[18]*Empire,* 19 February 1867, quoting *Western Daily Press* (England),
15 December 1866.
[19]H. Burton, in *The Peopling of Australia,* p. 39 (see p. 105).

was able to absorb this sudden and enormous influx of immigrants
indicates the swift economic development which took place during
those years. The news of gold brought most of these immigrants;
and it was the news of gold which had established Mrs Chisholm's
society on a firm financial basis. But though many of her emigrants
might indeed have found their way to Australia without her aid,
through her society she helped them to emigrate in comparative
comfort and independence, and to establish themselves where
their labour was needed.

There is no doubt that those who emigrated on her ships were
good colonizing material, and skilled tradesmen predominated
among them.[20] Such immigrants raised the moral standard of
colonial society, and their own moral well-being was increased
by their freedom from want in the new land.

As well as the many relatives who rejoined each other by her
good offices, the passenger lists show the large numbers of complete families who emigrated in her ships. She hoped that such
families would form 'bush partnerships', and a letter to her from
a squatter near Braidwood, New South Wales, shows how many
of them might have prospered. He was in urgent need of labour
and asked Mrs Chisholm to send him an emigrant family. 'This
is the wages I will give to anyone that will take care of 1,000
sheep: £26 a year with a weekly ration of 10 lbs. flour, 10 lbs. good
meat, and some for his dog, and 1 lb. for every 100 over the 1,000;
and 2 lb. of sugar, 4 oz. tea and if he or any of [them] will sleep
in the watchbox and move the hurdles, I will give £10 a year
more and if he will braid cabbage-tree hats I will buy them of
him. My son gave for four in Sydney £2 8s. . . . If any more rations
is required for the family flour [they may have] meat 2d. per lb.,
tea 2s.; sugar 4d.; a garden ploughed and fenced, and seed given
for the first season, and a cow lent for milk and butter for the
family, and a pig in the bargain . . . It is very frequent here for
families to manage two or three flocks, and some fetch in cows and
milk, or scare birds, so that all able are gladly employed. I know
of many families, by being industrious have a nice little herd of
cattle and horses of their own.'[21]

An agricultural labourer's wages in England at this time were
about 7s. to 8s. a week, increased by about 4s. or 4s. 6d. by piece-
work and rations. His food 'in Dorsetshire, was vegetables flavoured

[20]See Appendix F.

[21]*The Times*, 24 December 1852, 'A Voice from the Bush'. This letter
was written after the extreme shortage of labour, caused by the Victorian
gold discoveries, was felt in New South Wales.

with bacon fat, or bread and cheese; in Somersetshire, bread and butter, or bread dipped in cider; in Cheshire potatoes or gruel thickened with treacle'.[22] It is not surprising that the Australian conditions were attractive.

Altogether, Caroline Chisholm achieved what she had attempted in the Family Colonization Loan Society. The only noteworthy failure was the non-repayment of the loans, but because of voluntary contributions, many of them, like those of the London merchants, prompted by the interest aroused by the gold discoveries, the financial success of the venture was assured. In practice the society fulfilled the most important needs of emigration.[23]

One way to estimate the success of Mrs Chisholm's society is to compare the achievements of Dr Lang's company with that of the Family Colonization Loan Society. Lang's six ships took 1,424 emigrants to Port Phillip and Moreton Bay. His people were of excellent colonizing stock, but his proposed company was extinguished amidst financial chaos and bitter recrimination. Moreover he did not give his emigrants the good ship-board conditions which Mrs Chisholm provided, and he certainly did not provide for their reception in the colony as she did. Her society had an advantage in that the gold discoveries gave it a great impetus towards success. But even before the news of gold reached England the Family Colonization Loan Society was beginning to prosper. A comparison of the success of Mrs Chisholm's scheme with the comparative failure of the other private emigration societies founded during the 'fifties is significant, for these others, too, should have been able to exploit the gold rush.

There was, for instance, the Highland and Island Emigration Society founded under the sponsorship of Sir Charles Trevelyan 'to assist the destitute inhabitants of the northern parts of Scotland to emigrate in groups of families by means of advancing sums of money to defray the expense of passage etc. to those members of families who from age or other causes would be ineligible for free passages under the Regulations'.[24] In its encouragement of family emigration it was very similar to Mrs Chisholm's society, and it also advanced loans to its emigrants. Its foundation may well have been influenced by the principles put into practice in the Family Colonization Loan Society. Unfortunately, like

[22] T. E. Kebbel, *The Agricultural Labourer* (1870), pp. 30, 35.
[23] See above, p. 59.
[24] *Report*, Immigration Agent, 9 June 1853, V. & P. Leg. Council Vic. (1853), i (1), 589.

Mrs Chisholm's emigrants, the people sent out evaded repayment of their loans. But, unlike her emigrants, their worth did not compensate for this. Edward Grimes, the Victorian Government Emigration Agent, had not a good word to say for them. They were of 'ignorant and indolent habits' and the society soon fell into disrepute.

Another society which functioned for a short time during the early 'fifties was Sidney Herbert's Society for Promoting Female Immigration. This, too, was unsuccessful, chiefly because of the poor character of the women and girls it introduced.[25]

Undoubtedly, as T. A. Coghlan considers, Caroline Chisholm's Family Colonization Loan Society was the most important private immigration society in existence at the beginning of the 'fifties.[26] In it private emigration is seen at its best; the immigrants were of a high standard, and their welfare was carefully considered, both on board ship and after their arrival in the colony. But, like all the other private emigration societies, it had one inherent weakness, and this was in financing the venture. In its early stages it was only the Chisholm's valiant struggles which kept it solvent; and the interest in Australia which was aroused by the gold rush was the turning point in its fortunes. Even after it was well established, however, economies still had to be made, and as soon as the voluntary contributions ceased it was impossible to continue the despatch of emigrants.

No private emigration organization could afford to maintain any large volume of emigration. On the other hand the government could, and did, maintain a large volume, notwithstanding the fact that when the land fund was exhausted, assisted emigration had several times to be suspended.

The Victorian Committee on the Present System of Immigration which reported in 1853, and which was greatly influenced by Mrs Chisholm's work, complained of 'the inability of the Commissioners to procure Immigrants, while at the same period crowds were offering to come and pay a great portion of their own passages by Mrs. Chisholm's ships'.[27] The Duke of Newcastle, Grey's successor at the Colonial Office, made answer: 'The Committee have been deceived as to the state of the facts. Mrs Chisholm is a lady whom it is impossible to name without adding an expression of respect and admiration; and it appears that

[25]*Ibid.*
[26]T. A. Coghlan, *Labour and Industry in Australia*, ii. 598.
[27]*Report*, The Present System of Immigration, V. & P. Leg. Council Vic. (1852-3), ii (2), 896.

much to her credit she had despatched about 1,000 emigrants to the Colony in the course of a year and a half preceding Mr Chisholm's evidence before the Committee but the number of emigrants despatched by the Commissioners in the course of the single year 1852 was 34,000 . . . They had in their office at one moment as many as 18,000 applications.'[28] The commissioners' assertion is borne out by all contemporary records and accounts of the extraordinary numbers of emigrants who made applications for passages to Australia after the news of the gold discoveries reached England. An article in *Household Words* speaks of 'the dense throng of impromptu sheep-shearers, ready-made agriculturists and shepherds by inspiration'[29] who crowded the Park Street office of the Land and Emigration Commissioners. Even in 1849 'the great increase in the number of applicants permitted the Commissioners to demand some payment, and the charges were graduated according to ages and occupations'.[30]

This Victorian committee, therefore, would seem to have been carried away by its enthusiasm for Mrs Chisholm's work, for between 1846 and 1852 while Earl Grey was in office it has been estimated that 60,680 immigrants arrived in Australia in government ships.[31] There was little or no difficulty in recruiting emigrants, but it was undoubtedly difficult to attract good types. Indeed, the deliberate policy under Grey was that the emigrants should not be able to become employers of labour on their own account for several years.

This decision to give Australia large numbers of immigrants was a result of the colony's persistent demand for labour. And this demand was made most loudly, and most persistently, by the squatters. Mrs Chisholm touched the heart of the matter when she made the accusation that 'the Board of Commissioners are but the agents of the squatting interest or men of capital in the Australian colonies'.[32] The way in which the squatters held sway over the Colonial Office is illustrated by T. F. Elliott's answer to Robert Lowe's fierce criticism of Grey because of the favourable terms given the squatters by the Waste Lands Occupation Act. Elliott pointed out with some asperity that the Hon. Francis Scott, the accredited agent of New South Wales,

[28]Despatch from the Duke of Newcastle, 19 September 1853, *V. & P.* Leg. Council Vic. (1853-4), ii (1), 186.
[29]*Household Words*, viii (1853), 42 ('The First Stage to Australia').
[30]Madgwick, *Immigration into Eastern Australia*, p. 195.
[31]Statistics compiled by T. A. Coghlan, *op. cit.* i. 368 and ii. 598, 627.
[32]Chisholm, *The A.B.C. of Colonization*, p. 4.

had favoured the squatters' claims, and 'if there are counter interests they should have made themselves heard'.[33] With some reason the Colonial Office considered that when the colony's representative gave them certain advice it was proper that such advice should be followed. The squatters produced the wool on which the economic wealth of Australia was based, and they held the leadership of colonial society. There was a certain justice in the fact that immigration was tempered to suit their needs, but there was injustice in the fact that the small settlers could not gain a proper hearing.

Mrs Chisholm herself, before she left New South Wales, had considered that it was the poorer immigrants who were urgently needed to supply the labour market. But, as on the question of introducing families with large numbers of small children, she changed her mind. By the time the Family Colonization Loan Society was established she was railing against the 'pauper emigration sponsored by the Government'.[34] She may have been disillusioned by the way in which the government administered assisted emigration after it was renewed in 1848; but her later disregard of the need for poorer immigrants was probably influenced by her increasingly hostile attitude towards the squatters. The squatters disliked immigrants who possessed enough capital to establish themselves as settlers within a short time, and Caroline Chisholm had become convinced that these were the most valuable colonists. The steadily increasing numbers of such immigrants heralded the challenge to the squatters' power which was to be made when the gold immigrants gave battle for possession of the land.

The emigrants 'eligible under the Regulations', and repeatedly demanded by the colony, were those suitable for agricultural and pastoral needs. When the colonists complained because of the small numbers of such immigrants the Colonial Office always made answer that those sent were the best available. The people who would have made the best emigrants were able by their own initiative to make their living in Britain. This factor must always be remembered when any criticism of the quality of government emigrants is made. Even Mrs Chisholm's emigrants, though praised by the colonists, were chiefly skilled tradesmen unused to agricultural and pastoral pursuits. Indeed, in the persistent and some-

[33]Morrell, *Colonial Policy of Peel and Russell*, p. 343, quoting a minute by Elliott, 21 December 1846.
[34]Chisholm, *The A.B.C. of Colonization*, pp. 4, 27-8.

times unwarranted criticism of emigration as conducted by the government, the colonists betrayed a certain contrariness. They had outgrown their dependent childhood, and were passing through a period of uneasy adolescence. As adolescents they were hypercritical of the parental control still exercised by the home government. Dr Lang's extravagant accusation that Earl Grey deserved 'both dismissal and impeachment' for his 'gross mis-government' was an extreme expression of this attitude.

If Mrs Chisholm had been able to maintain her emigration on a larger scale she would probably not have been able to maintain the high standard of emigrants, because such were available only in limited numbers, and most of these preferred to emigrate to North America. Emigration as conducted by the government and by Mrs Chisholm was complementary, for while the government could maintain a large volume of poor quality emigrants, Mrs Chisholm catered for smaller numbers of a superior type.

Together, Caroline Chisholm and the government did much to supply the demand for labour in the Australian colonies, and despite the colonists' protests that they did not want artisans or mechanics, all Mrs Chisholm's immigrants, and nearly all government immigrants, found instant employment. During the later 'forties and early 'fifties the supply of immigrants never equalled the demand; artisans and mechanics could always find employment and the demand for agricultural and pastoral labour was unceasing.

A Forthright Radical

MELBOURNE

The *Ballarat* arrived in Port Phillip Bay on 12 July 1854.[1] Mrs Chisholm had been away from Australia for nearly eight years, and during those years the colonies had grown swiftly — so swiftly that she found many novelties in colonial society when she returned. She had never visited Victoria before, and the stories she had heard of the effects of the gold discoveries made her eager to see the conditions for herself. A week before the *Ballarat* arrived the *Argus* published a leader which praised the work of 'our benefactress' and urged the public to give her a rousing welcome. When the ship came sailing up the bay, a large crowd assembled to greet her, but unfortunately the *Ballarat* was late in docking and many left before Mrs Chisholm arrived.[2]

Preparations for a public welcome were quickly made, and a *soirée* was held in the hall of the Mechanics' Institute on 31 August.[3] On the day the meeting was held the *Argus* delivered itself of another pontifical leader again headed 'Our Benefactress'.[4] This leader criticized the national character, particularly the 'contemptible' ingratitude shown to so many great men and women — among them Caroline Chisholm. This publicity seems to have had a good effect, or else the *Argus* was unduly pessimistic, for the meeting held at the Mechanics' Institute that evening was certainly a success. The hall was full, and there was 'a fair number' of women present. Lauchlan Mackinnon read and presented to Mrs Chisholm an address from the Immigrants' Aid Society,[5] and prominent men such as J. F. Foster (the Colonial Secretary) and J. T. Smith (the mayor of Melbourne) made eulogistic speeches. The *soirée* had an unmistakably mid-Victorian flavour, for tea was served and at the end of the hall a band

[1] *Argus*, 13 July 1854.
[2] *Ibid*. 15 July 1854.
[3] *Ibid*. 27 July, 30 August 1854.
[4] *Ibid*. 31 August 1854.
[5] *Ibid*. 1 September 1854.

played, while Mrs Testar sang in 'her usual tasteful manner'.[6]
In an excess of zeal the *Argus* reported this welcoming *soirée*
twice. The first report published the day afterwards seems adequate, but the next day a much more detailed one is given with
the explanation that there had not been room for a full account
the day before.

It is perhaps significant of the waning strength of the Family
Colonization Loan Society that it was not until towards the end
of September that a meeting of the committee was held at the
Town Hall to consider the best means of testifying the gratitude
of the society towards its foundress.[7] This meeting was a fiasco
for only three members of the committee, including the mayor,
arrived — a failure which seems to have been caused by the
inadequate notice given.[8] A second meeting, which was fully
attended, was held five days later at the Mechanics' Institute.
It was then decided to have public gathering to consider a testimonial to Mrs Chisholm; a sub-committee was appointed to draw
up resolutions to be submitted to this gathering, and 'to ascertain
Mrs Chisholm's views on the mode in which she was willing to
accept the testimonial'.[9]

Members recorded 'their deep sense of the unwearied exertions
of Captain Chisholm . . . in the re-union of families . . . which
they feel has been to him a labour of love, as such exertions are
to Mrs. Chisholm in England. Long after the hours usually devoted
to business has Captain Chisholm laboured night after night, and
in some instances until the morning, after being incessantly
occupied during the day, absolutely performing the work himself,
and what would occupy two clerks in order to keep down the
expenses of the Society'.

It was well said and richly deserved, for it was Captain Chisholm and no one else who had assured the success of his wife's
scheme of family colonization in Australia. After this resolution
was made his name is hardly mentioned in the press during the
twelve remaining years which he spent in Australia. With the
return of his wife he seems to have been well content to retire
into obscurity. It was she who was always the initiator, and he
who faithfully carried out her schemes. Though he worked so
devotedly for the Family Colonization Loan Society there is
more than a hint of weariness in the words in which he tendered

[6]*Ibid.* 2 September 1854.   [7]*Ibid.* 20 September 1854.
[8]*Ibid.* 21 September 1854.
[9]*Ibid.* 26 September 1854.

his provisional resignation in June 1852.[10] He was anxious to give more attention to his children, and he seems to have hoped that his wife would abandon some of her public work when she returned to Australia. This hope was not at once fulfilled.

When Mrs Chisholm was sounded as to what kind of testimonial she would like she was not at all helpful. The press reported that 'the reply of the disinterested and most independent lady was to the effect that she would decline to give any hint upon the subject'.[11] She had refused gifts before when she was in the full possession of youth and strength, with the expectation of several years strenuous work ahead of her. Now she was in her middle forties and she had to think of her children's future. But years before she had dedicated her 'talents to the God who gave them', and her religious vow had been strengthened almost to the point of obsession.

Her admirers were not daunted. At first it seems to have been proposed that a suitable home for Mrs Chisholm and her family should be purchased,[12] as she was then living 'in a humble cottage in Flinders Lane'.[13] As well as this, such provision was to be made 'as will enable her to devote her time to the public good'.[14] Eventually a motion was made in the Legislative Council: 'that an address be presented to His Excellency the Lieut.-Governor praying his Excellency will be pleased to place on the Estimates for the ensuing year the sum of £5,000 as a testimonial to Mrs. Chisholm expressive of the recognition by the Government and the people of the important services rendered by Mrs. Chisholm in the cause of colonization, conditional on the sum of £2,500 being raised by private subscription.'[15]

At first the committee deferred canvassing until the commercial depression was relieved. Then, at the end of January 1855, it was announced that a canvass for the testimonial was to begin. This change of plan was made because it was discovered that Mrs Chisholm, despite her refusal to ask for monetary assistance, was now 'poorer than hundreds of those [she] had befriended'. She had 'laboured at positive and constant pecuniary loss'[16] for many years. Indeed, the testimonial committee had to advance the family 'a small sum of money to put them in a position of earning

[10]*Ibid*. 1 July 1852.   [11]*Ibid*. 2 October 1854.
[12]*Ibid*. 9 October 1854.
[13]*Ibid*. 2 October 1854 (leader).
[14]*Ibid*. 9 October 1854.
[15]V. & P. Leg. Council Vic. (1854-5), i. 87.
[16]*Argus*, 29 January 1855.

their livelihood'. With this sum she and her husband opened a
large store.[17]

The £2,500 was collected, but when the Legislative Council
came to the point of voting the £5,000, John Pascoe Fawkner made
a determined effort to reduce the amount on the ground that
Mrs Chisholm, like Dr Lang, had been guided by sectarian
motives. What was more, all she had done 'had been mainly for
the advantage of New South Wales and, in that case, let New
South Wales, and not Victoria, vote her a gratuity'.[18] Be it
remembered to Fawkner's discredit that he had been a member
of the Victorian committee of the Family Colonization Loan
Society and should have known a good deal better.

After four divisions Fawkner's amendment was lost. He, William
Taylor and William Forlonge were the three opposers of the
measure. Their most creditable reason for opposition was that
the colony's finances were not sufficiently stable to permit such a
gratuity being given to a private individual. This argument against
the grant had been made when it was debated the previous year.
The government was then in debt to the banks for £300,000 but,
despite this, the colony was declared to be in a good state and
the Treasury well able to grant the £5,000.[19] The tone of Fawkner's
opposition makes it clear that his concern for the colony's welfare
was a secondary consideration. He was activated by his characteristic suspicion of the motives of others.

In spite of the disgruntled trio the £5,000 was paid to Mrs
Chisholm by the Treasury during 1855.[20] There is no mention
of the presentation in the press or any other contemporary record.
The colony was in such an uproar at this time that it is not remarkable that Caroline Chisholm's activities were overlooked.

THE GOLDFIELDS

The *Argus* might berate the public as it would in its efforts to
arouse enthusiasm for Mrs Chisholm, but events were moving
too fast during the gold era for an individual famous in an earlier
generation to be given due recognition. The leap in the Victorian
population statistics gives some indication of the socal revolution
which took place during the gold years. At the end of 1851 the

[17]*Ibid*. 4 April 1855.   [18]*Ibid*.
[19]*Ibid*. 1 November 1854.
[20]Treasurer's Finance Statement, expenditure 1 January—22 November
1855. Information by courtesy of Mr A. T. Smithers, Victorian Treasury.

population was 83,350; at the end of 1853 it was 198,496;[1] the vast majority of the immigrants were gold diggers, many of whom were radicals uprooted from troubled Europe and eager to found Utopia in the antipodes as well as founding their own fortunes. They altered the whole social complexion of the Australian colonies, particularly in Victoria where they disrupted the pastoral life and challenged the power of the squatters.

At this time the Australian colonies were preparing to set up the responsible government given them by the Australian Colonies Government Act of 1850. The new constitutions in Victoria, New South Wales, South Australia and Tasmania came into effect in 1856. The gold immigrants had a most significant effect on the experiment in self-government which was to be made in Victoria, for the radical element they brought into the life of the colony insistently demanded the recognition of political rights. This insistence forced democratic development and caused disturbances which in a slower, more balanced growth would have been avoided. For better or worse, the radical element in the population was well established by the time Mrs Chisholm returned to Australia.

Her active connection with the Family Colonization Loan Society seems to have ceased after she left England. She probably intended, as her husband hoped, to retire from public life and devote her time to her family, but the troubles of the gold diggers and her own inclinations proved too much for her. She determined to see the conditions for herself, principally so that she could make some provision for the numbers of unemployed,[2] whose ranks were constantly swelled by unsuccessful diggers. By investigating conditions on the goldfields, she hoped to facilitate the permanent settlement of families either on small farms or 'in the fields of labour'.[3]

By the end of October she was on the well-worn track to Bendigo in 'an ordinary covered cart'[4] pulled by two horses provided by a friend.[5] It had been suggested that the government should pay her travelling expenses, but she was convinced this would be unwise, for if she accepted government assistance she would then be a government servant and might have to withhold

---

[1]Victorian Statistics, V. & P. Leg. Council Vic. 1853-4, i (2), 937; *ibid.* ii (2), 199; *ibid.* (1854-5), ii (2).
[2]*Argus*, 1 November 1854.   [3]*Ibid.* 2 November 1854.
[4]*Ibid.* 3 February 1857, letter from Caroline Chisholm for information of British workmen.
[5]*Ibid.* 11 November 1854.

information from the public. One of her sons, presumably the eldest, Archibald, went with her.

The roads were as bad as they could be. There was 'enormous traffic' passing over them and 'the heavy loads, the cutting, narrow, sharp-edged wheels, plough up the road, and the wide range they are obliged to take in bad weather cuts up the road so much that foot-passengers suffer very much from the roughness of the same'.[6] Every other traveller bemoaned the difficulties of the trip to the diggings. Young Lord Robert Cecil described the road through the Black Forest as 'a mere pathway . . . not only a foot deep in dust and pitted with as many holes as a rabbit warren but . . . at times so narrow that the naves of both wheels grazed the trees on each side'. It was also intersected by large roots and dotted over with stumps half buried in the sand.[7]

The Bendigo diggings were over ten miles square, with the poppet heads where shafts fifty to sixty feet deep had been dug, and the yellow 'mullock' thrown up in great mounds beside them. The miners, the owners of sly grog shops and the various hangers on, lived in tents and log huts. The tents — Henry Lawson's 'little homes of calico' — were the distinctive mark of the goldfields. Some of them were well kept and comfortable — almost every one had 'its large fire-place and chimney constructed of logs at one end of it'.[8] The log huts were diversfied in design, and those built by the Irish bore a 'picturesque resemblance to the cabins of the Green Isle, being more remarkable for their defiance of symmetry than any others'.[9] Round the tents wandered fowls, goats and all manner of livestock.

There were many women on the goldfields, distinguished like the diggers by their bright 'jumpers' and cabbage-tree hats. When dressed in their best they wore 'a white wide-awake hat with broad ribbon; a neat-fitting polka or jacket made like the body of a lady's riding habit, and a handsome dress beneath'.[10] As independent as the diggers themselves, they were capable of chopping wood 'with great axes', or dealing with any of the trials and dangers of a pioneer's life. Not all of them were wives; many prostitutes made their way to the diggings and relieved the miners of their earnings. Such a one was Lavinia, who had come from Adelaide, and whom Lord Robert Cecil saw 'dressed in the

[6]*Ibid.* 2 November 1854.
[7]*Lord Robert Cecil's Gold Fields Diary*, introduction and notes by Ernest Scott (Melbourne, 1935), p. 7.
[8]Howitt, *Land, Labour and Gold* (1855), i. 377.
[9]*Ibid.*   [10]*Ibid.* i. 381.

most exaggerated finery, with a parasol of blue damask silk that would have seemed gorgeous in Hyde Park'.[11]

In spite of such women, and the sly grog shops which flourished, the diggers appear to have been a remarkably law-abiding lot. Throughout his short stay on the Bendigo diggings Lord Robert Cecil was impressed by this fact. Mrs Chisholm was agreeably surprised, too, for she had not expected 'such a fine body of intellectual men'.[12] The picturesque and flamboyant wickedness suggested in many tales of the gold days was much less obvious on the actual diggings than it was in Melbourne itself. Even there, in the centre to which the diggers returned to spend their earnings, there was less crime and violence than is usually supposed. By 1854 gold-digging had become an industry like anything else, and it was treated as such rather than as a romantic adventure bound to yield fabulous riches.

Bendigo was the largest of the diggings, and Mrs Chisholm seems to have spent more time there than on the other fields. She arrived at Castlemaine on 6 November, but the meeting to welcome her, held in the Castlemaine Hall, was only thinly attended.[13] No doubt the diggers were preoccupied with the agitations and arguments which were soon to culminate in the riots at Ballarat. From Castlemaine she went on to Maryborough, the Avoca and Ballarat,[14] but there are no reports of her from these goldfields — the press, like the diggers, was almost wholly concerned with the miners' grievances, and in the general uproar Mrs Chisholm's doings were overlooked.

By 9 November[15] she was back in Melbourne to tell what she had seen on her tour, and what should be done to help the miners. A meeting was held in the hall of the Mechanics' Institute on the evening of 9 November. She spoke for nearly an hour, and told a large gathering of her conclusions concerning the conditions she had found.

She made it clear that she must know more of the goldfields before she could advise immigrants whether or not to attempt to find work there. But, as was inevitable considering her strong feeling for family life, she vigorously disapproved of the numbers of husbands at the diggings who had left their families behind them. Those men entered 'their blankets at night more like dogs than men'.[16] She compared the amounts needed by diggers before

[11] *Lord Robert Cecil's Gold Fields Diary*, p. 15.
[12] *Argus*, 11 November 1854.   [13] *Ibid*. 6 November 1854.
[14] *Ibid*. 2 November 1854.   [15] *Ibid*. 10 November 1854.
[16] *Ibid*. 11 November 1854.

they ventured to try their fortunes on the different fields. Since hotel meals alone cost from 4s. to 5s. each the digger going to Forest Creek should have £10 in his pocket. If he were going to Bendigo he should have £20, and if to Simson's Ranges, £25 to £30. Single men could travel to Castlemaine in a day for £4 by Cobb & Co.

She considered Forest Creek to be the best diggings, for £4 to £15 a week could be earned by an industrious miner. On this field she found several diggers living together in parties of seven or eight, though they did not work together in such large numbers. Board and lodging at one of the hotels which catered for the miners cost on an average £2 a week. The conditions were not equal to those in a hotel or boarding house in Melbourne, for most of these places were kept by men and 'men are bad hands at making a pudding'.

If Forest Creek was where the best opportunities were found, Bendigo was the 'poor man's diggings'. As soon as they found themselves down on their luck the diggers returned to Bendigo, where living was less expensive.

Mrs Chisholm found it difficult to get the actual truth of the conditions from the miners; they were afraid that if she tried to make it easier for men and their families to reach the diggings wages would be lowered by the influx of labour. Nevertheless, in spite of their reluctance to talk, she had found that the great grievance of all the diggers was the difficulty in securing land on which they could settle and establish their families. Thus the land question immediately confronted her; but for the present she did not pursue it. Her practical mind had grasped the first need of the miners, and to this she now gave her attention.

The largest stumbling block which prevented the diggers' wives and families joining them on the goldfields was the vile conditions which prevailed on the roads. These conditions also enormously increased the diggers' expenses and difficulties. Apart from the bogs, ruts and general hazards of the track, there was the lack of accommodation. No matter what the weather, families had to camp by the roadside at night. Caroline Chisholm considered that 'one of the great wants would be accommodated by means of second-class hotels on . . . the road to the diggings'. Accordingly, she proposed that houses of accommodation should be established at several points. A bed would cost 1s., and a society of shareholders should be formed to erect the depots. Contributions of 5s. to £1 could be made to this society, and subscribers would receive tickets entitling them to an amount of lodging equivalent to their subscription.[17] The Passenger Act imposed a 5s. tax on every immigrant who landed, and she suggested that part of this money might be used to erect the shelters.

Mrs Chisholm was careful to point out that the establishment of such depots would not injure existing hotels, for they would cater for a class of traveller who had either not travelled before, or else had slept by the roadside. By means of the depots she hoped to make it easier for families to 'get inland to the goldfields'; they were 'intended to be the first link in the chain of country dispersion'.[18] As in Sydney during the 'forties, so now in Melbourne during the 'fifties, she realized that the immigrants must be dispersed inland; they could not be allowed to congregate in the city. After they had earned enough on the goldfields she hoped they would all settle on the land. For the moment she disregarded the fact that settlement was so difficult. The struggle for the lands waited upon the immediate need for the shelters. Her proposal was acclaimed, and the meeting recorded the decision to establish the depots.

By the middle of March the plans for what had become known as the 'shelter sheds' were completed, and the *Argus* gave all the details of the proposition.[19] The road to Castlemaine was the first route on which the sheds were to be established. They were to be built a day's march from each other — at Essendon, Upper Keilor, Aitkin's Gap, Gisborne, the Black Forest (two sheds), Woodend, Carlsruhe, Kyneton, Malmesbury, Taradale, Elphinstone, Castlemaine, Muckleford Creek, and Maldon. Each was to accommodate thirty single men and ten single women, as well as married couples with families. It was to have cart sheds and stables, two cooking houses, with other conveniences, and a house for the station keeper, who was to sell wood, water, candles and some stores at fixed rates. In this way there would be no interference with the rights of existing storekeepers on the road, and no necessity for travellers to burden themselves with provisions. A bed was to cost 1s. for an adult and 6d. for a child. The tickets entitling the holder to the accommodation of the shelter sheds were to be available in Melbourne, and also in England. Mrs Chisholm proposed to visit all the sheds at frequent intervals, and if the plan succeeded on the Castlemaine route

[17]*Ibid.* 10 and 11 November 1854.
[18]*Ibid.* 13 June 1857.   [19]*Ibid.* 19 March 1855.

it was to be extended to the other goldfields and to remote agricultural districts.

There are notices in the press of one or two meetings to discuss the shelter sheds during the next few weeks,[20] and then, at the end of April, it was announced that tenders were being called to erect shelters at ten points along the road to Castlemaine.[21] The plan had been modified. The sheds finally built were at Essendon, The Gap, Gisborne, Keilor, Keilor Plains, the Black Forest, Woodend, Carlsruhe, Malmesbury and Elphinstone.[22] The contractors were allowed to cut any necessary timber without charge on Crown Lands around the localities where the shelters were erected.

The report of the Victorian Government Immigration Agent dated July 1855 gives further information.[23] A portion of the Immigrants' Rate Fund was to be expended in their erection, but the total cost was to be limited to £3,800. Mrs Chisholm was to manage the society which organized the shelters and, with her friends, she had guaranteed to take charge of them and maintain them when erected. As her future fortunes indicate, she must have spent a great deal of the £7,500 testimonial in the maintenance of the sheds.

By the time the Immigration Agent made his report the shelters were being built, and by November 1855 they were said to be 'ready for the reception of travellers in a few weeks'.[24] At a meeting which the committee held at that time[25] subscriptions were asked so that proper equipment such as bedsteads and water casks could be provided. By that time it had been decided that each shed was to be placed in charge of a married couple; the tickets were to be transferable, and they were ready for sale.

Mrs Chisholm must have made many arduous journeys to see that the work was completed, and when the shelters were built she still journeyed to and fro so that the service provided should be properly maintained. In a letter in 1857 she mentions casually that she had been 'six times through the Black Forest last winter'.[26] Considering the Slough of Despond into which the track through the Black Forest was transformed in winter this was a remarkable feat for a women nearing her fiftieth year.

[20]*Ibid* 28 March 1855.   [21]*Ibid.* 28 April 1855.
[22]Plans and Surveys of Victorian Lands Department, made available by courtesy of the Secretary.
[23]*V. & P.* Leg. Council Vic. (1855-6), i (1), 381.
[24]*Argus,* 2 November 1855.
[25]*Ibid.*   [26]*Ibid.* 16 January 1857.

The shelter sheds were established and maintained, and many a weary wayfarer, whether a footsore young man, or a tired mother, must have blessed the name of Caroline Chisholm. The pity was that such shelters had not been erected earlier when many more could have been saved the hardships of the journey. But, as with the distressed immigrants in New South Wales, the government made no move before Mrs Chisholm intervened.

The shelters on the Castlemaine route were undoubtedly a success, but no others were erected. Mrs Chisholm's health was failing, and probably she did not feel equal to the task of establishing other sheds.

Those which had been built remained, and during the next fifty years they became a part of the life of the people. 'Chisholm's shakedowns' were well known, and 'a great boon to the weary traveller in those early days long gone by'.[27] The Essendon shed (probably the others were very similar) contained fourteen rooms besides the kitchen, and seems to have been larger than the original plan, but this is not surprising, because such a building would have grown with the years. But as the years passed, and the immigrants along the trail to the diggings became fewer, other uses were found for them. Before denominational churches were built they were used for church services, and also for public meetings.[28] Later, additional public buildings were erected, and the shelters fell into disrepair. None have been in existence for about fifty years.[29]

One other philanthropic work occupied Mrs Chisholm even before the shelter sheds were built. After the wild extravagance of the 'rush' years there was 'an increasingly depressed state of the labour market'.[30] A result of this was that there were numbers of young girls unemployed. The Benevolent Asylum and the Immigrants' Aid Society had insufficient funds to offer shelter to these girls and Mrs Chisholm wanted the 'co-operation of the public in forming a well-considered system of lodging-houses for them'. The charge for board at such houses would be, she hoped, 4s. a week, and she proposed to raise the amount necessary to

[27]James McJunkin, 'Essendon Past and Present', and George G. Bishop, 'Essendon from a Village to a City', unpublished notes in the possession of Essendon Council made available by courtesy of Mr L. W. Scott, Town Clerk of Essendon.

[28]Miss Barbara Armstrong of Kyneton has been able to provide a great deal of interesting information concerning the sheds.

[29]Information from the Shire Secretaries of Melton, Gisborne, Keilor and Metcalfe.

[30]*Argus*, 17 February 1855, letter from Caroline Chisholm.

rent one home for a year by the sale of tickets at 4s. each. These tickets would entitle a girl, or one of her friends, to one week's lodging. They would be an insurance against a time when their holder was out of work and had no place of refuge.

Mrs Chisholm intended to interview girls who were interested in the city itself, and also in the suburbs of North Melbourne, Collingwood, Richmond and Prahran. She hoped that she would be lent a room for this purpose in each of the localities. She hoped, also, to find two men who would be treasurers for the society which was to be formed and to hold meetings where the plan could be discussed.

It is uncertain whether this scheme was ever put into operation; there seems to be no further mention of it. Such lodgings would have been the equivalent of the Y.W.C.A. and Salvation Army Hostels of today.

UNLOCK THE LANDS!

Mrs Chisholm had heard the angry arguments which fore-shadowed the great struggle for the lands before she left New South Wales. The home government had tried to prevent settlement beyond the boundaries of the nineteen counties surveyed by Sir Thomas Mitchell at the beginning of the 'thirties, but it was impossible to hold the settlers within the bounds of the survey. The men who took their flocks and herds out on to the plains had no respect for map-drawn boundaries. Governor Bourke had been forced to go beyond his instructions and issue yearly £10 licences to squatters, and also to impose on them a tax varying with the amount of stock they held.

Slight as they were, these restrictions, and their insecurity of tenure irked the squatters, and by the 'forties they had formulated three demands. They wanted compensation for improvements, security of tenure, and a pre-emptive right to the lands which they occupied. Governor Gipps attempted a solution of the diffi-cult situation by drawing up what became known as the Occupa-tion and Purchase Regulations. He did this in April 1844, and the regulations aimed at counteracting the effects of the high price of land by encouraging the formation of smaller holdings. The squatters were not in the least grateful for the time and trouble Gipps had devoted to their affairs. The regulations were violently opposed. At that time Mrs Chisholm did not add her voice to the tumult, but she showed clearly that her sympathy was with the 'little man' in opposition to the large landholder. In her experimental farms at Shell Harbour she had attempted to give practical expression to this sympathy.

Notwithstanding the squatters' rage Gipps stood firm, but when the British parliament passed the Waste Lands Occupation Act in 1846 it 'embodied Gipps' concessions while thrusting aside his safeguards'.[1] The act embodied the idea of fixity of tenure for a different number of years depending on whether the land was settled, intermediate (partly settled) or unsettled. In all cases the squatter had to pay rent for the run, and an assessment for stock. The rental for the land was to vary with the amount of stock carried. In general the squatters were given the three rights which they had demanded — compensation, security of tenure and pre-emption. Security of tenure, together with the high price of land (£1 an acre), meant that their tenure 'was as lasting as fee simple',[2] for the price was too high for anyone but wealthy landowners to pay. Thus they secured a virtual monopoly.

It was the strict interpretation of the Waste Lands Occupation Act which precipitated the struggle for the lands. The squatters placed one interpretation on the terms of the act, and the New South Wales government another: 'On the one hand, the stockmen held that the Order *promised* leases for a fixed period (1, 8, or 14 years) with rights of pre-emption and compensation for improvements. On the other, the Government maintained that this was conditional, and that the privileges should not accrue to the squatters if they stood in the way of the development of general population and industry.'[3]

The battle between the opposing factions was fought in Victoria; it was there that the squatters were strongest, and also, because of the large goldfields population, that their rights were most strongly challenged.

The loose legal phraseology of the Waste Lands Occupation Act gave the squatters opportunities for evasion, which they grasped eagerly. There were such fierce quarrels concerning the length of lease, and the nature of the pre-emptive right, that Lieutenant-Governor La Trobe refused to issue the leases. Instead, it was suggested that 'licences renewable from year to year' should be granted, with a rental according to grazing capacity.[4]

Various methods of solving the difficulties were tried, but none were successful, and the squatters would not budge. Then came

[1] S. H. Roberts, *History of Australian Land Settlement, 1788-1920* (Melbourne, 1924), p. 186.
[2] *Ibid.* p. 188.   [3] *Ibid.* p. 205.   [4] *Ibid.* p. 210.

the gold discoveries and the rush of diggers into the country. Among those who downed tools and set off to seek their fortunes were most of the surveyors of the Crown lands, which meant that the survey of the lands where it was intended that leases were to be granted was delayed.[5] The squatters were inconvenienced by the loss of labour and the general confusion caused by the 'rush', but they held to their lands more jealously even than before, and their possessiveness was increased by the covetous eyes of the diggers.

Meanwhile the gold rush was at its height, and the harassed La Trobe had thrown the onus of the interpretation of the Waste Lands Occupation Act back on the home government. He wrote a long despatch to the Duke of Newcastle, then Secretary of State for the Colonies.[6]

The answer to this arrived in November 1853. The squatters were told that as far as the leases were concerned the length of the lease-terms within the limits fixed by the act was left to the decision of the government. 'The squatter was to have pre-emptive right limited to his homestead and the actual improvements with no power of exclusive purchase during the whole term of his lease. In return, he was to have security by lease for any number of years up to the maximum and compensation for his improvements.'[7]

This solution of the difficulty was a compromise and, given a fair trail, it should have been a workable one, but one of the most important factors in the situation was the imminence of the introduction of responsible government in the colonies. The execution of the compromise was not to be enforced by the home government, but was to be left to the colonies themselves. The fact that the squatters were powerfully represented in the New South Wales and Victorian Legislative Councils, with prospects of being as powerfully represented in the proposed Legislative Assemblies, was a portent of future conflict on the land laws.

It was not until several months after her return that Mrs Chisholm made a public statement of her views on the land question. This is not surprising, for before she returned she was ignorant of the squatters' monopoly. In England she consistently advised her emigrants to go to any of the Australian colonies

---

[5]Edward Jenks, *The Government of Victoria* (1891), p. 181.
[6]V. & P. Leg. Council Vic. (1853-4), ii. 241-304.
[7]Roberts, *op. cit.* p. 210.

they chose, to take up land as small settlers and then to 'multiply and replenish the earth'. Yet, especially in Victoria, this was just what they had not been able to do, and it was to Victoria that most of her immigrants came. After the news of the gold discoveries she had advised her people to choose one of the other colonies rather than Victoria, but this was because of the disorganization caused by the gold; it was not because she thought there was any great difficulty in settling on Victorian land.

It was not until she had made her tour of the goldfields and heard the miners' grievances at first hand that she began her championship of the cause of the small farmers. Her immigrants were of the small farmer class, and it was they, and their families, who were to advance the prosperity of Australia. Of this she was passionately convinced. Like many others she believed that the English type of small farm could be transplanted to Australia. It is true that the squatters were selfish in their monopoly of the land, but natural conditions often justified their demands for large runs. Because of the constant recurrence of drought, sheep-farming had to be conducted on a large scale and, for the same reason, in many areas agricultural farming was impossible. Mrs Chisholm did not properly understand the difference between English and Australian conditions.

The stand she made for the miners was uncompromising — on the land question she refused to see that the middle way between the two extremes of squatter and miner was the only hope of solution. Her anger against the squatters was a result of generosity of heart, but in this instance it would have been better if she had supported the moderate party which suggested 'selection on easy terms within certain surveyed areas'.[8]

In November 1854, at the meeting in Melbourne where she announced her plan for the shelter sheds, she gave her challenge to the squatters. She had found that the great grievance of the diggers was that they could not get the land. She declared vehemently that the lands should be unlocked, for as she said, 'I never could — I never would, have recommended any men to come to this country if I did not think this possible and that it would soon be done'.[9] She followed this two weeks later by an outspoken letter in the *Argus*.

'Our aim must be to make it as easy for a working man to reach Australia as America', she wrote, 'and we must hold out a

[8]*Ibid.* p. 234.
[9]*Argus*, 11 November 1854.

certainty of being able to obtain land. Nothing else will tempt the honest working man of the right sort to emigrate.'

Five days after this letter was published the miners made their stand at the Eureka Stockade, and the whole of Australia was shocked by the news. In a letter headed 'The Crisis' she deplored the incident which had 'stained the hands of the people with blood' and called on everyone to 'cast aside all party feeling or class interest'. 'We must alter our system if we wish to recover character and if Sir Charles Hotham [the governor who succeeded La Trobe] is a wise man he will at once call to his assistance that first minister of finance, the Plough!'[10]

At the New Year she gave a warning that 'if some steps are not specially taken to open the lands to the small capitalists they will in numbers leave us with their money and their energies for places where they can make more favourable and immediate investment'.[11] This warning was justified, for as the gold yield gradually dwindled many of the miners found they could not get land easily and they left the colony. There were 'rushes' to goldfields in Queensland and New South Wales, and in 1861, 10,000 to 12,000 men left for New Zealand. Nevertheless, compared with the actual increase in the population caused by the gold discoveries, the numbers lost in this way were negligible.

During the next few weeks she was seriously ill, and after that she was fully occupied for a time in organizing the erection of the shelter sheds. But in June she returned to the attack. Her letter this time was directly addressed 'to the members of the Legislative Council of Victoria', and it was published as a sub-leader in the *Argus*.[12] She condemned the government immigration system which she said had 'brought the Colony to the verge of bankruptcy', and suggested once again her land-ticket system. This system, she thought, would encourage immigrants and open the land to small settlers. Mrs Chisholm considered that the land-ticket system would solve the demand for labour which, in spite of the depression, still persisted. The scheme was thoroughly discussed in the *Argus*,[13] and the general criticism was that it would give an opportunity to speculators to traffic in the land tickets. Whether the plan was workable or not was never proved, for it was not tried.

The struggle for the lands was waxing fiercer. In June 1855,

[10]*Argus*, 9 December 1854.
[11]*Ibid*. 2 January 1855.
[12]*Argus*, 16 June 1855.
[13]*Ibid*. 21, 23, 30 June 1855; 6, 26 July 1855.

at the same time as Mrs Chisholm suggested her land-ticket
system, the squatters had formed themselves into a 'Pastoral
Protection Society'. They wanted protection from the Duke of
Newcastle's compromise, and from the suggested yearly licences.[14]
After heated debates in the first session of the new Legislative
Assembly, it was decided that the squatter should *not* have a
lease. Instead, yearly licences were to be granted. This was a
defeat for the squatters, but it was not a final one. They continued
to demand adequate compensation.

Echoes of the conflict are heard in four letters which Caroline
Chisholm wrote in January and February 1857, with the express
purpose of advising the working classes of Great Britain on Australian conditions. They were addressed to the president and
committee of the Family Colonization Loan Society and published
in the *Argus*.[15] When describing the needs of colonial life Mrs
Chisholm once again struck at the squatters. She 'did not advocate
or wish that every man should become a farmer', but 'children
ought to take precedence of sheep'. As for compensation for the
squatters, what could compensate the colony for 'the frightful
and demoralising effects of such a system as the one we have
now working?[16] But the squatters were not sensitive to Mrs
Chisholm's rebukes.

The fight between the squatters and the free selectors went
on, and it was raging fiercely when Nicholson's ministry came
to power in 1859. In the next year a land act was passed establishing selection after survey and credit payments. Its terms were
open to all and therefore it was most favourable to those who
had money and local knowledge — the squatters. This generosity
was soon seen to be misplaced, and in 1862 an act sponsored by
Charles Gavan Duffy 'provided that 10,000,000 acres (the whole
of the colony's prime arable land) should be proclaimed to be
agricultural lands. Two-fifths of this area then occupied by pastoralists under licence, was to be made available for selection at
£1 an acre almost immediately'.[17] One-quarter of the proceeds
of land sales was to be devoted to immigration, and the selectors
had to fence or cultivate one acre in ten within a year of taking
possession. But again the squatters got the better of the well-
meaning legislators. By dummying, that is, by having land taken
out in another's name, they maintained their lands. Three years

[14]Roberts, *op. cit.* p. 233.

[15]*Argus*, 5, 8, 16 January 1857; 3 February 1857.

[16]*Ibid.* 16 January 1857.

[17]Fitzpatrick, *British Empire in Australia,* p. 141.

later, what was known as 'Grant's Act' stipulated that 'bona fide settlement must precede alienation',[18] and eight million additional acres were thrown open to selection. In 1869 an amendment gave free selection before, as well as after, survey and provided effective safeguards against dummying.[19] By this time the squatters had entrenched themselves, and though further extensions of their power were prevented by the act, it could not undo the mistakes of the past. It was not until the 'nineties, when resumption and closer settlement were adopted, that the power of the squatters began to wane.

THE LAST YEARS

Caroline Chisholm left the battle for the lands half fought. The letter she wrote in June 1857 was the last one published for over two years. At the end of 1857 her health broke down. This was the beginning of the kidney disease which was to cripple her for the last five years of her life. In November 1857 she moved from Melbourne to Kyneton.[1] One or two years earlier either she or her husband had bought Roger & Harper's store in Kyneton for their two elder sons. By 1856 both young men had made their home there. Major Chisholm[2] often visited them and himself sat on the Magistrate's Bench. Therefore, when Mrs Chisholm was well enough to travel, she took her four younger children with her to the little township. By this time the store in Melbourne which had been bought with the money advanced by the testimonial committee was probably not in the family's possession.

Kyneton welcomed Caroline Chisholm with open arms, and has always been very proud of its association with her. For a few months she was often seen driving about the town in a low vehicle pulled by grey ponies,[3] but later she became so ill that the Melbourne doctors advised her to go to Sydney as the 'only chance of recovery'.[4] Possibly they thought the extremes of temperature which are often experienced in Kyneton were

---

[18] Shann, *Economic History of Australia*, p. 215.

[19] Roberts, *op. cit.* p. 242.

[1] Argus, 25 November 1857; *History of Kyneton, 1836-1900* (extracts from the *Kyneton Guardian*).

[2] He was promoted in rank on 28 November 1854 (Official British Army List, 1856-7).

[3] *Kyneton Guardian*, 19 November 1936.

[4] R. Harris, *What has Mrs. Chisholm Done for N.S.W.?* p. 12, quoting one of her letters.

bad for her. In Sydney, under the care of the 'venerable and venerated' Dr Bland, who attended her 'without expectation of fee or reward',[5] she struggled to regain her strength.

The fact that Dr Bland attended Mrs Chisholm 'without expectation of fee or reward' is significant. The Chisholms were in dire need of financial help at this time. The £7,500 given by the government and people of Victoria in 1856 was now either exhausted, or else was being used for charity. She may have invested a little of it for her family, and she might have had to pinch and scrape in the intervals between the times when income was paid. Probably she used a great deal of the money to maintain the shelter sheds; possibly she also contributed to other charities. The living expenses of her own large family could not have been inconsiderable. Whatever had happened to the money, at this particular time, when she was broken in health, she was literally penniless.

The winter journey from Kyneton to Sydney almost killed her. For weeks she could not move from the Post Office Hotel, George Street. In her distress, she asked the help of Father Therry, the venerated and kindly priest who, nearly half a century before, had laid the foundations of the Roman Catholic Church in Australia. He was then the parish priest of Balmain, and in June 1858 she managed to scribble a note asking him to call. A month later 'the inflammation [had] abated', and she asked him, 'can you for a short time lend me fifteen or twenty pounds?'[6] He may well have made her the loan.

Her sons in Kyneton gave her a little financial assistance, but at the end of this year she was shocked by the news of the sudden death of the second one, William. The next months must have been very dark. Most of the time she was still too ill to move about and her friends seem to have forgotten her. But J. K. Heydon, the printer and publisher of the Sydney *Freeman's Journal*, visited her in May 1859 and was horrified by her distress. He wrote:[7]

[5]*Ibid.* Dr Bland had been transported to New South Wales in 1814 for 'killing his man'. After a fiery youth he became a member of the New South Wales Legislative Council in 1843, and was universally respected.

[6]Two very short letters from Caroline Chisholm to Father Therry dated June and July 1858. These are among the Therry Papers, Canisius College, Sydney. The Most Reverend Dr Eris O'Brien told me of their existence, and copies of them were sent to me by the Rev. J. W. Doyle, S.J. Dr Bland was a close personal friend of Father Therry and possibly was often the vehicle for his charity.

[7]This letter is endorsed by Father Therry, 'J. K. Heydon, Esq. May, 1859, Mrs. Chisholm'. It was found among the Therry Papers by the Reverend J.

My dear Father Therry,

I was greatly shocked yesterday, on calling on the celebrated Mrs. Chisholm, who has been the instrument of so much good to thousands in this colony, to find her in the deepest distress from sickness and poverty. Although extremely ill from disease of the kidneys and unable to get out, no clergyman has visited her for about four months. She has lately lost her eldest son by death in Victoria, and I believe with him her principal means of existence, for, if I understand the matter rightly, the Major, her husband, sold his commission to start his children in business. Ill as she is, she is endeavoring to support herself by giving lessons in English to China Men, at 1s. 6d. per lesson, and also by working for the confectioners. They have three young children at home, and have pawned a medal given her by His Holiness to get bread for them.

In the name of holy charity call on her with some relief, and to console her in her affliction. Now that the Archdeacon is away, I know no one but yourself to apply to in such a case. She resides in Albert street, a turning out of Pitt-street, Redfern. The Redfern omnibus puts down passengers at Hank's Post Office and the people there will show the way.

Believe me to remain

My dear Father Therry

Yours most sincerely

J. K. Heydon

I would make her case known in the columns of the *Freeman*, but I fear to hurt their feelings.

This was an appeal which Father Therry could not have denied.[8] His open-handed charity was proverbial, and it was probably

---

W. Doyle, S.J., who sent me a copy. Heydon was a devoted convert to the Roman Catholic faith and a man of wide interests. He was only an acquaintance of the Chisholm family, and he makes the natural mistake of thinking that the son who died was the eldest one. The 'Archdeacon' he refers to was Archdeacon McEnroe who was then visiting Ireland to find a President for St John's College, University of Sydney. (See Moran, *History of the Catholic Church in Australasia* [Sydney, 1895], p. 138.) Archibald Chisholm could not have *sold* his commission but he may have made some private agreement whereby he paid over part or all of his annual pension of £292 as it came to him. The Reverend J. McGovern comments on this letter: 'It is possible though not probable that in the Sydney of the day her plight could have remained unknown to the clergy. Perhaps the frequent changes of address — from one growing parish to another and the arrival of priests from Ireland who did not know her or her earlier work, may be some explanation; but this a pure conjecture.'

[8]The Reverend J. W. Doyle, S.J., very kindly looked through Father Therry's bank books and diaries for me. Therry would have found it quite possible to meet Mrs Chisholm's needs.

only because she had already called upon him that Mrs Chisholm
had not asked his help again. It was less than two months after
this letter of Heydon's was written that she gave a lecture on
the land question and manhood suffrage in the Prince of Wales
Theatre, Sydney.

She had made a fairly quick recovery since the day Heydon
saw her, when she had been too ill to leave her room. Therry's
help must have given her the food and rest which she so sorely
needed, and her natural vitality had soon conquered the worst
symptoms of her illness. But though she faced her audience
bravely, she could not quite overcome the insidious mental effects
of her disease. Once again she attacked the land monopoly of
the squatters, but her old fire was gone. The lecture was rambling
and disjointed with only brief flashes of her characteristic wit.
The *Sydney Morning Herald* regretted that 'the audience, although of a highly respectable class, was far from being a
numerous one . . . in all of not more than 300 or 400 persons'.[9]

A much larger audience attended the lecture on free selection
before survey which she gave over a year later. Significantly, the
admission to this was free, though probably the expenses of the
theatre were met by her.[10] She must have been in fairly good
health when she gave her next lecture. She spoke for nearly two
hours to a hall which was so crowded that 'many ladies had to
sit on the platform'. The *Herald* report indicates that it was a
vigorous, well-integrated address; but she was now living on her
past triumphs. She looked back continually to the time when she
had done her great work during the early 'forties, and she told
how she had warned the government then of the dangers of the
squatters' monopoly.

Though these two lectures are concerned with the unlocking
of the lands, the tenor of them suggests that she was out of touch
with the battle still raging in Victoria. Her illness, followed by
her removal to Sydney, meant that she had left the field of action,
for though the feeling against the squatters was strong in New
South Wales, it was never so violent as it was in Victoria.

She gave two more free public lectures, one in February 1861
at which she spoke in favour of the early closing of shops, and
another in June of the same year when she spoke on the subject

[9] *S.M.H.*, 9 July 1859.
[10] *Ibid.* 11 December 1860. When she gave her lecture in July 1859,
she had promised to give others if the expenses of the theatre were paid.
(*Ibid.* 9 July 1859.)

Chisholm lived in Sydney. She took no part in public affairs, and there is no record of her life at this time. Then, probably to complete the education of their younger children, she and her husband decided to visit England. She hoped that it would be only a visit, and that she would return to Australia in a few years. The country of her adoption had become far dearer to her than the country of her birth. But when she left Australia in June 1866[19] is was for the last time. There is no record of her departure in the press — not even a mention of her name in the published passenger lists of outgoing ships.

A few months after she returned to England a young man forged her name to a cheque for £100, and she gave evidence in the ensuing court case. She stated that she was then living in Liverpool.[20] In the same year she was granted a government pension of £100 a year.[21] During the next two or three years her third son, Henry, completed his education in Ireland; the fourth son, Sydney, was at school in England. The elder daughter, Caroline, was boarding at a convent in London, and the younger, Monica, was in a Belgian convent[22] (many of the poorer English Catholics sent their daughters to Belgian convents at this time because of their low fees).[23] How it was all paid for, and how the family lived it is difficult to imagine, but it is probable that she engaged in some form of journalistic work which, with her government pension, eked out their small resources. Major Chisholm was then over seventy and he could not have helped the family a great deal; but when Henry Chisholm completed his studies he returned to Australia where he earned enough to help with the education of his sister Caroline,[24] who was by that time also in a Belgian convent.[25] Very soon after she left school she married Edmund Dwyer Gray, who was later to be mayor of Dublin.

If Mrs Chisholm had been trying to earn a little money to support her children she was forced to desist. The crushing tiredness came upon her more and more often. At last, about 1871,

[19]*S.M.H.*, 16 February 1924, article by the late E. Dwyer Gray.
[20]*Empire*, 19 February 1867, quoting *Western Daily Press*, 15 December 1866.
[21]*Dictionary of National Biography*, under 'Caroline Chisholm'. This pension was granted from the Civil List on 19 June 1867.
[22]Information provided by Miss M. E. Chisholm, a daughter of Henry John Chisholm.
[23]Information provided by the Reverend J. McGovern.
[24]Information provided by Miss M. E. Chisholm.
[25]Undated press cutting in 'Caroline Chisholm Newspaper Cuttings, 1852-87' (ML).

too weak even to sit up, she became bedridden. Her husband and she were then living at Highgate in very poor circumstances. Her dingy room was so small that the bed had to be placed in a corner from where she could not look through the window. She lay there for five years.

Sometimes her days were lightened by the visits of her grandson, little Edmund Dwyer Gray. When she was well enough the two of them chattered together of the strange things to be seen and heard in far-away Australia. Nearly seventy years later he still remembered her 'wonderfully serene and tender face'.[26] Often when her swift memory was slow and her keen mind dull, she lay for days and nights between dream and waking. But there were times when her thoughts were clearer and she fretted against her dreadful imprisonment. She longed to see the bright day, and she remembered the airy places of the southern land she had known so well. The surge of nostalgia sometimes overcame her. Then she found consolation in the religion which had guided her through life. Towards the end she hated her imprisonment so much that her family managed to find better lodgings at Fulham. She was carried down the stairs from her old room into the street where she exclaimed in gratitude, 'Oh, thank God for the beautiful sky!' The ambulance moved off, but half-way on the journey she insisted that the horses should stop where she could look into a shop window.[27]

In Fulham her bed was placed in a wide bay window, from which she could see the sky and the world passing by. Her heart began to fail, and the people and voices of the present faded from consciousness. She drifted towards death, and the flickering light of memory touched the past. Perhaps chance visions came to her — an Irishman's tumble-down hut on the Bendigo goldfield; the *Slains Castle* sailing into the sunset, and Charles Dickens' vivid face. The light flickered for a moment, and then lit a picture of struggling bullocks dragging a dray through a storm of rain near Picton. And the rain blurred into the pugnacious gleam of Dr Lang's spectacles, and Govenor Gipps' black brows frowning as he grumblingly granted her the use of the Barracks. The long shafts of sunlight shone again through the church windows on Easter Sunday, 1841, and she heard her own words whisper

[26] *S.M.H.*, 26 January 1924, article by the late E. Dwyer Gray. He repeated this description to me in March 1944.

[27] E. Pearson, 'Caroline Chisholm', *Ideas and Realities* (1914), p. 88. This writer's description of Caroline Chisholm's last years was confirmed by the late E. Dwyer Gray.

down the years, 'I promise to know neither country nor creed, but
to serve all . . . I promise . . . I promise . . .' Her husband's hand
was at her elbow as she walked through a jostling crowd in a
Madras bazaar, and her loving memory turned towards his devotion and understanding.   But his face faded, and at the end it
was not the immense, shimmering distances of the plains she
remembered; nor the stiffling dust of the bush roads, not even her
own children. Suddenly she, herself, was a child again, playing
an immigration game with touchwood dolls and a basin of water;
she felt an old soldier's hand on her head, the grass of green lanes
brushed her feet, and she heard the soft voices of the countryside.
She struggled back from the overwhelming weariness,. and found
breath to cry, 'Take me home! Take me home!'[28]

She died a few hours later while the church bells rang out
over London; it was Sunday, 25 March 1877, and she was in her
sixty-ninth year. The brief obituary notice which appeared in
The Times[29] gave the outline of her life and work in about ten
lines; a few months later the Australian papers barely mentioned
her passing.[30] Her husband and children took her body home to
be buried at Northampton with the rites of the Roman Catholic
Church. Major Chisholm died a short time afterwards and lies
buried in the same grave, where the headstone is inscribed 'The
Emigrant's Friend'.

[28]*Ibid.* p. 89.
[29]*The Times,* 26 March 1877; obit. 28 March 1877.
[30]*Argus,* 2 April 1877; S.M.H., 2 and 7 April 1877.

8

The Sum of Achievement

As Sir Keith Hancock truly remarks — 'it is scarcely an exaggeration to assert that Mrs. Chisholm established the dignity of womanhood and of the family in New South Wales'.[1] Many amongst the approximately eleven thousand whom she provided for during her early work in New South Wales were members of families. She established them on the land, and continued to advocate the importance of the family unit in her Family Colonization Loan Society. In the work of her last years too — the shelter sheds built along the road to the diggings and her impassioned campaign against the Victorian squatters — there is the same emphasis.

The most astonishing thing about her is that she did such work at a time when women were still imprisoned in the strait-jacket of Victorian convention. And after her initial hesitation she did it with little consideration as to the proprieties of the matter. The only other woman whose work was comparable with Mrs Chisholm's was Elizabeth Fry. Mrs Fry had gone into the filthy, disease-stricken prisons to bring comfort to the prisoners and, together with John Howard, she had been largely instrumental in beginning prison reform. Hannah More had founded Sunday schools, but her work had been comparatively 'genteel' and on a much smaller scale than Caroline Chisholm's. Mrs Chisholm's work linked two hemispheres; it was arduous, unremitting and much of it offensive in a notoriously squeamish age. Nearly all of it was accomplished before Florence Nightingale set out on her epoch-making mission to the Crimea; but because of its dramatic quality it was Miss Nightingale's work which seized the public imagination.

To her contemporaries Caroline Chisholm was a phenomenon and to women like Florence Nightingale, who fretted against the taboos of the age, she was an inspiration. Florence Nightingale declared that she was Mrs Chisholm's 'friend and pupil'.[2] They

[1] W. K. Hancock, *Australia* (Sydney, 1945), p. 39.
[2] R. Harris, *What has Mrs. Chisholm Done for N.S.W.?* p. ii. Also quoted by G. Elliot Anstruther, *Caroline Chisholm, the Emigrants' Friend* (1916),

may have met, though there is no known record of it. Certainly Miss Nightingale contributed £5 to the testimonial given Mrs Chisholm before she left England, and the example of Mrs Chisholm's work was quoted to good purpose when Florence was struggling to win her mother's consent to her outrageous plans. Florence's devoted Aunt Mai rather amusingly expressed poor Mrs Nightingale's view of the matter when she explained: 'Your mother . . . would, I believe, be most willing that you undertake a mission like Mrs. Fry or Mrs. Chisholm, but she thinks it necessary for your peace and well-being that there should be a Mr. Fry or Captain Chisholm to protect you from doing anything which *she thinks* would be an impediment to the existence of Mr. Fry or Captain Chisholm.'[3] But the rebel Florence would have none of this and was determined to strike out on her own without male protection.

Aunt Mai, perhaps, put her finger on the reason why, for the most part, after the Victorian world had recovered from the first shock of realizing what Mrs Chisholm was doing, the criticism of her was not more severe. Major Chisholm, in effect, was a chaperon! And when any estimate of Caroline Chisholm's achievement is made, his self-sacrificing devotion must be remembered. Without her 'dear Archy', Mrs Chisholm could never have accomplished so much.

It is rather remarkable that unlike the militant Miss Nightingale, Mrs Chisholm was never a crusader for women's rights. She saw what she had to do and did it with as little fuss as possible. But it was not simply natural humility which made her silent on the subject of feminism. In spite of her own career, she believed that a woman's place was in the home, and she considered that it was the 'design of nature' for women to be supported by their husbands. She felt the inconvenience of the Victorian attitude towards women. Yet she never denounced this crippling handicap.

Considering her own achievements and accomplishments there was a certain feminine inconsistency in this, but despite the press pronouncement which described her mind as 'masculine'[4] Caroline Chisholm was very feminine. She carried out her work much in the manner of an excellent housewife who dealt with each crisis as it arose, and had little time to spare for philosophical

p. 17. Sir E. Cook, *Life of Florence Nightingale* (1913), i. 123, gives a footnote to the effect that there was a correspondence between the two women in 1862.

[3]Cook, *op. cit.*

[4]*Bendigo Advertiser*, quoted by *Argus*, 27 November 1854.

speculations concerning her own destiny. She was an essentially normal woman, a happy wife and mother as well as a world-famous personality, and she felt none of the agony of frustration which drove Florence Nightingale to write in pent-up fury: 'Jesus Christ raised women above the condition of mere slaves, mere ministers to the passions of man, raised them by his sympathy to be ministers of God. He gave them moral activity. But the Age, the World, Humanity must give them the means to exercise this moral activity, must give them intellectually cultivated spheres of action. There is perhaps no century where the woman shows so meanly as this.'[5]

This was the cry which the suffragettes were to echo, but there is reason to think that Caroline Chisholm would have considered such an outburst unseemly. Nevertheless the example of her work helped to inspire Florence Nightingale's valiant struggle, and to encourage all those in revolt against the thraldom of Victorian womanhood. She was the forerunner of the emancipated women of the twentieth century and in the development of her own philosophy she exemplified the impact of the conditions of the time upon an open and intelligent mind.

Her achievement was made possible by her great gifts of idealism, courage and common sense allied with executive ability and personal charm. Her tolerance was so wide, and her love of humanity so strong that she gave of her best to all who asked her help no matter to what class or creed they belonged. From this love of humanity stemmed her resolve to devote her life without material reward to the service of mankind. She remained steadfast in this resolve through long years when she must often have been wearied and discouraged by criticism and misrepresentation of her motives. And she did not hesitate to impoverish her family so that her ideal might be achieved. The sacrifice of her personal comfort, and that of her husband and children, was justified by the happiness she helped to give to thousands.

Besides her belief in the divine inspiration of her work, and her conviction that she was capable of carrying it out, she possessed another quality which helped to assure success. This was her good-humoured acceptance of the faults and failings of mankind. Though she was an idealist and sometimes, as in her expectation that all the loans made by the Family Colonization Loan Society would be repaid, over-optimistic, her idealism was balanced by

[5]Louisa Garrett Anderson, *Life of Elizabeth Garrett Anderson* (1939), quoting words written by Florence Nightingale in 1852.

an astute understanding of human nature. She knew, even though she might regret the knowledge, that 'mercenary pursuit is the prevailing passion of man'.[6] She knew, too, when she began her work that she could not 'expect grateful thanks from all . . . having a very fair knowledge of human nature I knew what I had to expect'.[7] She expected the criticism and misrepresentation which were persistently directed at her in the early days of her work, and at intervals during her later years; her good temper and tolerance gave her the strength to combat them and the charity to disdain recriminations.

She began her work with no evident bias against the established customs of the nineteenth-century rich man's world. But her own generous spirit made her the instinctive champion of the unfortunate, and as she worked for them it followed that she came into opposition with the land-owning class, some members of which were not above exploiting immigrant labour.

After only a year's experience, there are indications in the report which she then made that her attitude towards the government and those in authority was hardening. She made fearless criticisms of the bounty system, and did not hesitate to accuse the British and colonial governments of negligence and incompetence in the administration of that system. During the following years, as she worked among the immigrants, her immigration theories were evolved, and she became the avowed champion of the small settlers against the squatters. She talked with and understood her immigrants, learnt their hopes and fears and difficulties. She wrote: 'the servant in Sydney, the shepherd in the Bush and the small settler are known to me; I have visited their homes — witnessed their trials and wants — seen their struggles and exertions'.[8]

She returned to England as the advocate of the small settlers, she favoured agricultural farms, and believed that 'agriculture is socially better than pasturage because it brings the people together'.[9] To Mrs Chisholm, no matter how practical-minded she might seem, economics were always a secondary consideration. There is no indication that she ever realized the inescapable truth that large areas of the Australian hinterland are unsuitable for agriculture, but make very valuable pastures.

[6]Chisholm, *Emigration and Transportation*, p. 15.

[7]Chisholm, *Female Immigration*, p. 53.

[8]Chisholm, *Prospectus*, p. iv.

[9]See her evidence before the House of Lords, Committee on Colonization from Ireland. *Report*, H. of L. (1847), xxiii. 46.

By the time the Family Colonization Loan Society was founded she had travelled a long way on the radical road. She was a champion of the labouring classes, and had tilted against the squatters. She was the friend of Charles Dickens, the man who in his fictional work cried out against social abuses; but she was, like Dickens, distrustful of Chartist methods, though she supported some Chartist aims.[10] This attitude was probably partly the result of the practical realization that for many there was no chance of prosperity in England, whereas there was every opportunity for advancement in Australia; agitations for political rights thus seemed unnecessary. But the chief reason for her dislike of Chartist agitators seems to have been her dislike of violence. A few years later she was to be horrified by the stand made by the miners at Eureka, though she sympathized with their cause.[11] Caroline Chisholm was no revolutionary. She wanted reforms and on occasion expressed herself very forcibly; but she abhorred any violent overturning of established conventions.

When she had been back in the colony for a few months, she was expressing herself vigorously on the land question, and the invective with which she pursued the squatters was in marked contrast with her former characteristic reasonableness. Where she thought injustice, and particularly injustice to the small settlers, was involved it was characteristic of her to refuse to compromise. In this she followed the dictates of her heart rather than her head, for a more moderate attitude on her part might have brought her to a true understanding of the land problem.

Not only did she take an uncompromising stand against the squatters in Victoria and trounce the British and Victorian governments for their handling of the immigrants, but she had the temerity to criticize those who attempted to stem the flow of Chinese immigration. Mrs Chisholm was suspicious of the agitation against the Chinese because she thought it might be used as 'a political dodge to divert attention' from the land question. She regarded it, too, as evidence of 'the monopolizing spirit of capital and power' which 'has locked up India and would now shut the gates of China against the will of Providence and the right of man'.[12] This was radicalism with a vengeance, but it was also deplorably muddled thinking. The reference to the locking-up

[10]Harris, *What has Mrs. Chisholm Done for N.S.W.?* p. 5; *Household Words*, iv (1852), 529; *S.M.H.*, 5 July 1859.
[11]*Argus*, 9 December 1854, letter 'The Crisis'.
[12]*Ibid.* 13 June 1857.

of India was to the failure of the renewed agitation, led by the squatters, for the introduction of coolie labour. Though some Indians had been introduced by labour-hungry landowners during the 'forties, the Colonial Office had refused to give assistance to coolie immigration. Sir James Stephen first condemned the proposal,[13] and Earl Grey finally refused his consent.[14] The great majority of the colonists supported the British government in this decision, but the squatters — the very 'spirit of capital' — were the section of the colonial community which wished to unlock India and let loose coloured labour upon a country which was beginning to realize the possible economic and social dangers of the introduction of such labour. Unfortunately, there are no records of Mrs Chisholm's attitude to the introduction of coolie labour when it was mooted in the early 'forties, and she made this rash accusation against the 'spirit of capital' in the heat of controversy; but it is expressive of the uncompromising standpoint which arose from her religious conviction. She refused to modify her Christian principles to placate any party, and if she lived to-day she would probably be reviled as a traducer of the White Australia Policy.

She approved the ballot and expressed 'her belief that on universal suffrage, vote by ballot, and the payment of members rested the salvation of the monarchy'.[15] Thus she gave her blessing to a good half of the Chartist programme, and expressed her shrewd opinion that democratic concessions would have the effect of popularizing the throne. Two years later she asked that every man should be given equal rights in the face of the law;[16] she insisted, too, that every home should take in and read its own newspaper,[17] and she cried out against the 'small ill-ventilated and filthy houses' in which 'too many' of the working classes had to live.[18] Yet this outspoken radical still felt obliged to approach her audience almost diffidently, for there were 'serious objections to a lady speaking before the public'! She explained that she was giving the lecture because she 'did not want her experience to die with her but if she had one good thought she wished to impart it'.[19] Doubtless her audience was satisfied that the breach of propriety was justified.

[13]Morell, *Colonial Policy of Peel and Russell*, p. 90.
[14]Madgwick, *Immigration into Eastern Australia*, p. 239.
[15]*S.M.H.*, 5 July 1859.   [16]*Ibid.* 8 June 1861.
[17]*Ibid.* 22 February 1861; 5 July 1859.
[18]*Ibid.* 8 June 1861.   [19]*Ibid.* 5 July 1859.

Nevertheless, in these last years when she was in most other respects an extreme radical, there is still no indication that she had any sympathy with feminism. The conclusion to be drawn from this, and from the general development of her outlook, is that she was not an original thinker. Throughout her life her opinions were formed by hard experience rather than swift abstractions. Like Charles Dickens, she was not a leader of radical thought, but a fearless fighter against abuses upon which others looked with apparent indifference.

After she returned to England, she was forgotten in the busy world in which only a few years before she had won fame. She had never sought material reward. Indeed, she had consistently refused it, and her repeated refusals probably contributed to the indifference and forgetfulness, for after a few half-hearted protests, the public was well enough pleased to accept her services without reward.

Many of the emigrants whom she had helped soon forgot that they had once been in need. They had not troubled to repay the loans her society had made to them, and when they were prosperous they did not like to be reminded of their debt to her. They let it be understood that they had paid their own passages, and after a few years they almost believed it themselves.

Besides the forgetfulness caused by this natural human weakness the record of her great services was probably deliberately disregarded by the squatters. They had heard enough from Mrs Chisholm, and some of the indifference and neglect meted out to her in her later years in Sydney is probably accounted for by the animosity she had aroused with her outspoken condemnation of the land-owning interests.

But perhaps the most cogent reason for the way in which she was so soon forgotten was the break-neck speed at which the Australian colonies were developing. Even when she returned to Victoria the gold discoveries had brought such a flood of new people into the colony, and so hastened the pace of what had been a leisurely pastoral society, that the *Argus* had to whip up public interest in her arrival. By the 'sixties the unhappy days of sex disparity were gone, and the after-effects of convictism were almost gone. The colonies were filled with a lusty, thrusting life which was the natural outcome of their economic and social development. Mrs Chisholm's work was done when she left Victoria; there was no further need to stimulate immigration. In this very completeness of her work there was, perhaps, another

reason for public forgetfulness. In those hurrying years there
were no reminders that she was missing from public life, because
there was no longer any need for her services.

Caroline Chisholm probably realized this and, as she lay dying,
the realization must have given her comfort. In the long weariness
of her last illness the sharp memory of old conflicts faded. She
felt no bitterness; she even remembered Dr Lang only as 'a great
and good man'.[20] Before she left Sydney she had given testimony
to the value of his work in one of her public lectures,[21] and on her
side at least there was no ill-feeling. Whether he had also forgiven
the old quarrel is not so certain, but with all his faults Dr Lang
was a valiant fighter for the democratic ideals in which Mrs
Chisholm so steadfastly believed. Her last years were spent in
poverty and physical suffering, but Caroline Chisholm must have
known peace of heart. She had kept faith with her ideal of service
and knew that her work had been well done.

[20]The late E. Dwyer Gray told me this.
[21]*S.M.H.*, 11 December 1860.

Appendices

APPENDIX A

Statistics of Mrs Chisholm's Female Immigrants, 1842

Eneas Mackenzie, *Memoirs of Mrs. Caroline Chisholm*, pp. 82-3

Since the establishment of the institution [the home], 735 young women have been provided with situations, at wages varying from £10 to £18 a year. Of this number 291 have been distributed in the country districts, of whom only 211 had been in service at home; 108 were orphans who had received their education in charity schools; 394 were Roman Catholics, 107 of whom could read, whilst 81 could read and write; 238 were Protestants of the Established Church, of these 42 could read, and 35 read and write, and 103 were Presbyterians, 35 of whom could read, and 21 read and write : total number of Irish 516; English, 184; Scotch, 35. To the number of 131 was taken by parties who never before kept servants; 13 have broken their agreements, whilst 26 employers have broken theirs; 8 have had charges of drunkenness brought against them, 2 of which were proved; 5 were charged with thefts, none of which could be substantiated; 2 were guilty of insolence : 1 obtained a situation by a false character, and 19 were removed from their situations by the secretary; 13 left their places without giving notice; 17 were discharged without notice by their employers, and 2 after eight o'clock in the evening without any charge being proved against their characters; 19 left their places without proper notice, and have not been paid their wages; in Sydney 81 have changed their situations; in the country, 11; pecuniary assistance has been offered to 47 persons, and 263 have received donations of provisions. The amount of subscriptions received is £156; the expenditure, £154; cash in hand, £2; subscriptions due, £41; debts none.

APPENDIX B

Voluntary Statements

(taken from those published as an appendix to Mrs Chisholm's pamphlet *Emigration and Transportation Relatively Considered*)

Statement No. 3 — Widow D. —— Perthshire

It's a good mistress I have, Mrs. W— long may she be spared. Don't say I am married. £20 and double rations, milk and everything here, done real well. Am with Mrs. J. W—— say how happy I am with this noble lady; say everybody can't expect to find the same luck; she is from the city of Glasgow. It would be thought strange at home how I should get married, but it's two or three times I might have been married. I was a widow from twenty-two. It's very remarkable but it was my luck. I am sure I'll recommend my master and mistress, it's good and kind they have been to me. I fancy, I need not care because they are rich but there is one Mr. ——, of Glasgow, — but no, I need not care, he is a great gentleman — it's long since I saw him, — no, it's the poorer relations at Perth I would send to; let them know it's a good country to live in, — at home it was a hard difficulty, — I could no more live now than I could fly on the living I had at home; the living was coarse at home; here meat, bread, milk, eggs, butter, cheese in plenty, sugar and tea as much as I can use; plenty milk, plenty cows. I never need take a hoe in my hands now to hoe turnips; it's not much toil with what I get. You will give a long description of this place. It's a very good country for good girls — at home they toil for sixpence a day. Fine country this, good wages, higher than £10 and £15 a year. They don't toil much for it, they win it with all manner of ease, compared to what they get in Scotland. Mention this, my Lady, and, if you please, mem, read it over that I may see it's correct — That's very nice, very nice, mem — that will do. How astonished they will be when they hear I am married!

New South Wales, 19 December 1845

Statement No. 4 – George B., London

I have been working for my own benefit about ten years in this colony, am single, — it's sharp work to meet with a wife here, — rent a farm, pay £10 a year for twenty acres, have a dray (waggon) and a good team of bullocks, ten cows, twenty all sizes; make a good living; come from London, parish of Cripplegate. My parents lived at London Wall, opposite a chapel; my father was a carpenter, and my brother Thomas was apprenticed to a man named Robinson, a carpenter, — he lived in Ford or Fort Street, Cripplegate. William was a shoemaker. I had also two other brothers, Edward and John; two sisters, Ruth and Martha. Oh, if they will come write to me, and as sure as I receive your letter I'll go to Sydney to meet them. If Edward would come I would give him a home, and go to meet him, or indeed, anyone of them. I would put them in the way of doing. Never heard from one of them. I left England in 1827. There is a living, and an easy one, to be got in this country. Of course a man must work, but it is easier to make out a living than at home. Have not long left Sydney. See, I have purchased for myself one chest of tea, one bag of sugar, one hundredweight of salt, three good shirts, and a new hat, jacket and other clothing. Have just taken a load of wool to Sydney, 30 cwt., distance 190 miles, got seven shillings the cwt.; was three weeks on the journey. Have now on my dray as return carriage one ton at four shillings the cwt.; it's not so far I have to take it. Manage my farm, and go three times a year to Sydney. It takes me about £3 to clear all road expenses up and down.

Emu Swamp, on the road to Bathurst, 19 December 1845

Statement No. 5 – Ellen W., London

I arrived in 1833. I am married to George W——; my maiden name was T——; we are doing well; I wish to have out my sister, she was apprenticed from St. Giles' parish; she now belongs to Islington where you will most likely hear of her. Her mistress's name is Cox; she did live at No. 12 Pleasant Row, Islington. Her name is Emma; she is about twenty-two years of age; will give her a comfortable home. Now mind you tell her that her sister Mary Ann is married well, and lives in the Goulburn District. My brother is doing well. Neither of us have wanted for anything in this country. Two of my brothers were sent as parish apprentices to the Cape of Good Hope. We pay eight shillings a week rent but it is well we get on. Oh, what a difference there is between this country and home for poor folks. I know I would not go back again, — I know what England is. Old England is a fine place for the rich, but the Lord help the poor.

Sydney, 11 March 1846

Statement No. 11 – Patt D. —— Kildare

It is six years since we arrived in the ship ——; we brought two children with us, and left one at home, named P. D——; he is about ten years of age. Oh; how we was pushed to get out when the money was to be paid; the fact was we could only find money for one. Well, what did we do ? There was a poor woman who wanted to get to her husband, a prisoner in New South Wales, and she had one child, so we agrees to take her child as our own, and she goes out as a single woman in the same ship; for this she gives us £1, besides the pound she gave us to pay for her child, and this saved us from leaving two children at home instead of one as it paid the agent.

We are, thank God, well-to-do now. We have seventeen cows. Well, I sends home £5 for this boy, and it is above three years I did this, but it is never a line I had; it was by —— I sent it and it's all the particulars I give you. Then now, when the emigrant ship —— was going home we gave him £2 to give our child for clothes, and a note of hand for £10 if he obtained a passage for our child. Well, he returns in a ship without the child, and not a bit of proof about the child; then he demands the £10, according to the promissory note, but we goes bang to Court, and the gentlemen, long may they live, made him give us the £2 back again; this £2, you see, he charged us for coach expenses. We leaves our child wi' a poor widow woman, one Betty Hurley; she did live in Barrack-street, thirty-two miles from Dublin. Don't rest till you find him, and may God reward you if you send my poor child to me.

New South Wales, 29 January 1846

Statement No. 13 – J. S. —— Cork

I arrived in 1833 by the *Java*. I am in the service of Mr. P—— and get 7s. a week, and my food and lodgings. I have saved about,—— here, look at the paper I have from the Savings Bank ——

Last year's Account, 1844	£43	4	11
October ditto, 1843	32	18	6
	£76	4	5

And I have more from this year's wages. I save every farthing to make a home for my wife. It is not my intention to leave my present service, having a fine master; indeed I never had a bad one. Men's wages run from 7s. to 10s. a week with food and lodgings. Girls' wages run from 4s. 6d. to 5s. 6d. a week. There is a scarcity of men-servants now, but more particularly women. My wife lives at Bandon, County of Cork, her name is Mary ——; my children's Elizabeth, Johannah, Ellen. As a token I give you a letter received from my wife. As another token, my wife, her sister and husband came to see me when I received sentence of death, for taking fire-arms from a constable in a Tithe row . . . I was sent here as a lifer. I am now on my Ticket — not yet received my emancipation. The row I was engaged in took place at Ballawerthen, twelve miles from Bandon. This was about 1832. J. K—— was sent here with me for the same offence. Here it is all quiet — Catholics and Protestants live here quiet : never saw a fight betwen a Catholic and a Protestant here on the score of religion. Look at my character —— they are both down together to help me get my wife; and now Parson R—— said to me, "Tell Mrs. Chisholm to get her out', and the Priest signed my paper; that's proof of what I say. It is a quiet, comfortable country.

New South Wales, 19 February 1846

APPENDIX C

Caroline Chisholm to Earl Grey

(C.O. 201/390. f. 225. Public Record Office, London; copy in the Mitchell Library, Sydney.)

> 29 Prince's Street,
> Jubilee Place,
> Mile End, London.
> 25 January 1847

My Lord,

It may not be unknown to your Lordship that I interested myself for a period of eight years in New South Wales in trying to ameliorate the condition of Emigrants on their arrival there, and other classes of the community who wanted employment, and that your late predecessor in Office was pleased to tender to me his thanks in his Despatch No. 84, of the 31st of May 1844 to the Govt. of New South Wales, for the services which I had rendered to Emigrants. The knowledge which I have thus gained, of the capabilities of the Colony, and of the character of the inhabitants, from my having travelled into the remote interior, in my exertions to settle individuals and locate families, emboldens me to address you at present on the important subject of Emigration, and on the evils that press so heavily upon the social and moral advancement of that Colony.

During the present lamentable distress that afflicts parts of the United Kingdom, particularly Ireland, I cannot in duty refrain from bringing to your Lordship's notice for the information of Her Majesty's Government, the numerous and daily Applications which I receive, from Country labourers and whole families for a free Passage to New South Wales, and Port Phillip, and more particularly from the relatives of those who had emigrated to Australia some years ago, and who have written to me at the request of their friends, — the majority of these are from Ireland. On Monday last, the Applications for that day [*sic*] amounted to three hundred, and when I retrospectively look to the vast and suitable field which New Holland offers for the enterprising and industrious Emigrant, I cannot but grievously lament, if the earnest solicitations of these poor people are not conceded to, viz., a Free Passage to N. S. Wales.

One of the evils which I would take the liberty to press upon your Lordship's notice, and that of Her Majesty's Government, is the frightful disparity of the sexes (men being out of all proportion in number to women), and from which flows misery and crime, I dare not dwell upon, and to this unnatural anomaly of the human race in that Colony, may be traced in a great degree the gradual but certain extermination of those unfortunate tribes, the Aborigines of New Holland; they, the original holders of the soil, demand the speedy and parental interference of a humane Government.

With a hope of removing to some extent this crying and national evil, I beg most respectfully to say that I would feel disposed to co-operate in finding a remedy, by making a selection of young women of good character as free Emigrants to Australia.

I beg most deferentially to remark that the present policy [*sic*] of sending women under penal sentence to New South Wales only adds infinitely to the moral evil, and it is with gratification I have to observe that I never met but with one man who did not express extreme desire to be married to a woman of good character, and it is a most erroneous opinion that such women make suitable wives enough for reclaimed convict men; nature and moral religion both shrink from the idea of such characters as mothers of children — no one is more sensitive upon that point than the reformed prisoner received back into the social order of society, and often in my travels through the Bush did I come upon the solitary and cheerless Hut of the unfortunate Emancipist living alone, or at times find two young men associated together, because they could not meet with respectable females to whom they could offer otherwise a comfortable home; and I also frequently fell in with Natives of Australia — descendants of Europeans, similarly situated — no helpmate to cheer their habitations. It may be also observed that respectable Emigrant Parents object to their daughters serving in the same establishment with this class of females.

The demand for domestic Servants by respectable families in Australia, and by the yeomen of the country, renders it easy to provide for such young women, as may be disposed to emigrate, soon after their arrival, more particularly as the demand for servants in the interior is on the increase : The protection necessary to be afforded to those young females on their Passage out, as well as on their arrival in the Colony, and after dispersion in the interior, is a subject of such paramount importance to their welfare, that it will afford me deep and sincere satisfaction to impart that information and knowledge which I have gained relative thereto from experience.

I have the honor to be,

My Lord,

Your very Obedt. Humble Servt.

CAROLINE CHISHOLM

[Minuted at foot]

27 Jany.   *Mr. Hawes*

I suppose this must be referred to the Land and Emigration Commissioners.

—J.S.

Jy. 27

B.H.

Yet with an instruction that if they can devise any practicable measure for affecting the object in view I shall be anxious to consider it. — Mrs. C. must be thanked for the communication expressing my sense of the benevolence of her object and my desire to promote its accomplishment, at the same time informing her that her letter has been referred to the Commissioners and requesting her to communicate with them.

(C.O. 385/22. Public Record Office, London)

To Mrs. Chisholm

Madam,   4 February 1847

I am directed by Earl Grey to acknowledge the receipt of your letter of the 25 Ult. in which you urge the present state of affairs in Ireland as bearing directly on the question of relief being afforded to some of the poorer classes of that Country by means of Emigration, and you suggest that, with this view, H.M's Govt. should grant free passages to New South Wales and Port Phillip, and especially to those who are desirous of joining their friends and relatives in the Colony, of whom you represent the number to be very large.

You likewise express your willingness to co-operate with any scheme that may be devised for selecting young women of good character, who should be sent out as free Emigrants to Australia, in order to remedy the present evils arising out of the great disparity of the Sexes.

For the remarks you have offered on these and other topics adverted to in the same letter, Lord Grey desires me to convey to you his sincere thanks, and to express to you the sense which he entertains of the value of your observations, and of the spirit of benevolence by which they have been dictated. His Lordship has every wish to promote the objects you have brought under his notice, and he directs me to add that he has caused a copy of your letter to be sent to the Colonial Land and Emigration Commissioners with whom his Lordship would suggest that you should [sic] place yourself in communication.

I am, etc.

[unsigned]

APPENDIX D

Caroline Chisholm to Miss (later the Baroness) Burdett-Coutts (Miss Coutts was a granddaughter of the founder of Coutts & Co., the remittance bankers for the Family Colonization Loan Society. The original is in the Mitchell Library.)

East India Road,

Poplar

Dear Madam,   14 March 1854

The deep respect I feel for your character as one really anxious for the Elevation of the poor, and the kind support you have given my plans made me anxious for an opportunity of seeing you before I left England, and I shall therefore have great pleasure in dining with you on Friday the 24th as you have kindly allowed me to name a day.

The great demand for ships for the *Service* has been the cause of much annoyance and vexation to me for when freights are on the rise there is a great temptation to break contracts — I am glad to say that for my party I have under [the] circumstances made a satisfactory arrangement, though not a very good one for myself — £100 — a higher sum than has ever been paid by a Lady for herself, a cabin 7 feet by 7 for my boys with 2nd-class accommodation below, but taking their meals with me £40 each. For the young girls £21. Families — £25 each adult. There is a large number of these young women and some children on board for whom it would be desirable to have a person who would instruct and attend their Morning and Evening devotions. A number of wives with their children are following their husbands and as this large party differ from me in their Religion I cannot do more than make their state known to you, trusting that you will meet the expense necessary for their satisfactory emigration.

A highly respectable man and his wife made application to me who have been on the London Mission, but as I never question anyone on religious subjects I made no enquiry in this particular case — thinking some offer might be made I have let the matter rest till now.

Yours Sincerely and Gratefully
CAROLINE CHISHOLM

APPENDIX E

Some Ship-Board Regulations of the Family Colonization Loan Society

(See Trelawney Saunders, *The Story of the Life of Mrs. Caroline Chisholm*, pp. 22-9.)

Ship Regulations :— The following extracts from the 'Rules and Regulations' enforced on board all the Society's vessels will show that every attention is paid to the morality, health, comfort, and safety of the passengers. These Regulations are all carried out under the superintendence of the Surgeon.

'The Groups are to choose six persons from their body to be called the Group Committee whose duty will be to preserve order on the Lower Deck, and see that deck kept clean, to attend during the issue of provisions, to see that each mess has the proper allowance; and to keep a register of the Brands on the various casks or provisions, that they may know they are consuming the provisions put on board for their use. The appointment of the first Committee (to act for one month only) devolves upon Mrs. Chisholm; at the expiration of that period the Groups can elect others.

'For the more effectual preservation of order and regularity, all complaints to be made to the Surgeon, through the medium of the Group Committees, in order that he may apply to the Captain should it become necessary with a view to remedy the cause of complaint.

'No smoking allowed on the Poop, Lower Deck, or abaft the Main Mast on the Upper Deck.

'Single men not to go abaft the Main Hatchway on the Lower Deck (except during meals).

'One side of the Poop Deck to be reserved exclusively for the Captain's use and comfort, and that of his officers.

'The Passengers to leave the Poop Deck at half-past eight in the evening, and the lamps to be extinguished at ten o'clock with the exception of three large ones on the Lower Deck and one on the Poop, which will be left burning all night. No lights of any kind permitted in the Cabins, and those over the tables must not be removed.

'No clothes may be dried in the Cabins, or between decks.

'Any Fire-arms, Gunpowder, Lucifer Matches, or combustible materials of any kind, discovered in the possession of the Passengers will be immediately taken away from them by the Captain, and retained by him until the termination of the voyage.

'The Scuttles not to be opened except by the Carpenter of the ship, who will do so when ordered by the Officer of the Watch. Provisions will be issued at the following hours :

Water, daily, at half-past six in the morning; and all Provisions at ten o'clock in the morning of the days specified in the "Ration Regulations".

'The Odd Messes, viz. 1, 3, 5, etc., will *Breakfast* at eight in the morning, *Dine* at one in the afternoon, and *Sup* at five in the evening. The Even Messes, viz. Nos. 2, 4, 6, etc., will *Breakfast* at nine in the morning, *Dine* at two in the afternoon and *Sup* at six in the evening. By this arrangement, all confusion will be avoided.

'The Emigrants are to prepare their food for cooking, and take it to and receive it from the Cook appointed in the Emigrants' service. This duty should always be done by a man from each mess, as it is not proper for respectable females to go forward among the ship's crew.

'Passengers are strictly prohibited from giving any Wine, Spirits or Beer to any of the Ship's Company or Passengers' Cook.

'The Surgeon will attend on the Lower Deck daily at the hours of ten in the morning and five in the evening. It is requested that all applications for Medicines will be made at those hours, except in cases of emergency.

'As ventilation and cleanliness are essential to the health and well-being of every person on board it is earnestly recommended that the Bedding, etc., from the several Berths be brought on deck, twice in each week (viz., Tuesdays and Fridays if practicable), aired, and the Berths well cleaned.

'The washing of Passengers' clothes and articles in use must always be concluded before nine in the morning.'

Notice of Departure:— At least one month's notice is always given of the sailing of the vessel to which Emigrants may have been nominated. To those resident in the country every advice is given by Mrs. Chisholm as to the best and most economical plan to be adopted in removing their families to the metropolis for the purpose of embarkation.

N.B. The Society engages none but A1 ships, and each vessel carries an experienced Surgeon.

Price of Passage :— The exact sum to be charged as passage-money cannot be positively stated until a ship is engaged. Children between one and fourteen half price. Infants nothing. The reason of any fluctuation in the charge arises from the variation in prices at which vessels can be procured at different periods. Any advantages resulting from favourable circumstances is always given to the Emigrants.

Cooking :— The provisions being prepared by the Emigrants and delivered as directed in the 'Ship Rules & Regulations' will be cooked by an Emigrants' cook, provided to perform that duty by the Society.

Children :— It will be at the discretion of the Surgeon to issue three times a week, to children under seven years of age, 4 ounces of Rice, or three ounces of Sago, in lieu of Salt Meat.

Medical Comforts :— For the information of the Committee of the Society, the Surgeon of the vessel is required to keep an account of the issue of medical comforts, with the names of the parties receiving them.

Luggage :— The bulk of luggage (*free of charge*) allowed to each adult passenger is fifteen cubic feet; ten in the hold, and five in the cabin with half that amount for children. This includes the cabin box, which must not be more than 1 ft. 6 in. long and 1 ft. 10 in. broad, and 1 ft. 2 in. deep. (A carpet bag is far more useful than a box.) The cabin box (or bag) is to contain sufficient linen or other articles for fourteen days' use, as no other packages can on any account be allowed in the cabins. The remainder of the baggage marked 'Wanted on the Voyage', will be so stowed in the hold that it can be got at once a fortnight (or oftener) during the passage, for the purpose of making any required exchange of apparel. All packages of baggage must be distinctly marked with the name of the passenger, and also with the words 'Wanted on the Voyage', or 'Not wanted on the Voyage' and they must be at the docks, ready for shipment, at least *Five* days prior to the day appointed for sailing. Persons residing in the country can have printed baggage tickets forwarded upon application, by enclosing *Two stamps* for the same, and stating the number they require. The Society does not make arrangements for extra luggage.

APPENDIX F

Occupations of Family Colonization Loan Society Immigrants arriving in New South Wales from the United Kingdom, 1855

These immigrants came in the *Bangalore, Abdallah, Washington Irving, Lord Burleigh, Nimrod* and *Light-of-the-Age,* the statistics being taken from the *Votes and Proceedings,* Legislative Assembly of New South Wales, 1856-57, ii. 449. Records for the two ships which arrived in 1854 — the *Hanover* and *Marchioness of Londonderry* — are not available.

Farmers and agricultural labourers, 82
   (comprising 58 labourers, 13 gardeners, 7 farmers, 3 carters, 1 herdsman).
Domestic servants, 137 (130 female, 7 male).
Building trades mechanics, 64
   (comprising 31 carpenters, 9 bricklayers, 9 painters and glaziers, 7 plumbers, 4 plasterers, 1 locksmith, 1 brickmaker, 1 sawyer, 1 mason).
Clothing tradespeople, 85
   (comprising 38 dressmakers, 18 milliners, 9 needlewomen, 7 tailors, 6 shoemakers, 3 drapers, 2 bonnet makers, 1 hatter, 1 tailoress).
Food and drink tradespeople, 13
   (comprising 5 bakers, 3 millers, 2 butchers, 2 grocers, 1 brewer).
Printing tradesmen, 9
   (comprising 6 printers, 2 bookbinders, 1 engraver).
Miscellaneous — male, 55; female, 6
   (comprising 8 smiths, 6 cabinet-makers, 4 engineers, 3 coopers, 2 stationers, 2 turners, 2 ship's stewards, 1 coachtrimmer, 1 wheelwright, 1 coachmaker, 1 coachpainter, 1 tallow chandler, 1 hairdresser, 1 porter, 1 warehouseman, 1 wood sorter, 1 tanner, 1 skinner, 1 wireworker,

1 carver and gilder, 1 carpet weaver, 1 cattle dealer, 1 land agent, 1 cattle doctor, 1 brushmaker, 1 distiller, 1 organ builder, 1 boat builder, 1 police officer, 1 iron moulder, 1 packer, 1 tinplate worker, 1 tobacco manufacturer, 1 bootcloser, 1 saddler and 3 nurses, 2 schoolmistresses, 1 governess).

Occupations of Family Colonization Loan Society Immigrants arriving in Victoria between October 1852 and July 1854

This classification is made from the passenger lists of the *Scindian* (arrived 16 October 1852), *Nepaul* (19 October 1852), *Chalmers* (24 November 1852), *Ballengeich* (6 December 1852), *Caroline Chisholm* (27 May 1853) and *Ballarat* (12 July 1854). Passenger lists for the *Slains Castle* (25 January 1851), *Blundell* (29 September 1851), *Athenian* (1 March 1852) and *Mariner* (29 June 1852) are not available. These figures can only be regarded as approximate, as there appear to be many mistakes and omissions in the lists, which make it impossible to compile any record of the number of families and individuals who arrived in Victoria under the auspices of the Family Colonization Loan Society.

Farmers and agricultural labourers, 111
   (comprising 76 labourers, 29 farmers, 6 gardeners).
Domestic servants, 18 (13 female, 5 male).
Building trades mechanics, 43
   (comprising 32 carpenters, 4 builders, 2 painters, 2 plasterers, 1 mason, 1 bricklayer, 1 plumber).
Clothing tradespeople, 54
   (comprising 20 drapers, 18 tailors, 4 shoemakers, 3 bootmakers, 3 milliners, 3 umbrella makers (female), 1 hatter, 1 embroidress, 1 needlewoman).
Food and drink tradespeople, 35
   (comprising 8 bakers, 7 butchers, 6 grocers, 3 millers, 2 milkmen, 2 brewers, 1 greengrocer, 1 cheesemaker, 1 cheesemonger, 1 dairyman, 1 fisherman, 1 confectioner, 1 barman).
Printing tradesmen, 20
   (comprising 13 printers, 5 compositors, 2 bookbinders).
Miscellaneous — male, 178; female, 10
   (comprising 43 clerks, 11 warehousemen, 9 smiths, 9 engineers, 7 seamen, 5 stationers, 5 accountants, 4 bookmakers, 4 jewellers, 4 travellers, 4 shopmen, 4 merchants, 3 ironmongers, 3 watchmakers, 2 surveyors, 2 saddlers, 2 coachmen, 2 musicians, 2 surgeons, 2 cellarmen, 2 piano makers, 2 cutlers, 2 brushmakers, 2 artists, 2 mechanics, 2 druggists, 2 stonemasons, 2 wheelwrights, 1 harness maker, 1 cabinet maker, 1 oilman, 1 brazier, 1 porter, 1 veterinary surgeon, 1 coal dealer, 1 manufacturer, 1 cowkeeper, 1 general dealer, 1 solicitor, 1 stable keeper, 1 tobacconist, 1 bookseller, 1 french polisher, 1 storekeeper, 1 lapidary, 1 tinplater, 1 dyer, 1 die-sinker, 1 shepherd, 1 teacher, 1 last maker, 1 pewterer, 1 lodginghouse keeper, 1 mercer, 1 cashier, 1 turner, 1 miner, 1 gentleman, 1 pawnbroker, 1 law stationer, 1 steward, 1 coachmaker, 1 wainwright

and 4 housekeepers, 3 shopkeepers, 1 schoolmistress, 1 tobacconist, 1 governess).

Occupations of Family Colonization Loan Society Immigrants arriving in Adelaide, in the 'Slains Castle' and 'Blundell', 1851 (See Votes and Proceedings, Legislative Council of South Australia, 1852)

Agricultural labourers (21) and gardeners (2), 23

Building trades mechanics, 8

(comprising 4 carpenters, 2 bricklayers, 2 housepainters and plumbers).

Butchers and bakers, 2

Shoemakers, 4

Typefounders, 2 and printers and engravers, 2

Miscellaneous — male, 23; female, 30

(comprising 11 general labourers, 5 engineers and smiths, 2 sawyers and 5 other trades

and 27 female servants, 2 governesses and 1 female artist).

Index

Illustrated London News, 102
Illustrated Magazine of Art, 128-9, 132n.
Immigrants' Aid Society, 158, 168
Immigrants' Rate Fund, 167
Immigrants' Shelter of Family Colonization Loan Society (Melbourne), 140-1
Immigration Barracks (Sydney): branch homes, 26, 29, 47; Female Immigrants' Home, 12-18; government use, 10, 11, 27, 36; registry office, 21, 40; school, 27; scope expanded, 26
Immigration Board, 10, 38, 99
Ireland, 28, 70-1, 88, 93, 105, 122

Java, 195
Jerrold's Weekly Newspaper, 83
Jewish Ladies' Benevolent Loan and Visiting Society, 128
Jones, William, 5
Jones, Mrs William, 5, 74, 132

King William, 119
Kyneton, 175-6

Land: Caroline Chisholm (advocates small-holdings) 44, 46, 50, 51, 97, 101, 162, 172, 173, (attacks squatters) 107-8, 155, 172-3; squatters' opposition to small-holdings, 45, 51, 98, 101, 105, 137, 155-6; struggle for land, 169-75
Landor, Walter Savage, 130
Lang, George, 51
Lang, Dr John Dunmore, 65; arrival in Sydney, 51-2; attacks Caroline Chisholm, 66-8, 87, 89, 93-5, 122; attacks Earl Grey, 93-4; character, 52, 53-4, 66, 74; dealings with Colonial Office, 76, 90-6; efforts to promote Protestant migration, 52-3, 66, 87-93; in England, 87-96; hatred of Roman Catholics, 65-6, 67-8, 88-9; membership of Legislative Council (N.S.W.) 43n., 54; pamphlets and lectures, 89-90; see also British Banner
La Trobe, Charles Joseph, 140, 170
'Letters to the working classes of Great Britain', 174
Lindsay, W. S., 127-8
Lloyd's Weekly Newspaper, 94
Lowe, Robert, vi, 146, 155

Macarthur, James, 51, 65, 76

Macarthur, William, 51, 65, 76
Mackenzie, Eneas, 5n., 6n., 7n., 76, 117, 118n., 125
Maitland, 29, 30
Mariner, 123, 124, 126
Melbourne, 119, 138-9; see also Victoria
Melbourne Benevolent Asylum, 168
Mereweather, F.L.S., 36, 43
Mitchell, Sir Thomas, 106, 169
Moreton Bay, 29, 45, 57, 86, 89
Murphy, Rev. Francis, 24, 27, 101, 102, 134

Nelson, Richard William, 34-5
Nepaul, 123, 129
Newcastle, Duke of, 154, 171
New South Wales: 1, 4, 8, 9, 10, 42, 48-9, 61, 64, 83-4, 169; Legislative Council, 43-8, 51, 55, 91, 143-4, 171
Newspapers, 41, 102-3
Nicholson, Dr Charles (later Sir Charles), 38-9, 43n., 65, 86, 174

Occupation and Purchase Regulations, 169; see also Land

Parramatta, 26, 29, 86
Passenger Acts: (1852), 127; (1855), 147
Pastoral Protection Society, 174
Pius IX (Pio Nono), 123
Poor Law Amendment Act (1834), 69; New, 109
Punch, 130-1

Reform Act (1832), 69
Robertson, Robert, 34-5
Roman Catholics, 13, 28, 29, 53, 66-8, 87, 89, 91

School for Girls (Sydney), 179
Scindian, 123, 129, 143
Scotland, 70, 88, 91, 102, 122
Scott, Hon. Francis, 87, 94, 155
Select Committees (House of Lords): Colonization from Ireland, 85-6, 97, 100, 101; Execution of the Criminal Law, 85; Transportation, 72-3, 77, 90
Select Committees (Legislative Council of N.S.W.); Distressed Labourers, 43, 46, 51; Immigration, 61, 62, 63, 64
Select Committees of the Legislative Council of Victoria, on Immigration, 139, 154-5
Shaftesbury, Earl of (formerly Lord Ashley), 102, 103, 106, 144